"Even dictators need excuses. Hitler was in want of one. After early October 1939 he had decided to invade the neutral countries of Holland and Belgium. The excuse was needed not so much because Hitler shrank from the international conscience, but because he had to overcome the opposition of his own generals. Two incidents, the bomb outrage in the **Bürgerbräukeller** in Munich and the so-called **Venlo** incident in early November, gave Hitler the excuses he needed."

B.G.J. (Bob) de Graaff, Dutch Historian

Cartoon from *The Times*, London, November 1939

GEORG ELSER
The Zither Player

TOM FERRY

CONSULTANT EDITOR: PETER KOBLANK

First published in 2016
Copyright © 2016 Tom Ferry

All rights reserved.

Title: GEORG ELSER: THE ZITHER PLAYER
Author: Tom Ferry
Consultant Editor: Peter Koblank

A Cataloguing-in-Publication record is available from the National Library of Australia.

ISBN: 978-1517710217

Printed by CreateSpace

Contents

ACT 1
1 | August 5, 1939: Schnaitheim-Munich — 11
2 | August 10, 1939: Munich — 17
3 | September 1, 1939: Munich — 23
4 | September 1, 1939: The Hague — 27
5 | September 3, 1939: Munich — 35
6 | September 3, 1939: the Hague — 41
7 | September 5-6, 1939: Munich — 46
8 | September 18, 1939: The Netherlands — 49
9 | September 20, 1939: Munich — 55
10 | October 12, 1939: Munich — 60
11 | October 20, 1939: The Netherlands — 63
12 | October 20, 1939: Munich — 70
13 | October 30, 1939: The Hague — 75
14 | October 30-31, 1939: The Hague — 85
15 | November 1-2, 1939: Munich — 90
16 | November 4-5, 1939: Munich — 94
17 | November 5-7, 1939: Munich-Stuttgart-Munich — 99
18 | November 7, 1939: Venlo — 108
19 | November 8, 1939: Venlo — 114
20 | November 8, 1939: Friedrichshafen-Konstanz — 118
21 | November 9, 1939: The Hague-Venlo — 122

ACT 2
22 | November 9, 1939: Konstanz-Munich — 131
23 | November 9-10, 1939: Venlo-Düsseldorf — 134
24 | November 10-11, 1939: Munich — 139
25 | November 10-17, 1939: Berlin — 143
26 | November 12-14, 1939: Munich — 149
27 | November 19-20, 1939: Berlin — 157
28 | November 17-December 8, 1939: Berlin — 174
29 | November 21, 1939: Berlin — 178
30 | November 22, 1939: In the Press — 187
31 | November 22-23, 1939: Berlin — 193

Contents

ACT 3
32	November 25, 1939: Berlin	203
33	December 1-6, 1939: Berlin	207
34	December 7-10, 1939: Berlin	212
35	December 9-10, 1939: Sachsenhausen	219
36	Late December, 1939: Berlin	222
37	1940: Sachsenhausen	225
38	June 30, 1942: Sachsenhausen	232
39	June 30, 1942; Sachsenhausen	236
40	February 15, 1943: Sachsenhausen	238
41	1943: Sachsenhausen	240
42	July 20, 1944: Sachsenhausen	243
43	February 20-April 2, 1945: Sachsenhausen-Buchenwald	249
44	March 7, 1945: Dachau	259
45	April 3-8, 1945: Buchenwald-Schönberg	264
46	April 7, 1945: Dachau	268
47	April 9, 1945: Schönberg-Dachau	273
48	9.00-11.00pm, April 9, 1945: Dachau	278

END
49	April 9-May 2, 1945: Dachau-Tyrol	283
50	May 5, 1945: Naples-Isle of Capri	287
Afterword		292
Appendix		299
Acknowledgements		323
Bibliography		322
Postscript		325

Abbreviations

NSDAP	National Socialist German Workers' Party [Nazi Party]
SA	*Sturmabteilung*—the paramilitary wing of the Nazi Party [Brown Shirts]
SD	*Sicherheitsdienst*—Security [Intelligence] Service of the SS and the NSDAP
SS	*Schutzstaffel*—initially the paramilitary protection squadron for Nazi Party leaders
SIS	British Secret Intelligence Service

"When the curtains were falling thunderously on the last moments of the Nazi regime, Hitler suddenly remembered the existence of the zither player—and as if possessed by a sudden and inexplicable shame, this murderer of millions attempted to conceal his execution of the assassin who had long since been forgotten by the world."

Hans Bernd Gisevius.

ACT 1

1   August 5, 1939
Schnaitheim-Munich

MARIA is more lovesick than ever as we embrace by the river. She runs her fingers through my hair. The heat of her passion belies her sixteen years. All morning she has been a Martha, ironing my shirts, polishing my shoes, checking I've packed ample underwear. Naturally she wanted to know the reason I was leaving. I gave her the name of a furniture company to convince her of my story. Whether or not there's an opening for a cabinetmaker in that company I have no idea. All I know is Maria and her family must be protected and remain oblivious to my true intentions.

"Write to me Georg," I hear her call.

I don't dare look back or slow my pace as I push the handcart across the bridge to the railway station. Acting as if I am going about my normal business I off-load my wooden trunk on the platform and return the handcart to the stationmaster's store. When the attendant at the booking window croaks the obligatory homage to the one in high places I give him the innocent look of insanity as I purchase my one-way ticket.

There are only a handful of passengers aboard the two-carriage train, as is normal in the midafternoon. Seeing no one who I know, I am saved from making polite conversation and sit alone by a window with my trunk stowed in the luggage bay. When the castle fortress overlooking Heidenheim vanishes from view I close my eyes and try to empty my mind. If that was the last time I will ever see or touch Maria Schmauder I want to stay in denial.

I change trains at Ulm and doze to Augsburg. From there the line is fast and flat to the Bavarian capital. When I see the city outskirts glint in the afternoon sun I pull from my pocket the letter with the address of my lodging. On my previous stays in Munich I have had trouble finding an affordable room not infested with fleas or having some other irritation. This time I took the precaution of placing an advertisement in a Munich newspaper simply worded, 'Gent seeks clean furnished room'. Scores of offers came by mail, giving me plenty to choose from. After the most promising offer fell through, due to no fault of my own, I posted my acceptance with a full month's board to a Frau Baumann residing at Blumenstrasse 11/19.

The ride from Munich's main station takes little more than ten minutes. Though the driver demands a hefty three marks I make no complaint as I haul my trunk from the back of his van. The apartment building rising up before me looks little different from any of the others along Blumenstrasse. Leaving my heavy load in the lobby, I climb the stairway to apartment No.11, and in the hope this will not be another debacle I reach for the doorbell. Within half a minute a slim blue-eyed woman opens the door. Her prominent cheekbones suggest intelligence, while her age would be not too dissimilar from my age of thirty-six years.

"Frau Baumann?"

"Yes. And you must be Herr Elser. We were expecting to see you last Tuesday."

"I was delayed through illness."

"Nothing contagious I hope. Have you registered with the police?"

"Not yet."

"You must register today if you are to stay with us. How else will the police keep track of the population?"

"I believe I have twenty-four hours to register. I promise to register first thing in the morning."

"Please do so without fail. We don't want any trouble. Do you have any luggage?"

As I haul my trunk up three floors I start to wonder if renting a room from Frau Baumann is a gross mistake despite her intelligent looks. And when she informs me breakfast will cost 20 marks on top of the 35 marks per month I have already paid in advance, my temperature rises even further. But the room is clean and well ventilated, of good size and decently decorated, while the central location on Blumenstrasse will be convenient to my work. The only drawback I foresee is lack of space to tinker.

After Frau Baumann demonstrates how to turn off the tap to avoid a drip and a stain on the basin, she hands me a clean towel and a new cake of soap. Once she has removed herself from my room I take off my coat, necktie and slip off my well polished shoes. I need to put up my feet as three months ago a large stone fell on my foot, almost crippling me. It took nine weeks for the bone to knit. Though no sooner had my doctor pronounced me fit to return to work I was violently ill with fever, vomiting and diarrhea. For four torrid days and nights I was confined to bed with Maria and her mother waiting on me hand and foot. I still feel less than one hundred per cent but I was determined to travel today. Though, had I not paid my rent in advance I might have prolonged my recovery, convalescing another week in the comfort of the Schmauder household.

After an hour lying flat on my back and with the time at 7.15 pm I roll off the bed to unlock the padlock and lift the lid of my trunk. I need to change my clothes as when I arrived this afternoon I felt like a stuffed turkey wearing a dark blue formal suit with a white starched collar. Knickerbockers and an open necked shirt with a sleeveless knitted pullover will look far less conspicuous in this city on a mild Saturday night.

Once I have changed and hung my suit on a hanger in the cupboard, I straighten the bedspread and relock my trunk. The last thing I need is Frau Baumann sniffing through my things like an Alsatian wolf dog. She seems a woman who lives by the letter of the law, no matter what the consequences.

With the key to my trunk in my pocket, I pull the door shut and head to the sitting room. I find Frau Baumann perched on a straight-backed chair knitting what looks like a sock for an elephant. A short balding man, who I can only presume is Frau Baumann's husband, is sunk deep in an armchair with a pipe hanging from his mouth like a meat hook. Both act as if I do not exist—as if in a deep trance. I soon realize I have walked in on another Nazi pep talk.

___Thus, they turn for help to where the Jew, as the Devil incarnate, rules. Who would have thought that once proud Albion would beg for support for months in Moscow? In recent weeks, we have seen people abroad trying to make a distinction between the German people and its leadership, just as they did in the period just before the takeover of power. Then they said: The German people are being raped! It wants nothing to do with Nazism! Today, they promise wonderful things to the German people if they will only desert Adolf Hitler.

However, the German people have learned from the past. It knows that such promises are lies. The German people and its leadership are united. It is ridiculous to attempt to separate the people from Adolf Hitler.

The Führer is with the people, and the people are with the Führer!

"Who was that?" I ask.

Frau Baumann's lips stay buttoned as her companion levers himself from his armchair to switch off the Volksempfänger. He then turns his cheerless eyes on me as if I have asked a question *so* stupid I do not deserve an answer. After taking his pipe from his mouth he utters two words.

"Julius Streicher."

"I have not heard of that name before. Is he an accomplice of Herr Hitler?"

"I am gobsmacked you have not heard of Herr Streicher! He is an old campaigner for the Führer and organized the first highly successful boycott of Jewish businesses back in 1933. He runs the inspirational weekly paper, *Der Stürmer*. If you need bedtime reading I can lend you back issues."

"I will let you know if I do. Right now I'm going out for a bite to eat."

"What time will you return Herr Elser?" asks Frau Baumann.
"Maybe about ten?"
"We will wait up for you," she offers.
"No need. If you give me a key I can let myself in."
"We prefer to wait up."
"In that case I will try not to be too late."
"We hope not. My husband and I are not night owls."

Without any further exchange I depart Baumann's cosy little Nazi nest to cross Blumenstrasse to the Viktualienmarkt. As the time is closing in on 8 pm and as the sun is setting in the west, the stallholders have already packed away their leftovers. Being too late for a market meal, and not wanting to sit with the glassy-eyed lager drinkers, I continue on to Marienplatz where stands the monstrous neo-gothic Rathaus. Without stopping to gawk in wonder I descend to the basement restaurant, the Ratskeller.

Though packed to the stony arches with rowdy customers I soon attract the attention of a waitress and order weisswurst with mustard, a pretzel and a glass of beer. I could have gone the whole hog and ordered ratsherrenschmankerl but I need to be frugal with my savings. At last count 375 marks is all I have to last until November 8. After that date I will need to look for work, not in Germany but in Switzerland. This is the plan I have dovetailed into my mind. Whether my plan is realized only time will decide.

With the white pork sausage still swilling in my stomach, I pay my bill and head back into Marienplatz. From there I walk the short distance to the Church of Saint Peter. For several minutes I stand gazing up at the clocks on the tower and the spire that disappears into the darkness. As the church doors are locked preventing my entry, I wander only a little further in the streets of the old city before heading back to Baumann's apartment. I do not want them up too late on my account—at least not on my first night.

"Back already," says Frau Baumann as she opens the door.
"I'm afraid I am."
"I trust you found somewhere suitable to dine."
"I did, and took a short walk afterwards."
"The city sights are impressive at night," remarks Frau Baumann.

"They are, though I did happen to see a department store in need of some repair not so far from the Church of Saint Peter."

"I presume you're referring to Uhlfelder's old department store on Jakobsplatz," interjects Herr Baumann, rising abruptly from his chair. "That valuable property is up for sale due to the owner emigrating to India."

"India? That seems a strange move for a successful businessman," I remark.

"We thought the same. Most Jews emigrate to the UK or the USA after their stay in Dachau during the orderly transfer of their assets to non-Jewish citizens."

"I confess I have my doubts about the fairness of this procedure."

"You do? I can assure you everything is done strictly in compliance with the asset management principles of the Office of Aryanization," explains Herr Baumann.

"Even so____"

"Even so what! The procedure could not be better. Those Jews who can afford to emigrate—will emigrate. Those less well off must make the most of living in a concentration camp. And it is only right Uhlfelder pays for all the broken glass and damage done to his premises before he goes to India."

"But____?"

"But nothing! You forget the Jews are only paying back what they stole from us in the first place!" Herr Baumann explodes.

"I will consider what you have said in bed," I answer, thinking he might burst a blood vessel should I continue to speak my mind.

"You must remember Herr Elser, the Jews are a defilement of our community and a threat to national security," adds Herr Baumann for good measure, as he knocks the ash from his pipe into his smokers' stand.

When Herr Baumann returns to his chair and his wife returns to her knitting, I head to my room.

"Remember breakfast is served at 7.30 am, Herr Elser," I hear Frau Baumann call as I close my door.

2

August 10, 1939

Munich

THIS is already my fifth day in Munich. After registering with the police I have kept mainly to my room, spending much time in bed. When Frau Baumann queried my shiftless state I explained I have enrolled in a polishing course that is yet to commence. Since then she has found odd jobs for me like shopping and splitting wood in the basement. Otherwise I do as little as possible. I am happy not to read books or newspapers. Nor have I bothered Herr Baumann for copies of *Der Stürmer*. I have more important things to occupy my mind than pages of lurid cartoons of Jews.

For instance, the considerable sum I have paid for my board still troubles me. Every day I must seek out cheap meals in the back streets to compensate. Had I not paid in advance I would have moved out yesterday — though there is something even more pressing on my mind. Now that my two toolboxes have arrived — thanks to Maria Schmauder's father shipping them by rail — I have no legitimate reason not to start my work tonight.

Inside one of my toolboxes I have packed a small brown vulcanized case, like the sort a child would take to school. In this small case I have assembled a modest selection of my hand tools. After double-checking I have everything I need, including a flashlight, I lock the padlock on my trunk and slip the key into my coat pocket. Dressed in well-worn clothes that suggest I am nothing other than an honest tradesman, I am ready to leave.

As is usual at this hour of the day the reluctant night owls are perched in their sitting room. Frau Baumann's knitting needles are clicking while her balding husband is busy tweaking the dials of his humming Volksempfänger.

"Please excuse me, but tonight I am starting my polishing course, so don't wait up as the course goes all night," I say crossing the room like a spirit.

"Good night Herr Elser," I hear Frau Baumann call, as if what I said has not registered.

Her husband does not have time to pipe up before I disappear out the door.

Once in the street I breathe in the fresh night air. With my small case tucked under my arm I stride along Blumenstrasse going in the direction of Isartorplatz. After the Viktualienmarkt, I turn into Frauenstrasse to reach Zweibrückenstrasse, the broad avenue that sweeps down to the Ludwig Bridge and the river. Since I arrived in Munich last Saturday I have not once crossed the Isar. When I do it will be like I am crossing the Rubicon.

The clock on the tower of Müllers public baths on the far bank reads 7.25 pm as I cross. I glance down at the glistening flow but do not dare to stop. Up the incline of Rosenheimerstrasse, not so far from the river, I come to the arched portal in the high wall where italic letters spell out: Bürger-Bräu-Keller.

Not giving myself time to hesitate or to reconsider anything I have decided in the past, I step through the entry doors and stride across the vestibule. I soak up several minutes washing and drying my hands in the men's washroom before making my grand entry into the Bürgerbräu restaurant. I know my way around as I was here during Easter this year and during November of last year. I also know every day of the week customers can enjoy a moderately priced hot meal washed down with Bürgerbräu beer.

Not wanting to appear a person with something to hide I take a seat at a vacant table towards the middle of the dining room. As there are more vacant tables than diners I do not have long to wait to be served. The young waitress who comes to take my order is better stacked than the one who served me on my last visit. She has an impish look and wears her long plaits curled up on her head, as do most of the waitresses here.

"Sauerbraten with roggenbrot and a glass of beer," I order.

"You don't want a jug of beer?" she queries.

"No, only a glass as I am a teetotaller, and I do not wish to drink a whole jug."

The young waitress gives me a quizzical look, notes my order on her pad and leaves. What I said to her about being a teetotaller is not that far from the truth as I once had a girlfriend who belonged to a temperance union. That was almost ten years ago while I was still living a restless life far from my mother's control.

When the same waitress brings my meal I cannot help asking her a simple question.

"What is your name?"

"Why do you want to know?" she asks back.

"Because you have a pretty face."

"Gerda," she answers, before rushing away with her face as red as a beetroot.

When I finish my meal at 8.30 pm I still have a centimetre of beer left in my glass, entitling me to remain seated at the table. It is another two hours to closing time so I have more time than I need to drink the rest of my beer. I try not to think too much about the work ahead of me tonight or the night after and the night after that. How many nights my work takes is not important. I once had a roommate who always said, 'the end justifies the means'. He turned out to be a Communist and had a sudden end in 1933.

Rather than thinking of the future I try thinking of the past. But by staring at the beer left in the glass only brings my father into my mind. And he is someone I take no pleasure in thinking about. He cannot hold his liquor—as they say. My dear mother after toiling all day in the field always had a mop and bucket ready when he came in late, and while she suffered my father's drinking affliction downstairs, his children cowered in their beds upstairs. We could hear him abusing her until he passed out. Only then did we get to sleep.

"Would you like another glass?" I hear the same young waitress say into my ear.

"Nay," I say and she leaves me be.

I check my wristwatch to read 9.25 pm. I still have at least another hour to wait about. When I was here before I observed the opening and closing times of the doors to the hall. They are open during the day and locked at night between 10.30 pm and 11.30 pm. That being the case I still have time to think about Hilda Lang. When I was living in Konstanz Hilda was the girl who took me to the temperance union meetings, warning me of the perils of grog—as if my father was not warning enough! Once a month the adherents held their social get-togethers, often playing childish games like würstchenschnappen. Hilda was a seamstress and she was astonished when I made her a folding sewing table. I recall how I walked her home late one night from a temperance union meeting. We paused in a doorway in a dark city street. Without saying a word I held her chin and kissed her lips. Though she was devout, attending the Catholic Church every Sunday, one kiss was all it took to___

I glance at my watch: 10.25 pm. Time to make a move! I drink the last drop in my glass, pay at the till and leave. With my small case in hand I go to the men's washroom, as this will be my last opportunity for some time tonight. After leaving the washroom I pass the cloakroom to reach the hall, hoping no one will challenge me for going the wrong way at this time of night.

When I push through the double doors I find the great hall is still partially lit, though nobody is about as far as I can tell. The chandeliers that hang from the decorative plaster ceiling have been extinguished, though the lights under the long galleries on each side of the hall are still burning. I do not stop until I reach a gallery staircase tucked into a corner of the hall. At the top of the staircase I pass behind a row of tables and chairs to reach a door at the end of the gallery. The door is unlocked as expected, though the room is stacked with empty cardboard boxes. This is unexpected as on my previous visit this room was empty. I have no idea where the boxes have come from, what they contained or who put them there. While this is unsettling I realise the boxes will be useful to screen me should someone happen to open the door while I am inside.

Once the boxes are redeployed and I've stepped into the workpants I had packed into my small case, I stretch out on the floor behind the cardboard boxes. This is where I must lie and wait until all the hall lights have been extinguished, all the doors have been locked and all the staff have left for the night.

As I lie on the floor in total darkness I would have had total silence if not for the periodic flushing every ten minutes of the automatic urinals in the men's washroom on the floor below. I am sick of hearing the urinals flush by the time I hear the sound of the hall doors being locked. I also sense the hall lights have been extinguished, but to be safe I remain concealed for another twenty minutes before I dare come from my hiding place.

In the nightlight that seeps through the windows on one side of the hall I make my way back along the gallery, passing behind the row of tables and chairs to the candidate pillar. Of the eight great pillars in the hall this is the pillar I selected after my first visit in November last year. This is the same pillar I observed to stand directly behind the speaker's podium erected for the reunion rally. The pillar has considerable bulk, being about seven metres in height with an ornamental ionic capital at the top.

With the dark silhouette of the pillar looming before me, something odd happens—my teeth start to chatter. This is something I did not anticipate. I cannot comprehend if I am exhilarated or petrified by the enormity of the task I have set myself. Not waiting for enlightenment I drop to my knees, open my small case and take out my flashlight. I need to start without delay. Any hesitation now could annihilate my decision to act.

Fearing the beam from my flashlight will glow through the windows and betray my presence I take a blue cloth from my pocket to wrap over the lens. With the flashlight dimmed I make a thorough inspection to determine where and how to make an opening in the wooden panelling to reveal the inner structure of the pillar. Making minimal sound, I remove a skirting board and prise off several timber moulds. With that done I make neat saw cuts in the panelling. This work takes over three hours, but one slipup in the initial stage could multiply errors down the line. And besides, I have no need to rush my work. There are still three months to go before the annual reunion rally of the Nazi leaders here on November 8.

With the skirting board and the timber moulds reattached my saw cuts in the panelling are concealed and the pillar looks exactly the way it looked before my intervention began. I pack my tools back into my small case and use a soft cloth to remove any trace of sawdust on the floor and the surrounds.

Returning to the storeroom I wave my flashlight in the darkness. It crosses my mind to flatten a cardboard box to soften the floor, but I decide against the idea. A flattened box would be an obvious sign an intruder had slept the night.

Lying on my side with my head propped on my small case I doze on and off, checking the time whenever I wake by placing my flashlight against my wristwatch. From my previous observations the hall doors are not unlocked until between 7.30 and 8.30 in the morning. As the temperature drops I fold my arms across my chest and draw up my knees into the foetal position. Morning cannot come soon enough.

My night ends when I wake at 7.25 am. I hear the sound of the doors being unlocked ten minutes later, though to be doubly safe I do not leave the storeroom for another twenty minutes. Before leaving I remove my workpants and lay them folded in a corner, trusting no one will think anything of blue workpants should they be found. With my small case in hand I go down the staircase at the end of the gallery and leave the hall by a door that takes me past the kitchen to the beer garden. From there I can reach the street at the rear. By acting in a self confident manner no one will suspect me of being up to something should I meet someone on the way out. At least this is my theory.

From Kellerstrasse I cut back to the Ludwig Bridge, cross the Isar and hurry along Zweibrückenstrasse to a kiosk at Isartorplatz. Newspaper, tobacco and flower sellers are manning their stalls. Motorcars, buses, trams and bikes are on the streets. The people of Munich are out of bed and going to work—all oblivious to the work I have commenced on their behalf. To celebrate the start of my vital work I treat myself to a cup of coffee.

3
Munich
September 1, 1939

HERR Baumann has had his ear up to the Volksempfänger all through breakfast listening to the latest bulletins on the Polish situation. With his wife on kitchen duty he attacks me with his prognosis of the overnight invasion.

"First the Poles refuse our ultimatum for a plebiscite to settle the border dispute. Next day they have the nerve to attack a German radio station at Gleiwitz. What option did the Führer have other than send in the Wehrmacht?"

"We only ever hear one side of the story," I return across the table.

"I hope you are not suggesting the Führer is being less than honest?" Herr Baumann retorts.

I make no reply, preferring to apply myself to spreading a healthy dollop of plum jam onto a thick slice of toasted sauerteigbrot.

"Our Führer would not misinform the German people on such an important matter as our national security," offers Frau Baumann as she comes from the kitchen bearing a bowl of hard-boiled eggs.

"But why would the Poles bother to attack a German radio station? What would be the point? What would they hope to gain?" I ask, unable to hold my tongue.

"Whatever the reason might be the Führer knows what is best for the German people," concludes Herr Baumann before popping an egg into his mouth.

I might have provoked him further had I gone on to say:

But this idiotic act of aggression will bring the British and the French down on our heads, unleashing an almighty conflagration.

Instead I am happy to fill my stomach, eating as much as I possibly can while I still have the opportunity. Ten minutes later I am ready to make my grand announcement.

"I regret to say this will be my last breakfast with you."

"Oh! Are you returning to your hometown Herr Elser?" asks Frau Baumann.

"Not yet. I must finish the polishing course first."

"I will miss you not being here to split wood for me," admits Frau Baumann.

"I will miss doing that too, though I could always call by whenever you need me."

"I would pay you of course," offers Frau Baumann.

"Any payment from you would be greatly valued," I reply, causing her husband's eyes to revolve as if his coffee is poisoned.

"Please vacate your room by 10 am," he snaps as I get up from the table.

"I will be gone before 9 am, though if I may be permitted to leave my luggage here until midday that would be appreciated."

"Of course you may Herr Elser," replies Frau Baumann, not waiting for her husband to reject my reasonable request.

I vacate my room at 8.45 am, leaving my trunk and my two toolboxes in my room, the only place Frau Baumann could find to store them. Once in Färbergraben I head in the direction of the Karlstor. As I draw near to the old city gateway I see technicians reeling out wires to connect loudspeakers hung from the central archway. With no inclination to discover the reason for this installation, I avoid busy Karlsplatz and make a detour taking me past the Jewish Synagogue, now but a pitiful pile of rubble. After that scene of wilful destruction I cross the tramlines running along the broad Maximilianplatz. Reaching Briennerstrasse I take the first right turn into Türkenstrasse, a narrow street that runs as straight as a die.

After several cross streets I come to No.94, a five-storey apartment building with shops beneath. I am happy to see the 'room for rent' sign is still on display. No one was at home when I came by yesterday. I climb the stairs to the second floor and ring the doorbell of apartment No.11. Baumann's apartment is also No.11 I recall. What a coincidence, I think as I ring a second time.

"Hello!" I hear behind me.

I turn to see a woman with brown hair tied in a long plait has come up the stairway nursing a bunch of rhubarb. I also notice she is heavily pregnant.

"Frau Lehmann?" I inquire.

"Yes."

"I have come about the room to rent advertised on the sign in the street."

"One moment and I will unlock the door."

"Let me hold your rhubarb while you find your key."

"Thank you. I must warn you the room is small and breakfast is not included in the four marks per week."

"I am only a light eater so breakfast is not so important to me."

"Of course you are always welcome to make yourself a bowl of haferschrot," Frau Lehmann adds, as I follow her inside.

"What is your name?" she asks, half turning towards me.

"Georg Elser."

"Well Herr Elser, put the rhubarb on the table and I will show you the room."

We backtrack to a room like a closet near the front door. There is barely space to fit my wooden trunk let alone my two toolboxes even when stacked one on top of the other. A musty smell suggests poor ventilation, though there is a tiny bedside table, a desk and a coat hook on the wall.

"This will be ideal for me," I say without hesitation. Frau Lehmann's amiable manner is more than enough compensation for any physical defects the room may have.

"I hope you will be comfortable here. My husband, Alfons, is an upholsterer and leaves early for work each morning," Frau Lehmann informs me as if this is something important for me to remember.

"Shall I pay you for my first week's rent now?" I ask, keen to secure the lodging.

"If you wish, though Alfons would kill me if I don't first ask your occupation."

"I'm a skilled carpenter currently involved in inventive work," I submit.

"Alfons will be pleased to hear you are honestly employed."

Encouraged further, I eagerly hand over four marks and promise to return with my baggage.

I return to the streets to retrace my steps back to Baumann's apartment. As I draw near to the Karlstor the humdrum of the city is broken by an ear-piercing screech followed by a great eruption issuing from the loudspeakers. People stop as if paralysed. The tyrannic tone is unmistakable. The Führer is on the warpath making a public broadcast. While many are trapped in the open I keep moving in the back streets to escape the claptrap. But escape is impossible. More loudspeakers are installed at the old gate at Sendlinger Tor, and probably at every other public place in the city to announce the inevitable war of Nazi design has begun. When I climb the stairs to Baumann's apartment I imagine I will be free of the din. Nay. Reaching the landing the blare of the Volksempfänger is coming under the door like hot wind.

___German defence forces will carry on the battle for the honour of the living rights of the re-awakened German people with firm determination I expect every German soldier, in view of the great tradition of eternal German soldiery, to do his duty until the end. Remember always in all situations you are the representatives of National Socialist Greater Germany!**

Long live our people and our Reich!

Only after the gypsy dictator has climaxed do I dare sound the doorbell to retrieve my regime changing gear.

4 September 1, 1939
The Hague

___Long live our people and our Reich!

Jan Lemmens disconnects the crystal set that sits on his workbench. The frenetic voice of the German Chancellor is still ringing in his ears as he returns to polishing the big red car. The duco is sparkling like a vintage red when a tall lean figure comes through the open doorway from the street.

"Is she ready to go?"

"Oh! Mr Best, you gave me a start," says Lemmens.

"Sorry, old boy."

"I've changed the engine oil and topped up the water in the radiator but I still have to whiten the whitewall tyres, Mr. Best."

"Leave it for another day. They look fine to me. You Dutch are all the same — damn perfectionists."

"If you say so, Mr Best."

"I have a business meeting in half an hour's time and I'll be damned if I'm going to roll up in a tram. Put the bill in the mail, will you Jan?"

"I will, Mr Best."

"Good man."

"Shall I back her out for you, Mr Best?" asks Lemmens.

"If you would. Better you dent my mudguards on your doorposts than me."

Lemmens gets in behind the wheel and turns the key to set the twelve cylinders into motion. The Ford Lincoln Zephyr inches out of the garage in reverse.

"Did you hear the news, Mr Best?" asks Lemmens, once he has safely parked the car by the kerb.

"I presume you are referring to the plight of the Poles. Herr Hitler might have bitten off more than he can chew this time."

"Do you think so, Mr Best?" asks Lemmens, holding the door open for the owner.

"I jolly well hope so. Though I may need you to drive me places. But not today, Jan."

"Just say the word, Mr Best."

"I will. How's the wife?"

"Good for someone gone eight months."

"Give her my regards."

"I will, Mr Best."

Without saying another word Best climbs into the driver's seat, slams the door and drives off down the street. Jan Lemmens stands on the kerb watching until the gleaming red car turns right and is out of sight.

Ten minutes later Best is nosing the Lincoln into a parking bay in front of the grandiose seaside institution of Hotel Kurhaus. A dark bank of threatening cloud is already hanging over the North Sea as Best mounts the steps like a man half his age. The doorman tips his cap and holds the door open as Best strides into the glass-vaulted lobby. He checks his hat and coat in at the cloakroom and proceeds to the palm-laden restaurant. As diners are in short supply Best has little difficulty in tracking down one Englishman. At a table with a fine view of the gathering storm sits a dark-suited man with a head of neat thinning black hair, black eyebrows and a black moustache cut precisely to align with the extremities of his mouth.

"Richard Stevens," he introduces himself, rising to his feet.

"Payne Best," responds Best, as they shake hands.

Once the two settle into their chairs, Stevens is first to resume the pleasantries.

"I was told to keep an eye out for a tall chap with a monocle, so when you came through the door___"

"You knew you had your man?"

"Exactly. Is Payne your Christian name?"

"No, I was christened 'Sigismund' by my wise and loving parents. Payne Best is my double-bung surname. But I prefer to be simply known as, 'Best'.

"Best is best you might say," remarks Stevens.

"You could."

"And Payne is a pain?"

"You have a sense of humour I see, but at other people's expense."

"I did not mean to offend."

"No offence taken, old boy."

"Ready to order gentlemen?" inquires the tuxedoed waiter from Java.

The Englishmen order a light luncheon: a dozen oesters natuurlijke each, followed by coq au vin, washed down with a bottle of Spätburgunder from the Rhineland.

"I hear you are married," remarks Stevens after the waiter has left with the order.

"Your intelligence is good. May is my second wife in fact. She is Dutch and paints quite well for a woman. And what about you?" Best inquires.

"My wife keeps a low profile."

"She sounds an ideal woman. So how did you find India, doing your bit for God and country?"

"India is what you make it. Some hated it. Others, like me, loved it."

"Did you shoot many?"

"Many what?"

"Tigers."

"Not me. I played hockey mainly, and was pretty darn good, until my shin splints gave me curry."

"Bad show."

The conversation is paused when the waiter from Java returns with the oesters natuurlijke and the bottle of pinot noir. Neither man has an appetite for polite conversation once food and wine is on the table.

When the plates are cleared and after the two Englishmen have emptied their glasses and used their serviettes to dab their chins, Best offers his companion a cigarette from his half smoked packet of Pall Malls. Stevens accepts and both light up like they have done this before. After Best has blown a dense smoke screen across the table, he is ready to ask Stevens a question.

"Do you think Chamberlain will?"

"Will what?"

"Declare war."

"I only follow orders, not speculate on the future," replies Stevens.

"Aren't you speaking to Whitehall daily?"

"Yes, but with 'C' riddled with cancer things are in an unholy mess in Broadway."

"Poor old Hugh Sinclair. He's given his life to the SIS."

"Coffee gentlemen?" asks the same tuxedoed waiter from Java.

Stevens wastes no time in sending the waiter away with an order for two lang sort kaffe.

"Perhaps we should get down to tin tacks," says Stevens.

"Like what?"

"My understanding is they want us to work more closely together if war is declared."

"When I worked with Dansey during the 1914-18 war we knew more about the Huns than they knew about themselves. I ended the war with an OBE. I must have been doing something right you would think," responds Best.

"So you want to run the show?"

"Not necessarily. I'm just saying I probably know the lay of the land in Europe better than you. Do you speak German?" asks Best.

"Fluently".

"Any other languages?"

"French, Russian, Greek as well as Arabic, Hindustani and Malay. My mother was Greek so Greek is my second language," replies Stevens.

"No Dutch?"

"I'm working on it."

"You have a few up on me. I manage to get by with Dutch, German and French," concedes Best, stubbing out his cigarette as if to signal he has tired of the linguistics competition.

"I can see nothing wrong with pooling our resources, if only in the field of communications," Stevens observes.

"Nor I, old boy."

"So who is picking up the tab today?"

"We could always go Dutch?"

"Seems appropriate," concludes Stevens.

There is a spit of rain as they descend the hotel steps. Best gives Stevens a lift back to a large three-storey residence on Nieuwe Parklaan, a wide avenue in the salubrious suburb of Scheveningen, no more than two kilometres from Hotel Kurhaus.

Once Stevens is out of the car Best can think more coherently on the merit, if any, of hitching his 'Z' organisation to the so-called 'Passport Control Office', another undercover operation of British intelligence that Stevens now heads in The Netherlands. As both intelligence networks ultimately report back to the same people in London, Best can see nothing wrong in playing his cards close to his chest for a little longer, at least until the dust settles on collaboration.

Not that far from the city centre and the Binnenhof, the sprawling complex of buildings housing of the Dutch Parliament, Best parks his car in Nieuwe Uitleg. A canal and a row of houses flank the cobbled tree-lined street. He has a short walk to his office in a three-storey merchant's house built in a past era. A brass nameplate beside the front door reads 'Pharmisan.'

Best hangs his hat and umbrella on the hallstand, lights a cigarette, and settles at his office desk to thumb through his mail. Giving his full attention to private business matters involving the import and export of pharmaceuticals is difficult when he is expecting a stranger to call. An hour later a chubby faced, balding man dressed like an eager salesman is ushered into Best's office by his Dutch business partner, P. N. van der Willik.

"Please take a seat, Dr. Fischer," says Best, once his partner has left.

"Danke."

"Cigarette?"

"Nein—but I would welcome a drink."

"Dutch gin?"

"Ja. Anything."

Best goes to the sideboard to pour a glass for the German and one for himself.

"You're probably wondering why I phoned yesterday to bring you here today," says Best as he hands Fischer his glass.

"I thought you might be offering me a job in your company. I'm good with money. Though I suspect you are interested in my excellent work for Dr. Karl Spiecker."

"Even with your doctorate in economics, employing someone who has fled Germany to avoid facing a charge of embezzlement would be rash, to say the least."

"I was not going to wait around for a Nazi court to decide my fate," Fischer mutters.

"Sorry to raise your past misdeeds, old boy, though you are right about my interest in your involvement with Spiecker. But I understand you spent time in Switzerland after you fled Germany before your met with Spiecker," states Best, as he opens up a manila folder lying on his desk.

"But I did no skiing in Switzerland. I had to spend a few months in hospital in Berne after an operation before the Swiss deported me to France in June 1935."

"What date did you say you fled Germany?"

"I didn't, but I'll tell you anyway—January, 1935. Exactly six months after the Röhm-Putsch.

"Oh—the Röhm-Putsch! Hitler certainly showed his true colours in that vile bloodbath. Who knows what evil he is capable of with his wild ideas for an Aryan-Nordic master race?"

"This is my fear also, and this is why Dr. Spiecker founded the German Freedom Party and continues the fight against Nazism while in exile."

"How you came to meet Spiecker?"

"I was introduced to him by Dr. Emil Ludwig."

"Emil Ludwig? Was he not the writer who made a name for himself with interviews of Mussolini, Stalin, Mustafa Atatürk and Masaryk, the first President of Czechoslovakia?"

"I remember Ludwig as an intense Jewish man from Breslau so that would not surprise me."

"And after being introduced to Spiecker did you became involved in his activities?" asks Best as he prepares to light a cigarette.

"Ja. I knew of Dr. Spiecker when Chancellor Brüning made him a special envoy to the Reichstag with the tough job of combating National Socialism. When Hitler came into power Dr. Spiecker lost his post and had to migrate to France. To his credit he continued his work against the Nazi Party and Hitlerism from Paris. When he asked me to join his party I willingly agreed. He gave me the task of making contact with military officers."

"I presume you're talking about dissident military officers opposed to Hitler."

"Ja. I am. Another war would be a catastrophe for Germany."

"And did you make contact with any rebellious military characters?"

"After much effort I managed to make a connection with a Luftwaffe intelligence officer and introduced him to Dr. Spiecker and two other like-minded party men at the Carlton Hotel in Amsterdam. This was in January 1938 before I was moved on to The Netherlands. As you may be aware the French government is unsympathetic to German refugees in France."

"Did you come straight to The Hague from France?"

"Nein. I lived in Amsterdam at the Eden Hotel in Warmoesstraat, a small shabby hotel, but ideal for Germans escaping from the Nazis. Now I live with two fellow refugees in The Hague — Paul Schreiber and his wife Suzanne Menzel. Paul is a painter and they are planning to make a movie. I have been helping them by trying to raise the finance for their project."

"Well good luck with that. But getting back to this Luftwaffe fellow I understand he has come up with useful intelligence."

"Ja. He has. Dr. Spiecker sent me to London to deliver his intelligence to Mr. Stead."

"Stead! I assume you're referring to Mr. Wickham Stead, the former editor of *The Times* newspaper and now the self-appointed enemy of the Nazis."

"I only know that Mr. Stead is in cahoots with Dr. Spiecker."

"And what was the nature of the intelligence you took to Mr. Stead?"

"He provided the date of the German invasion of the Sudetenland and the date of the invasion of Poland. Both dates have now proved to be correct."

"With the invasion of Poland last Friday it appears Spiecker is now fighting for a lost cause."

"Not so. Though the German people have fallen under the spell of Hitler, there are high-ranking officers with no enthusiasm for this war."

"We are aware of the undercurrent of discontent in the military. But is there an appetite in the Wehrmacht to take a firm stand against the Nazi leaders?"

"There is—from what my Luftwaffe friend has said. He has his ear to the ground."

"Can you set up a meeting with him?"

"Possibly."

"How soon?"

"I will need to get back to you."

"Do that. Any meeting will need to be held here or in Amsterdam," advises Best.

"That may not be possible."

"No?" returns Best, rising from his desk.

"I will check."

"Well let me know."

"Ja, I will," answers Dr. Franz Fischer, scoffing down his last drop of Dutch gin before the Englishman sees him to the door.

5 September 3, 1939
Munich

ALL is quiet in Lehmann's apartment this morning. My new landlady and her man have not stirred from their bedroom giving me free run of the bathroom to wash my hair. I stayed in bed all yesterday after a long night of work at the Bürgerbräukeller. Today I'll resist the temptation to repeat my idleness even if today is a Sunday. After shaving and dressing casually I have a bowl of haferschrot in the kitchen without hindrance. No doubt Rosa and Alfons Lehmann will come to life once they hear me leave the premises.

I have no destination in my mind when I step into Türkenstrasse, though instinctively I turn to the left towards the old city. After going two blocks I turn right into Schellingstrasse, a street I've not yet walked. All the expensive cafés are closed and even if they were open I suspect they would not serve a Swabian on the loose with barely a bean to his name. At the corner with Schraudolphstrasse Nazi flags hang like dirty linen from upper windows of an Italian restaurant that bears the name Osteria Bavaria.

When I reach the next intersection in Schellingstrasse I turn left into

Arcisstrasse, a long street that leads to a broad open space flanked by Greek style buildings. As I gaze across the new stone pavement I notice two lines snaking through two pure white temples. I join one of the lines to discover the attraction that requires two armed sentries to stand like statues each side of the entry steps. As I draw near I observe how the twin temples are mirror images, each being square in plan with white marble columns supporting a white marble roof with a central opening to let in rain and sunlight. Once inside the temple every eye is cast downwards into the stone depression where are rowed eight black cast iron caskets.

"Who or what is inside these ugly caskets?" I ask the fat woman ahead of me.

She rolls her eyes and turns away as if not to know me.

"The blood martyrs of the Beer Hall Putsch," barks the old man behind me, having overheard my question.

"The blood martyrs?" I query.

"The sixteen with the Führer who willingly sacrificed their lives at the Feldherrnhalle in 1923. The sixteen who died for the resurrection of the German people," says the old man with his hat pressed against his chest.

Hearing this hocus pocus, I break free from the line of brain dead pilgrims and hurry from Königsplatz, going into Briennerstrasse. I turn left into Türkenstrasse and do not break my stride until I have come to the shopfront of the ironmonger, Suckfüll. Peering through the plate glass at the objects in the window display, I forget my close encounter with the blood martyrs to think on higher planes. Purchase of any one of these precision tools would set me back a packet, though I know I will have to fork out something soon on screws, bolts, nuts and washers to complete my apparatus. But not today.

The time is a little past midday as I approach Alter Simpl, a tavern halfway along Türkenstrasse, only a block from Lehmann's apartment. As the doors are open for business I step inside for the first time. Inside the walls are half-timber panelled and hung with rows of neatly framed cartoon pictures. Sunshine streams through two high arched windows onto the well-worn wooden furniture. I take a seat at one of the several vacant tables and place my order with the waitress. I have barely dipped my spoon into my ochsenschwanzsuppe when a bearish fellow looms up beside me.

"You're sitting at my table," he growls.

"Sorry, I did not realize this table was reserved," I reply.

"I have an unofficial reservation."

"There are three other chairs," I advise, expecting his hairy fist to land on my chin.

"Jörg Brög," he says, offering me his hand to shake instead.

"Georg Elser."

"Your accent is Swabian," he observes as he eases his bulk into the chair opposite.

"I come from the one horse town of Königsbronn."

"In the Brenz Valley?"

"Aye, though I should not have called it a one horse town as my father once had a team of horses and a wagon."

"A wagon! What's his business?"

"Timber merchant."

"Has he motorized now?"

"Nay. He is more immobilized, than motorized."

"I am sorry to hear that."

"What about yourself. What is your calling?" I ask.

"Master carpenter."

"We have something in common then."

"What's that?"

"I'm a cabinetmaker."

"Carpenter, cabinetmaker, what's the difference?"

"These days one must be flexible and take whatever work is on offer. Are you going to order?" I ask.

"No need. The waitress brings me what you're having every day of the week."

"Ochsenschwanzsuppe?"

"Right."

Brög's blue eyes brighten when the waitress brings his bowl of soup with a slice of weissbrot. His fuzzy white beard is so vast it grows out of his ears.

"So what brings you to Munich, my friend. Are you escaping from a woman?" asks Brög as he drapes a napkin down his grubby overalls.

"Nay. I am here to assassinate the Führer."

"I hope you joke!"

"Yes—I do."

"You must not say such things in public or to strangers. Who knows what will happen to you? Take for example that Swiss crackpot, Maurice Bavaud."

"What do you mean?"

"Don't you read the newspapers?"

"Nay."

"Bavaud came to Munich to shoot the Führer during the annual Nazi march from the Bürgerbräukeller last November. But all he managed to do was to run out of money and board a train bound for Paris without a ticket."

"I am glad he got away."

"He did not get away, my friend. The ticket inspector turned him over to the Gestapo when he found the young guy still had his pistol in his pocket."

"There must be a lesson in there somewhere," I conclude.

I let Brög enjoy his ochsenschwanzsuppe before I attempt to speak again.

"My real purpose for being in Munich is to work on my invention."

"Invention! What is the nature of your invention?"

"It is hard for me to explain, though when my invention is realized people will wonder how they managed to live without my invention."

"Sounds a worthwhile investment."

"I hope so. My difficulty has been finding a workshop where I can tinker."

"Tinker? I may be of some assistance to you. My workshop is next door at Türkenstrasse 59. I work independently but sometimes I need an extra hand."

"If I scratch your back you will scratch my back. Is that what you are saying?"

"Exactly, my friend. If you are interested, call in sometime. But don't come until after 3 pm, as I like to take a nap after lunch."

To fill in time to 3 pm I take a long walk around the block, letting the ochsenschwanzsuppe settle. After passing by the straight edge edifices of the State library and the university buildings, I continue to the Siegestor, another stone gateway to the old city. As I walk back through the streets I think Brög's offer is like an answer to prayer, with his workshop being so close to where I am living. The location will save much time in the final weeks of the assembly of my apparatus, I muse as I step off the kerb.

"Watch it mister!"

I stop in the nick of time—clutching hold of the handlebars to prevent the rider crashing to the road. I hang on longer than I need, intrigued by her permed hair falling across her pale face, her mouth embalmed in bright red lipstick.

"Is this the way to the Englischer Garten?" the young woman asks in poor German.

"Just keep going in the direction you are going and you will get there," I reply, though I have never been to the English Garden.

"Then let go of my bike!" she pleads as a tear drops from a doleful eye.

I reluctantly let the beauty go—giving her seat a good shove to send her on her way. She peddles off with a wobble, her pleated skirt rising above her knees, her handbag strung diagonally over her shoulder. As I stand watching her disappear I think how odd to see a young English woman cycling in Munich.

Not wanting to appear overeager I arrive in front of the five-storey building at Türkenstrasse 59 a good fifteen minutes after 3 pm. The wicket gate in the double doors is unlocked when I try the lever handle. On the other side of the doors a covered passage leads to the yard at the rear of the building. Brög is grumpy when I find him waking in a back room, but after splashing his face with water from a bucket his good nature returns.

"Take a look around. See what you think," he says, waving his hand in the air.

My eyes dance about from carpenter's bench to electric circular saw, to drop drill and grinding wheel. There is not much more I could have wished for.

"Here will be ideal for me to tinker on my invention," I enthuse.

As Brög gives me a bone-crunching handshake I decide to go for broke.

"I see you have a handcart. I need to move some stuff out of my lodging and into your storeroom. I trust this will not be an imposition."

"If you must, you must, I suppose. I'll go and get the key," answers the master carpenter.

Once I have the storeroom key in my hand, I waste no time in wheeling Brög's handcart down the passage and along the street to my lodging. I leave the handcart in the lobby and climb the stairs. My sudden entry into the apartment surprises the couple. Rosa is slumped on the sofa looking more pregnant than ever. Alfons is alongside her holding her hand being a good husband, while looking more downcast than usual.

"Is anything the matter?" I ask.

"Have you not heard the terrible news?" asks Alfons.

"Nay."

"Britain has declared war on Germany."

"Well it was only to be expected," I answer, realizing my decision to act is now more imperative than ever.

6

September 3, 1939
The Hague

BEST scurries down the stairs in his crimson smoking jacket as if the house has caught fire. Going into his library he twiddles the knobs on the Zenith wireless set until he has tuned into the BBC World Service.

"Are you there May! Come quick! Hurry!" he calls out several times.

Not waiting for his good lady, Best settles into his desk chair as the droll voice of Prime Minister, Neville Chamberlain, crackles from the speaker:

This morning the British Ambassador in Berlin handed the German Government a final Note stating that, unless we heard from them by 11 o'clock that they were prepared at once to withdraw their troops from Poland, a state of war would exist between us. I have to tell you now that no such undertaking has been received, and that consequently this country is at war with Germany. You can imagine what a bitter blow it is to me that all my long struggle to win peace has failed. Yet I cannot believe that there is anything more or anything different that I could have done and that would have been more successful. Up to the very last it would have been quite possible to have arranged a peaceful and honourable settlement between Germany and Poland, but Hitler would not have it. He had evidently made up his mind to attack Poland whatever happened, and although he now says he put forward reasonable proposals which were rejected by the Poles, that is not a true statement. The proposals were never shown to the Poles, nor to us, and, although they were announced in a German broadcast on Thursday night, Hitler did not wait to hear comments on them, but ordered his troops to cross the Polish frontier. His action shows convincingly that there is no chance of expecting that this man will ever give up his practice of using force to gain his will. He can only be stopped by force.

We and France are today, in fulfilment of our obligations, going to the aid of Poland, who is so bravely resisting this wicked and unprovoked attack on her people. We have a clear conscience. We have done all that any country could do to establish peace. The situation in which no word given by Germany's ruler could be trusted and no people or country could feel themselves safe has become intolerable. And now that we have resolved to finish it, I know that you will all play your part with calmness and courage.

At such a moment as this the assurances of support that we have received from the Empire are a source of profound encouragement to us. The Government have made plans under which it will be possible to carry on the work of the nation in the days of stress and strain that may be ahead. But these plans need your help. You may be taking your part in the fighting services or as a volunteer in one of the branches of Civil Defence. If so you will report for duty in accordance with the instructions you have received. You may be engaged in work essential to the prosecution of war for the maintenance of the life of the people - in factories, in transport, in public utility concerns, or in the supply of other necessaries of life. If so, it is of vital importance that you should carry on with your jobs.

Now may God bless you all. May He defend the right. It is the evil things that we shall be fighting against—brute force, bad faith, injustice, oppression and persecution—and against them I am certain that the right will prevail.

"Was that you shouting Siggy?" asks May, arriving not a moment too soon.

"Did you hear dear? We're at war!" exclaims Best, jumping up from his desk.

"You sound pleased."

"I am in a way."

"Then you're sicker than I thought. I'm thankful to be Dutch and to live in a neutral country."

"Don't count on it May. Herr Hitler will use any trick in the book to walk into Holland, just as he walked into Poland last Friday."

"Well I'm not staying in for him. I have an appointment."

"With whom?"

"I told you last week. Queen Wilhelmina is sitting for me."

"Another picture?"

"You idiot!"

With an incredulous glare May plants her cavalier hat on her head and storks out of the room. The sound of her slamming the front door has barely dissipated when the telephone rings. Best instantly lifts the receiver.

"Best."

"Did you hear the broadcast?" asks Stevens.

"I would think the whole world heard — apart from my wife."

"We need to talk."

"About what, old boy?"

"Whitehall has been on the teletype wanting to know if we have had any peace feelers."

"Already! And whose request is this? The PM?"

"Possibly."

"Are we talking about peace feelers from within Germany?"

"I would think from anywhere."

Best takes his time to pull a pack of Pall Malls from his top pocket and shake out a cigarette.

"Are you still there?" asks Stevens.

"I am. In fact I did have a chat with a German refugee living under our noses."

"When was this?"

"Two days ago."

"Why the dickens did you not mention this to me before now?"

"I assumed you were in the loop."

"What loop? Perhaps you can send me a memo on the matter," snorts Stevens.

"I will. Don't fret."

Stevens rings off. Best lights his cigarette and sits down at his desk. On the edge of his desk a gold framed photograph of his wife, May, and his stepson, Enzo, taken last year on a motoring holiday in Switzerland, is aimed in his direction.

As he swivels back and forth in his well-padded leather chair, Best casts his eye over his considerable collection of books filling his floor to ceiling shelves. He soon concludes there is nothing on his shelves to help him with his quandary over Dr. Franz Fischer. On one hand Fischer, though a bit testy appeared earnest enough. He was able to answer questions with a degree of conviction. And having the confidence of Dr. Karl Spiecker of the German Freedom Party, must count for something. On the other hand Fischer could be a decoy. His involvement with Dr. Spiecker and his role in delivering not insignificant intelligence to Wickham Steed in London could have been a stunt to win the confidence of Whitehall.

Best is not ignorant of Mr. Steed and his antics. He remembers the article Steed wrote a few years ago on German biological weapons research where he claimed experiments had been carried out in 1933 by German secret agents in certain Paris Metro and London underground stations. Whether true or not, the article so alarmed the British government the stockpiling of vaccines was ordered urgently as a counter measure. Going further back to 1920, Best recalls how Steed endorsed the anti-Semitic document, *The Protocols of the Learned Elders of Zion,* in an editorial in *The Times* newspaper. In the same editorial he blamed the Jews for the war of 1914-18. He also claimed Jews were the greatest threat to the British Empire. Though when *The Protocols* were shown to be a forgery by a colleague, Steed retracted his endorsement almost immediately.

As he stubs his cigarette in a glass ashtray, Best is forced to admit to himself that while these are fascinating sidetracks into the character of Wickham Steed, they shed no light whatsoever on the bona fide of Dr. Franz Fischer. He recalls it was Claude Dansey, his chief, who had instructed him to initiate contact with the refugee, Fischer—even if it was Dansey's no.2, Kenneth Cohen, who telephoned the instruction—so it is not as if he is acting entirely off his own bat. Best concludes asking Fischer to set up a meeting with someone who might put him in contact with the German Opposition in the Wehrmacht can do no harm. And after all, a positive outcome could be the difference between world peace and a catastrophic world war.

7
Munich

September 5-6, 1939

THE Lehmanns are eating the last of their rhubarb pie as I go out the door at 7.30 pm. They have accepted my nocturnal ways and have given up asking questions. When I told them I sometimes sleep on a park bench all night to conduct an experiment they must have realized their lodger is unhinged. But as long as I pay my board they have nothing to worry about.

By taking a longer route over the Isar via the Maximilian Bridge, avoiding Odeonplatz and the Feldherrnhalle, I arrive later than usual at the Bürgerbräukeller. A waitress named Berta is on hand to serve me tonight. I need to remind her, like the other waitresses here, how I always drink only one glass of beer with my meal of sauerbraten with roggenbrot.

After Berta has taken away my plate I remain at the table, as is my habit. There are other customers, many men who prefer the company of their beer-drinking comrades rather than going home to their loving wives and their children. As I sit rotating my half empty glass waiting for another hour to pass, my mind ranges over the good progress I have made in the past weeks.

The secret door in the timber panelling that encases the pillar is now complete. I needed to purchase and fit pivot hinges at the top and the bottom of the panel in order to avoid the use of butt hinges. The knuckle of a butt hinge would have protruded beyond the face of the panel, making the hinge visible to anyone with good eyesight standing close by. After completing the secret door I spent several nights removing the plaster finish in order to expose the brickwork that appears to comprise the structure of the pillar. Tonight I will commence a major component of my work: the hollowing out of the pillar. I am not at all relishing this phase, with the possibility of unforseen obstacles like pipes or steel stanchions being embedded inside. But I do not want to cross my bridges yet. Once I have finished this testing phase I can progress to more technically challenging components of my project.

With the time now at 10.20 pm, I drink down the last drop in my glass, rise from the table and go through my regular routine to reach the store at the end of the gallery. After spending an hour in my hiding place, lying like a sick dog behind the cardboard boxes, I come out to start my work.

With the secret door open and the plaster removed, I use my dimmed flashlight to inspect the exposed brickwork. I have had no previous experience removing brickwork expect for the short time I worked for a carpenter named Grupp in Königsbronn. He normally made furniture, but after a contract to supply office desks to the Wehrmacht ended, he turned to fabricating timber windows for cottages. I helped Grupp with the onsite installation and when I rubbed shoulders with bricklayers I learnt something of brickwork demolition: a few swift blows with a sledgehammer. But this technique though quick and easy is not feasible in this situation. I need to use a little more finesse and do all the work in silence.

Taking a brace and bit from my small case I start by drilling a series of holes in the mortar joints around the first brick to be removed. Even the rotation of the drill in the cement mortar makes a grinding sound and the smallest sound echoes inside the empty hall. Nevertheless I persist and once I have drilled sufficient holes I use a lever chisel to break out the mortar between the holes. Occasionally I must give the chisel a tap with a hammer but only when the noise is masked by the sound of the periodic flushing of the men's urinals. As an added precaution I wrap a rag around the handle of the chisel to deaden the impact sound.

At 2 am with only three bricks removed I am ready to finish for the night. The muscles in my back are screaming. My kneecaps pop back into place when I straighten up. I place my tools inside the cavity formed by the removal of three bricks to be ready for my next night of work. I pack the debris of bricks and mortar into a lidded cardboard box to take back to my hiding place. Disposal of the rubble will be dealt with at a later date. After closing the secret door and after I have wiped the floor clean of all dust, I return to lie on the hard floor of the storeroom. The floor is not the most comfortable place to sleep, but within a minute I go out like a light.

I must have gone into a long deep sleep as the next thing I know I wake as if in a dream to see a dark figure silhouetted in the gloom of the open door. The phantom bends down, grabs a box and disappears, leaving the door ajar.

Did he see me? I am not sure. Perhaps he thought I was a corpse lying on the floor. To play safe I get to my feet, take off my workpants, dust down my clothes, run my fingers through my hair, pick up my case and step outside the room. I go a short way along the gallery and sit down at a table. A few minutes later the building manager comes into the hall and climbs the stairs to the gallery. By the time he approaches I have my notebook open on the table and a pencil poised above a blank page.

"What in hell's name do you think you are doing here?" he bellows.

"I am drafting a letter."

"But I was told you were in the storeroom. Why were you lying in there?"

"I was lancing a boil on my thigh to express the pus."

The manager gives me a loathsome look as if I am subhuman.

"I think you had better write your letter in the beer garden," advises the manager before he leaves.

I do just as he says without a moments delay.

8

September 18, 1939

The Netherlands

WHILE enjoying a breakfast of eggs and bacon, toast and marmalade, Best tunes his kitchen wireless set to the BBC. His day turns sour when he hears the aircraft carrier *H.M.S. Courageous,* has been torpedoed and sunk by a German U-boat with a loss of life of over five hundred Royal Navy personnel.

"This is a disastrous way for Britain to start the war," Best mutters.

"Can I get you another cup of tea Mr. Best," asks Maud, his live-in housekeeper.

"Not now Maud thanks all the same. I have a business lunch and need to dress."

"No golf today, Mr. Best?"

"No unfortunately."

By 10 am Best has bathed, shaved and is attired in an outfit Somerset Maugham would be proud to wear to high tea at the Savoy in London. He leaves the house and climbs behind the wheel of the Ford Lincoln

Zephyr parked outside. He has had little opportunity in recent weeks to drive at speed. Today the flat sealed roads of the Southern Netherlands present the perfect opportunity. But first he is obligated to pick up his co-driver.

Best wondered whether Dr. Franz Fischer would ever get in touch again after their meeting three weeks ago. He waited for over a week before he did. Fischer indicated his contact was prepared to meet him in Venlo, a large Dutch town close to the Dutch-German border. Fischer requested that Best book a hotel meeting room where they could meet incognito.

In view of his previous conversation with Stevens, Best thought it wise to mention today's planned excursion. The upshot is Stevens has agreed to sit on the sidelines and see how things develop. Even with eleven on his staff at the Passport Control Office, Stevens is currently up to his neck gathering intelligence on the anticipated imminent German invasion of The Netherlands. With Stevens being unavailable, Best has invited his Dutch friend, part-time driver and mechanic, Jan Lemmens, to accompany him.

The Dutchman is at the wheel when they pull into a Shell filling station on the southern outskirts of Eindhoven.

"Fill her up," Lemmens says to the petrol pump attendant.
"How far to Venlo from here?" Best asks his co-driver.
"Fifty seven kilometres."
"Less than an hour then," muses Best.
"If I put my foot down."
"I should stretch my legs," says Best getting out of the car.
"I'll check the engine oil," responds Lemmens.
"Again!"
"You know what they say: oil is cheap, but engines are expensive."
"Yes, yes! Just tell me where to find the latrine around here."
"See that tree over there."
Five minutes later Best returns to find Lemmens down on his knees.
"Tyres okay?" asks Best.
"Not too bad, Mr. Best," replies Lemmens, pocketing his tyre pressure gauge.
"Do you mind if I drive from here, old boy?"
"It's your car, Mr. Best."

Forty minutes later the Lincoln skids to a stop outside Hotel Wilhelmina, a three storey brown brick building on a corner opposite Venlo railway station.

"I am not sure how long this meeting will take. You can sit in or make yourself scarce," Best explains to Lemmens before they get out of the car.

"Don't worry about me. I am happy to hang about in the bar."

"On second thoughts you had better sit in on the meeting."

"If you insist, Mr. Best."

Best locks the doors of the Lincoln and leads Lemmens to the hotel reception desk. In due course a plump provincial woman emerges from the back office.

"Good morning ma'am. Sorry to disturb you, but I booked a meeting room by telephone."

"Your name?" asks the woman, opening the bookings book.

"Best. Payne Best."

"Ah yes, Mr. Best. Your room is No. 6 at the end of the passage. Turn right, then left. You'll find the room is unlocked and has already been cleaned."

"I hope so. And please bring a light lunch for three in forty minutes time, if you would be so kind."

"For three, Mr. Best?"

"Yes, another company employee is due to arrive any time now. He will be joining us for lunch."

Best and Lemmens gravitate to the hotel bar where a dozen or more locals have already gathered for refreshment.

"Let me shout you a glass of the local Trappist beer, Mr. Best," offers Lemmens.

"Well thank you Jan, but be on the lookout for a man dressed like a Franciscan abbot."

"Could that be him sitting in the corner smoking a pipe and wearing a beret?" suggests Lemmens.

"You might be right. But buy the ale first and wait for him to come to us," murmurs Best.

Lemmens does as he is told while Best finds a vacant table. By the time Lemmens returns and by the time their glasses are half drained, the abbot comes from his corner to mutter, "Do you have a light for a good friend?"

"Solms?" whispers Best.

The abbot nods his head.

"Room No.6," Best slurs, as he digs his hand into his jacket pocket for his lighter.

With his pipe on fire Solms returns to his corner, allowing Best and Lemmens time to finish their drinks before they saunter to the meeting room. A little later, as Best is drawing on his cigarette with Lemmens looking bored, Solms is knocking on the door. Once the German is admitted the three settle into leather armchairs around a Rietveld glass topped table.

"Fischer said I'd find a trustworthy friend at Hotel Wilhelmina." Solms begins. "He did not say there would be *two* men coming to the meeting."

"I can assure you my assistant is an honest Dutchman and you have nothing to fear from him," Best responds.

"I hope not! You cannot trust anyone. Gestapo agents are everywhere in Holland!"

"Settle down, old boy. Did Dr. Fischer mention to you our interest in the political situation in Germany?" asks Best.

"When he phoned he said he would not come today. Apart from that he said little else," replies Solms.

"He seems a nervy little fellow. How long have you known him?" probes Best.

"Two years, maybe."

"I believe he lived in Paris for awhile," says Best.

"So?"

"Did you meet him there?"

"Nien. I meet him in Holland a few weeks or a few months before I attended a big meeting at the Carlton Hotel in Amsterdam. I already knew his brother, Fritz, from Munich, though that is probably of no interest to you. I think whenever I have political discussions with Fischer we are in the company of Dr. Spiecker — whenever he was making one of his visits to Amsterdam, to Rotterdam or to The Hague to rally his few followers."

"Fischer mentioned Spiecker to me," remarks Best.

"That does not surprise me. Dr. Spiecker has been fanatical for many years to bring about the downfall of Nazism by spreading propaganda against Hitler's dictatorship. He leaves no stone unturned to spread the word, and no doubt you have heard of his broadcasts into Germany from a North Sea trawler. Some time ago I declared myself ready to assist Dr. Spiecker in his patriotic cause and I have already distributed thousands of his Letters of Freedom leaflets into Germany."

"You are taking a grave risk to involve yourself in this sort of covert activity. You could be convicted of treason by the Nazi government," warns Best.

"Treason! Why do you say this? Does being anti-Nazi make me a traitor to my country? I remind you, since September 1935 I have been a captain in the Luftwaffe Intelligence, active in newsgathering in France, commanding agents on the ground in Germany, Holland, Belgium, and in Italy as well! Does this make me a traitor—and not an honourable officer?"

"Not in my books," says Best.

"Danke for saying so," growls Solms.

"By being in Luftwaffe Intelligence you certainly have an excellent cover for your covert operations," observes Lemmens.

"Even so, I must always be on my guard, not taking chances, like I am today."

"Is this why you dress like a Franciscan fryer?" asks Lemmens.

"I not always dress this way."

"Perhaps we should come to the reason for our meeting," interjects Best.

"Good idea. I crossed the border today on the pretext of buying some Limburger cheese—not to waste time."

"Fischer told me you can arrange a meeting with military officers who share the convictions of Spiecker and are opposed to Hitler," says Best.

Solms leans forward and takes his pipe from his mouth, delaying his answer.

"Well, maybe I can, but I can say nothing."

"Nothing at all?" asks Best, as there is a knock on the door.

"Who's that?" splutters Solms, glancing about the room, looking for an escape route.

"See who it is Jan," orders Best.

Lemmens goes to answer. He finds the woman from reception has brought the light lunch Best had ordered. On the tray are three servings of the local speciality: hachée, a thick stew of beef and onion, ringed by mashed potato, plus an extra large ramekin of creamy Dutch pastries.

Once the light lunch has been consumed the big Bavarian is the first to resume the dialogue.

"I must be going," he says, wiping his fat lips on his sleeve.

"But can you arrange a meeting?" insists Best.

"I will need to speak to my chief before committing myself on this matter."

"When will that be?"

"Maybe we could meet here next week."

"Well let me check," says Best taking out his diary. "Yes I appear to be clear next Monday."

"Now I must really go," announces Solms, as he rises to his feet.

"Don't forget your beret padre," warns Lemmens.

"Heh!"

Solms reclaims his headgear from the glass tabletop and hurries out the door.

Best checks the time on his fog watch and while he is still seated at the table he makes a few notes in his leather bound diary.

"A comical character," remarks Lemmens.

"Only an errand boy, I'd say," replies Best, stubbing his cigarette in the ashtray.

With sufficient distance between themselves and the German the pair leave the room. Best pays the bill at the reception desk and they head to the street.

"Care for a drink before we hit the road, Mr. Best?" asks Lemmens as they reach the Lincoln.

"The light lunch was a little heavy on the belly, I admit. Where do you have in mind?"

"Have you ever been to the bar in Venlo called 'Hemingway'?"

"Hemingway? No, never, but the name is enticing. Lead on Jan."

9 September 20, 1939
Munich

THIS afternoon I helped Brög off-load lumber from the back of a truck into the workshop. Later he complained of backache and knocked off early. His problem has allowed me to tinker longer than normal. To speed my laborious night work I am making a long handled wire scoop. The function of this device is to remove debris from the chamber inside the pillar. All that I have left to do is screw the wire framework to the handle.

At 7.15 pm, with the wire scoop completed and inside my small case, I let myself out of Brög's workshop. The distance to the Bürgerbräukeller is almost twice as far from here as from the Baumann's apartment on Blumenstrasse. But I have done some bushwalking in my time and a little exercise never did anyone any harm. As I get into my stride along Türkenstrasse I recall Frau Baumann asked me to call in whenever I had the inclination to split her wood. Finding the time in my busy schedule has been a problem. Though I could do with a little extra cash to pay for incidentals.

When I turn left into Schellingstrasse the twin spires of the Church of Saint Ludwig rise at the end of the street. Though I am Protestant of the Lutheran persuasion, I have been inside any number of Roman Catholic Churches. Had I more time to spare I might have gone inside Saint Ludwig tonight.

Once I turn into Ludwigstrasse I soon reach Odeonplatz. The three evil arches of the Feldherrnhalle loom ahead. Ever since I learnt this is where the 'blood martyrs' met their Maker in 1923 this place has had a sinister odour. Though a detour to the left to avoid the Feldherrnhalle would take me straight past another grotesque Nazi landmark — the House of German Art. The master carpenter informed me the bullshit artist himself laid the foundation stone for this pile of pillars. Brög almost split his sides when he told me the bizarre story. When Hitler hit the stone with a silver hammer the hammer broke in two! Hitler's eyes watered, thinking this a bad omen. It was for the architect, Paul Troost, who had designed both building and hammer. He was dead within six months.

Chewing over this story again brings a callous smile onto my dial, causing total loss of my inhibition. I breeze past the Feldherrnhalle blind to the evil, cross the river Isar and reach the Bürgerbräukeller without tribulation.

After my regular washroom visit I take my usual low budget hot meal with one glass of beer in the restaurant. Tonight I must continue the infernal task of hollowing out the pillar. Sometimes I wish I had never started — though I know the sooner I have finished the sooner I can retire.

"Finished?" asks the waitress, arriving on cue to remove my plate.

Now all the waitresses treat me as part of the furniture. Even my flirtatious remarks bring only wooden looks. I never see Gerda these days. She must hide in the kitchen whenever she sees me coming. So without any other diversion to pass the time, and with a glass of beer my only companion, I rewind my mind to the first time I enjoyed a meal at the Bürgerbräukeller.

The date was November 8, 1938. I had come to Munich to see for myself the annual reunion rally of the Nazi Party. My aim in coming was to determine how best to implement my plan to rid Germany of the deadly menace.

I came by train from Königsbronn, changing at Ulm as is normal. As I recall I arrived at Munich's main station shortly before 7 pm. Finding suitable lodging was a hassle and I ended up sleeping on a hallway sofa in a guesthouse in Albanistrasse. According to a newspaper I picked up on the train the rally began at 8.30 pm at the Bürgerbräukeller. Without delay I walked to the venue from my lodging, though the closest I could get was the corner of Rosenheimerstrasse and Hochstrasse. The police had erected barriers in the street to control the onlookers. I was left to imagine the scene inside where Hitler would be haranguing the 'old fighters' — those who had missed out on becoming 'blood martyrs' in the 1923 Putsch.

At 10.15 pm a long convoy of flag decked Mercedes sped past. I presumed Hitler and his henchmen were inside the limousines. As the crowd dispersed and the barriers came down I crossed the street to the Bürgerbräukeller. The lights were still blazing with the doors wide open. I walked in without anyone stopping me or asking my reason for being there. Waitresses were still clearing the tables. Houseboys were mopping up the beer spilt on the parquetry. Some of the invited guests were still standing about intoxicated, slapping each other on the back, no doubt reliving past follies. I was happy to be totally ignored as I scouted about. Though repulsed by the lurid coloured banners emblazoned with the Nazi swastika hung from the eight pillars, I was able to memorize the hall's layout.

I was inside the hall for no longer than ten to fifteen minutes. As the restaurant was still open I went there for a meal at about 11 pm. While I was eating a man joined me at my table. We struck up a conversation and he shouted me a beer. He had a Swabian accent like mine and told me he was a slaughterhouse manager from Aalen, which is not so far from my hometown. After downing the beer I bid him good night and returned to my lodging.

The next morning I had breakfast at the same guesthouse and walked back to the Bürgerbräukeller. At 11 am I was again standing in a crowd on Rosenheimerstrasser. This time I had come for the annual Nazi march from the Bürgerbräukeller to the Feldherrnhalle. The marchers had assembled in the beer garden before they came through an archway in the wall and headed down the street towards the river. First came a fat buffoon of a man I did not recognize. Then came three men side by side — the one in the centre carrying the *Blutfahne,* the infamous blood stained flag. Next came the Nazi leaders themselves, in one crooked line. This was the first time I had seen them in the flesh. In the middle of the line was Hitler, marching with a rancid smile on his face, holding his side with one hand, as if he already had a stitch in the gut. On his right was Hermann Göring, the only one in a trench coat looking as if he thought he might catch a cold due to the grey weather. To the left of Hitler strutted the dark horse Rudolph Hess, looking ready to bolt given the chance. Beside him limped the weedy club footed Goebbels doing his best to keep up. Heinrich Himmler was way out on the extreme right, looking like he needed a blood transfusion. There were others but I could not name them and in a moment they had passed. Next came the rank and file, followed by row upon row of goons in black or brown shirts carrying flags. Unlike all those around me I did not cheer or raise my arm. The sight of grown men and women and even little children raising their arm in the Nazi salute sickens me to the pit of my Swabian stomach.

Nevertheless I followed the march across the Isar and into the old city as far the Isartor. Though I had no appetite to follow all the way to the Feldherrnhalle for the flag waving and the speeches. Instead I hastened to Munich's main station to head for home. I had seen enough.

When the appointed time arrives I drink my last drop from my glass and go to the washroom. I then steal to my hiding place as usual. Once the doors are locked and the lights extinguished I emerge like a phantom to continue my work. Extracting bricks one by one is a brute of a job, fit only for an idiot who takes pleasure in inflicting pain on his body. And the deeper I go into the cavity in the pillar the more my knees suffer. I have lost count of the nights I have been subjected to this torture. I try not to think how many more nights I must drill and chisel and scratch with my nails before the chamber will have the right dimensions for my apparatus.

Dealing with the debris is a risky operation. As the quantity mounts night after night I must come to my hiding place during the daytime to pack the broken bricks and mortar into my small case. I then take the case to the riverbank and tip the lot onto an existing pile of rubble behind Müller's public baths. I use the rear entrance and go through the beer garden with the air of a dim-witted tradesman. So far there's been no drama.

I stop work at 3.10 am, after working far longer than normal. As I scoop the last batch of debris into my lidded cardboard box I hear something I have not heard before at night when working—the patter of a paw.

Through the openings in the balustrade I see something in the gloom below. A dog is off the leash, trotting about, sniffing in corners as if searching for a truffle. When a flashlight comes through the part opened double door, I sniff double trouble. The mongrel stops at the foot of the staircase, then yaps and starts to climb. When the warden follows I stop breathing. Reaching the top he pauses to flash his light into the darkness. The hound runs free in the gallery, going from table to table, forever coming closer. I find in my coat pocket a lidded tin. Before the bitch is licking my face I throw out a portion of meat I saved from my evening meal. The stupid mutt snaps up the morsel and trots back to the warden wagging its tail.

Praise God! The warden and his black dog have gone! My hands tremble as I brush up the last of the dust and pack away my tools. I close the secret door and return to my hiding place. Lying frozen behind the cardboard boxes I shiver myself to sleep.

10
Munich

October 12, 1939

AFTER the black dog incident I went back the next night to overcome my terror. I have not been molested since, though I know at least two dogs are in the hands of the air raid wardens who have occupied a room in the building since the war began. With no enemy bombs yet falling my hope is they will continue in their lazy ways of sleeping all through the night.

Brög as usual is in the back room taking his nap after his midday meal. While he is out of the way I am busy at the bench assembling the containers to be filled with a deadly cocktail. I purchased the iron straps that hold everything together from the nearby ironmonger, Suckfüll. The explosive cartridges, detonators and rifle ammunition and everything else that I have stowed beneath the false bottom of my wooden trunk, will be deployed in due course. I am now near the end of my eternal struggle with only three bricks to extract before I commence installation of my apparatus.

As I insert and tighten the last few screws of my assembly I hear guttural sounds suggesting the master carpenter has woken from his after-lunch rest. Less than five minutes later he is standing at my shoulder.

"I see you work in iron as well as wood." Brög mutters.

"My ambition was to be a metal turner working a lathe in the local foundry."

"Until you decided to become an inventor?"

"My inventiveness came after I become a cabinetmaker."

"I suspect there is more to you than what first meets the eye—but stop fooling with your invention and come and give a man a hand with his wardrobe."

"How can I help?"

"You can hold this end while I go and find some clamps."

"Have you mixed the glue?"

"No, not yet. Maybe I should do that first."

"I think you should. When I worked for Dornier mixing glue and clamping was second nature."

"You worked at Dornier! Was that at the aeroplane factory on the Bodensee?"

"It was—near Friedrichshafen where the Zeppelin airships are built."

"Working for a firm like Dornier sounds a lark, unless you were the maintenance man."

"I worked in the propeller department."

"Propellers! Perhaps you made propellers that took Roald Amundsen to the North Pole or Charles Lindbergh across the Atlantic."

"That thought has never occurred to me. I was probably too busy cutting out the timber laminations, heating and mixing the special glue, clamping, then shaping and fine sanding the propellers to the specified dimensions."

"Sounds almost as tricky as building wardrobes. Perhaps you made the propellers for the Do X."

"What was that?"

"The Dornier Do X was the giant flying ship that made a big smash in the newspapers. It had twelve engines and flew to Rio de Janeiro and to New York, before landing back in Berlin like a big goose."

"When was this?"

"I think around 1930."

"I don't remember that, perhaps because I don't read newspapers as a rule. Besides, I only worked at Dornier for six months."

"Only six months! Why would you leave a job like that? Did you get the sack?"

"Nay. A fellow worker persuaded me to cross the Bodensee to join a music club in Konstanz. In those days I was young and restless, even a little reckless."

"I think Dornier lost a lot of money so it was probably best you left when you did."

"I did not know that. Do you want me to find the clamps and mix the glue?"

"Heh! Thanks for offering, my friend."

Using wooden dowels, animal glue and a little persuasion, Brög's wardrobe is assembled before 6 pm. While the master carpenter is still tinkering with the door handles, I casually carry the components of my lethal weapon to the storeroom to pack into my trunk to transport to the Bürgerbräukeller—though onsite installation will not happen for some nights yet. By kneeling on bare floorboards extracting bricks like teeth night after night, my knees have had more wear and tear than usual. When my right knee became ulcerated I sought medical advice. I explained to the doctor I am in the habit of praying all night for the Führer. He commended my devotion, but advised me to bathe my knees regularly, pray less and rest in bed for at least a week—all of which I have done.

I pack away my gear, padlocking everything before heading back through the workshop.

"Take care my friend," Brög tells me, still tinkering with his latest creation.

I go down the passage, pass through the wicket door and turn into the darkened street. The days are becoming shorter as winter is coming closer—reminding me it is now less than a month to my target date of November 8.

At the bakery I buy a brötchen to take back to my room. With some leftover Limburger cheese I keep on the windowsill the roll will be my evening meal. As I climb the stairs I am almost knocked over by Alfons coming down.

"Rosa's waters have broken!" he announces, as if this is something to celebrate.

11
October 20, 1939
The Netherlands

BEST expressed doubts to his minders in London after his first meeting with Solms. Despite his apprehension he was told to continue with the pursuit of the German Opposition and a second meeting was held with the Bavarian. With Lemmens not being present at the meeting—perhaps due to Best wanting more time behind the wheel—Solms was much calmer, and was able to answer technical questions on the Luftwaffe. At the conclusion he told Best a big conspiracy to remove Hitler from power was underway with high-ranking officers involved. But Solms could say no more as the ringleaders of the plot would only deal directly with Best.

A few days later, after Fischer had set up a secure communication channel, Best received a coded letter in which he was told a certain German general was eager to meet with him. But before any meeting could take place he must establish his bona fide as a British agent. For this Best was asked to arrange for the broadcast of a specific paragraph in the German News Bulletin of the BBC. Best arranged for this to happen on October 11.

Encouraged by these positive developments, Best contacted Stevens and raised the logistical problem of holding future meetings on Dutch soil with a dissident German general. With a German invasion expected any day, the Dutch armed forces had mobilized and established a cordon along the German border, making the staging of any meeting doubly difficult, if not impossible. Stevens suggested they discuss this problem with the Chief of Dutch Intelligence, General van Oorschot. The meeting went far better than either expected. Van Oorschot proposed a Dutch intelligence officer be assigned to assist them in dealing with the Dutch military to insure they had free passage. Also he requested that the nominated officer, Lieutenant Dirk Klop, be permitted to sit in on the meetings with the Germans and report back to him. His only proviso was the British officers must refrain from actions that might jeopardize Dutch neutrality. With this in mind Stevens has given Lieutenant Klop the alias 'Captain Coppens' to pass him off as a British officer. The deception is aided by Klop having an excellent command of the English language, due to him living in Canada for several years. His German is also up to the mark.

At 6 am, an hour before sunrise, the Ford Lincoln Zephyr is on the wet, slippery streets of The Hague, heading eastward towards Utrecht. Two Englishman, one Dutchman masquerading as an Englishman, and one German émigré are on board. With Jan Lemmens' wife expected to give birth any day, Best is behind the wheel. Beside him sits a bleary eyed Stevens who now wants to be in on the action. In the back Dr. Franz Fischer is slumped against the door, his felt hat pulled over his face. Beside him sits the spritely Lieutenant Dirk Klop, who is to be referred to only as 'Captain Coppens'.

After Utrecht, the pale rising sun lays a silvery path across the heathland dew as they approach the ancient city of Arnhem. Stevens, with a *Michelin* map spread open on his knees, helps to direct Best through the tangle of old city streets to connect them with the road to Zutphen.

"I must say Zutphen is some way from the border," remarks Stevens.

"The further we meet from the border the better," replies Best.

"They will not come to Zutphen," mutters Fischer.

"Did you say something Doctor?" asks Best, looking in the rear view mirror.

"They will not come to Zutphen!" Fischer yells back.

"Why do you say that?"

"Because Dinxperlo was the agreed meeting place," Fischer retorts.

"Maybe it was, but you and Captain Coppens will go to Dinxperlo to bring the Huns to Zutphen. Is that too difficult for you?" asks Best.

"Ja, ja. We will see."

At 8.05 am Best has the Lincoln crossing the bridge over the Ijssel and turning into the centre of Zutphen. After nosing through narrow streets to the Zaadmarkt, he manages to find a place to park opposite Café de Korenbeurs.

"Major Stevens and I will wait inside this café while you two go to collect the Germans. You should find a taxi around here somewhere I expect. Telephone me at the café if you have any trouble." Best instructs Klop.

"Leave it to me, Sir. We'll be back by 10 am if the Germans arrive on time," replies Klop.

Klop gives the sour faced Fischer a slap on the back and they head off to find a taxi, leaving Best and Stevens to enter the café. After removing their hats and overcoats they sit at a table by the window overlooking the street. Once they have been served the café breakfast Stevens sounds out Best on a few details.

"Tell me again who is coming to this meeting?"

"Not sure—but hopefully one will be a general. Fischer mentioned by letter that a General Deichmann of the Luftwaffe, a General Wietersheim or a General Ottenbacher were all possible candidates to attend."

"I must say it sounds promising."

"They have no excuse not to send a general as they know I am on the level. The paragraph they wanted read on the BBC was broadcast twice on the same day for good measure."

"And you said the man you met last time is not coming today." says Stevens.

"I did. Solms sent a message the Gestapo are on his tail and he needs to lie low."

"The Gestapo on his tail! He certainly sounds like a Luftwaffe man."

"He is also a big oaf. Between you and me I hope to never deal with him again, though after I quizzed him at our second meeting he seemed genuine enough. Fischer might even turn out to be real-deal as well," muses Best.

"Fischer? Hell! If he is not the genuine article, there will be red faces from the PM down," warns Stevens, looking more fraught than usual.

With that sobering thought percolating through their minds the pair drink their coffee and sit in sullen silence until Best breaks open a fresh pack of Pall Malls.

"Smoke?"

"Don't mind if I do," Stevens responds.

When the waiter comes to clear the table they order more coffee and take turns to use the bathroom. 10 am and 11 am come and go without any sign of Fischer and Klop. Another hour passes. More coffee needs to be ordered and more cigarettes smoked before Best is called to the café telephone.

"The Germans have only just arrived," reports Klop.

"We thought you had disappeared off the planet!"

" Sorry Sir. We'll be in Zutphen within the hour," Klop promises.

At 12.55 am a taxi pulls up outside the café. Seeing Klop sitting in the front seat beside the driver and two strange men sitting in the back seat with Fischer, Best bristles into action. He dons his hat and coat and hurries outside.

"Get everyone into my car and be quick about it," Best instructs the willing Klop.

When Stevens ambles out of the café he joins Best and Klop in the front seat of the Lincoln. Fischer and the two visitors are already packed into the back.

"Why the rush?" asks Stevens.

"I don't want to hang around this café any longer. The locals will get suspicious seeing six strange men in their town and report us to the police."

"Are we to conduct the meeting in your car?" Stevens taunts Best.

"If necessary — but I thought we might drive back to The Hague."

"No, no! Impossible! My friends need to return to the border by 8 pm tonight," Fischer protests.

"Calm down," mutters Best. "A roadside café may do us."

"Try driving south, Sir, there is bound to be something," says Klop.

"I hope so," quips Stevens.

There is nothing but fields of maize and piggeries until they reach the crossroads five kilometres south of Zutphen. After receiving a tap on the shoulder from Klop, Best pulls off the bitumen to park in the slush beside a red brick building. The six get out of the Lincoln and file inside Den Bremer, an ancient establishment that was serving travellers hot meals back when Abel Tasman was discovering Van Diemen's Land. A log fire is smoking in the fireplace of the dining room as two extra chairs are commandeered so all can sit around one table. When the innkeeper recommends rookworst with stamppot, Best is in no mood to differ.

"Perhaps while we wait you can introduce the visitors," Best prompts Fischer.

"But is this a safe place to talk?" he murmurs.

"This place is as safe as any we will find in these parts," replies Klop.

"Err — well this is Lieutenant Grosch and Captain von Seidlitz — both are good friends of mine," claims Fischer.

"Good to meet you both, but we were expecting a general," Best complains.

"Generals always give the sticky jobs to underlings," Grosch quips, causing Fischer to cackle.

A moment later two Dutch soldiers come into the café and sit at a nearby table.

"Did you see what I saw?" Stevens whispers to Best.

"I did. And if they hear us speaking German they will take us for a pack of German spies," Best whispers back.

"So what do you suggest?"

"I have a friend in Arnhem. We could use his house for the meeting. He owes me a favour."

"You had better ring him first to check he's at home. The café should have a telephone."

"Agreed. But I will ring once we have our fill of hot pork sausage. If we were to leave now we would only attract more attention."

The house of Best's friend takes two hours to find and it is not until 4.15 pm the six interlopers pile out of the Lincoln in a quiet back street in Arnhem. After everyone has disappeared into the house and found a place to sit at the polished mahogany dining room table, Best calls the meeting to order.

"Sorry for the run-around gentlemen, but one cannot be too careful. Now where were we?"

The next moment the owner of the house bursts in looking alarmed. Taking Best aside he whispers in his ear, "Police have surrounded the house and two men are at the front door asking about Germans. What am I to do?"

"Stay calm and I'll see what the problem is," whispers Best.

He signals Klop and they go together the front door to defuse the situation. After a lengthy conversation the two Dutch policemen agree to take Klop to their commander to straighten out the matter. Meanwhile Dr. Fischer has turned as white as a sheet and Stevens has his work cut out convincing the two German visitors not to jump out the window.

"My apologies for the interruption gentleman," Best says upon his return.

"Are we safe here?" squeaks Fischer.

"Absolutely. Captain Coppens has the situation well under control. It seems the police traced my telephone call from the roadside café," Best reveals.

"Under these circumstances and without a general being present is there any point continuing with the meeting?" queries Stevens.

"There must be something to be discussed," replies Best.

"We have not risked our necks to come all this way for nothing," retorts Lieutenant Grosch.

"Good to hear, and feel free to smoke because I intend to," announces Best, pulling a packet from his jacket pocket.

When Klop returns the atmosphere in the room is more conducive to serious discussion.

"Should I begin by telling you of the mood inside our military?" asks von Seidlitz.

"Why not?" agrees Best.

"Not so long ago our chief, General Wietersheim, attended an army commanders conference with Himmler in Konstanz. The mood was very tense as many commanders refuse to undertake major action against France or England. They disapprove of Ribbentrop's foreign policy and want every option to be explored before going headlong into war."

"And there are many like-minded officers. The conditions are such that only a small impetus is needed to set the ball rolling," amplifies Lieutenant Grosch.

"What do you mean exactly by 'set the ball rolling'?" queries Stevens.

"We are meaning a coup d'état against the Nazi government," beams Grosch.

"But for that situation to arise a firm undertaking is required from the British that peace will result from our action to unseat the Nazi regime," von Seidlitz clarifies.

"I suspect Britain would not wage a vindictive war against Germany once there is a genuine change within the German government. That said, hot heads like Winston Churchill could have a different attitude to the current Prime Minister," muses Best.

"The minimum terms His Majesty's Government would tolerate are real autonomy for the Czechs and the restoration of the independence of Poland. Of course everything will need to be referred back to Whitehall. In other words we have no authority to make any commitments to you," signals Stevens.

"We suspected as much and I'll inform General Weitersheim. There is every possibility he'll come to the next meeting," says von Seidlitz.

"Dr. Franz, you have not had much to say," remarks Best.

"I feel sick," he groans.

"Do you want to lie down?" asks Best.

"Just take me home."

"That lunch may be his problem, though I feel fine," offers Stevens.

"My gallbladder is my problem," moans Fischer.

"Poor chap! Perhaps Captain Coppens can take you to the railway station. There is bound to be a night train to The Hague," says Best.

"Remember Captain Coppens must return us to the border by 8 pm tonight," injects von Seidlitz.

"Captain Coppens is a busy man, but somehow he will fit you into his heavy schedule. Now I suggest everyone sit back and relax," advises Best.

"Should we now return to the purpose of the meeting?" asks Stevens.

"By all means, if there is anything left to discuss," says Best.

"If there is not, I will report our meeting as being preliminary in nature, but positive in purpose despite the interruptions. As for General Wietersheim please give our regards and advise him when he comes he must bring concrete proposals. Is that the way you see things, Captain Best?" asks Stevens.

"I could not have stated the position better myself."

12

October 20, 1939
Munich

WITH Frau Lehmann not coming into my room to dust, carpet sweep and make my bed everyday, I have more opportunity to tinker with my clock movements, batteries and other devices for my time-operated apparatus. Rosa has been in hospital for eight days straight after giving birth to her baby. And with Alfons at work for long hours or visiting his wife at the Red Cross hospital, I have had the run of the apartment for at least a week.

As I tinker at my desk in my tiny room I think back to the summer of 1925. Telling the master carpenter Brög last week how I resigned from my job at Dornier stirs memories of that experimental phase of my life. Though Dornier paid well and making aeroplane propellers was more interesting work than making fruit boxes, after six months, egged on by my fellow worker Leo Dannecker, I succumbed to the lure of the city. Konstanz, situated at the western end of the Bodensee and at the head of the Rhine, was predestined to be my abode and playground for the next seven years of my life.

The Bodensee was shimmering beneath a summer sun as we boarded the morning steamer at Friedrichshafen. We had barely cleared the harbour when we shed our shirts and lounged like tycoons in the deck chairs. The snow-capped Alps of Switzerland hung in the sky like a mirage above the rippling blue expanse. After Meersburg the steamer cut a course between the sailboats of the gentry to reach Konstanz a little past midday.

Like dills we carried our bags and tools about the streets until we booked into an overpriced hostel. But I was not too worried about the cost of things at that stage of my life. I still had plenty in my pocket, and in any case within a week we were signed on as cabinetmakers at the Schuckmann clock company.

Leo had originally told me he wanted to go to Konstanz to join a music club. But once we arrived he was more interested in chasing after girls than in playing his clarinet. Within a week he had two lined up to take to the picture theatre. I remember a double bill was playing: *The Last Laugh* and *Waxworks*. When we came out afterwards Leo suggested we all go back to our place. We made hot chocolate on the gas ring and sat around talking about nothing in particular until Leo and his girl fell into a clinch. My girl pulled me down on the other bed. I moved my hands over her breasts and was happy to leave it at that. Two weeks later we repeated the dose with the same two girls. The movie was titled, *The Hands of Orlac*. It was a horror movie that scared the daylights out of my girl, whose name was Brunhilde. She clung to me all the way back to our room and was keen for more action than the last time we had ended up on the bed. After we had gone all the way she looked up at me with her big brown eyes and told me she didn't mind having my baby. For the next month I lived with that fearful thought and I was happy to never see Brunhilde again.

Things hummed along like clockwork at the Schuckmann factory for over a year. I was receiving a modest, yet steady income, allowing me to taste the fruits of city life. So it came as something of a shock when the Schuckmann clock company closed down, throwing Leo and me out of work. For several months I wondered if I would ever find another job and took up smoking in earnest. I spent whole days in bed or paced the reedy banks feeding the ducks or roamed the Stadtgarten to gaze across the Bodensee to the Alps of Switzerland, unless of course I was at the employment office collecting my unemployment payment.

One of my consolations in those lazy days was meeting a girl named Anna. She reminded me of my sister, Anna, and cared for me like a mother. Perhaps this was why I liked her. Things turned out better than I thought they would, as within six months I was re-employed when the same clock factory reopened with a new owner, under the name Upper Rhine Clock Industries.

After Leo and I had gone separate ways I moved into a back room with another workmate named Fiebig. Living with him in the oldest quarter of Konstanz in an ancient house at Inselgasse 15 was more affordable but had drawbacks. Fiebig snored like a pig and stuck up posters on the walls of our room or anywhere he saw a need for the enlightenment of the working masses. Sharing a room with a card carrying Communist had a predictable outcome. Fiebig coaxed me to meetings of the local branch of the Red Front Fighters League—the paramilitary arm of the Communist Party, the KPD. When I paid my dues I received a badge in the form of a red clenched fist with the motto inscribed: *'protecting the friend, fighting off the enemy'*. Fiebig was a true believer and practically hero-worshipped Ernst Thälmann, the leader of the KPD. Sadly Thälmann came a bad third in the 1932 elections, even with the inspired slogan: *A vote for Hindenburg is a vote for Hitler; a vote for Hitler is a vote for war.*

Exactly when I met Mathilde Niedermann I cannot remember. All I recall is she was a waitress with an irresistible personality. We talked at every opportunity on every conceivable subject imaginable and in a short space of time we became intensely intimate. When I told Anna of my love for Mathilde she cried her heart out and said she never wanted to see me again. I failed to understand her bitterness as I told her we could always be friends.

I found new lodgings in a house at Gebhard-Strasse 4 across the Rhine. Mathilde lived conveniently close at no.25 in the same street in a room above the Bilgerbräu restaurant. Our regular lovemaking was interrupted when my little brother Leonhard came unexpectedly by train one weekend. My mother must have given him my new address as I had taken the trouble to write her a letter. Mathilde had a good idea on how to entertain young Leonhard, suggesting we all go to Mainau Island. The three of us caught the morning ferry on a rather misty day, as often happens on the Bodensee. Mathilde insisted I wear my dark blue suit so we could be photographed by a professional photographer on the island. Mathilde loved doing that sort of nostalgic family thing.

But the good times did not last. Only six months after reopening the renamed clock factory burnt to the ground, throwing everyone out of work. There was a strong suspicion of arson as the new owner was deep in debt. Some said he only wanted to get his hands on the fire insurance money and the police were called in.

My unemployment became a minor glitch when Mathilde mentioned she was pregnant. I did not want to be a father or even her husband and I told her to get rid of what was inside her. She took no action. Fiebig warned me abortion was a criminal offence in Germany under the Weimar government. He said things would change for the better once the KDP was elected. But I could not wait that long, and took Mathilde to a clinic in Geneva. We stayed overnight at considerable cost but to no avail. The woman doctor informed me it was against Swiss law for Mathilde to have an abortion, as she was now more than three months pregnant.

I was in the middle of my ugly breakup with Mathilde when I found work at Bottighofen, Switzerland, just eight kilometres across the border. The Schönholzer family factory was a small outfit producing a range of home furnishings. When I say small I mean small as Herr Schönholzer's son was the only other worker. As I was still living in Konstanz I obtained a permit that allowed me to cross the border daily or whenever I needed. The brand new pushbike I purchased for that purpose was a joy to ride even if it put a sizable dent in my meagre savings. When weather permitted I habitably disappeared after lunch to swim in the Bodensee. Any work time I lost during the day I made up in the evenings to keep Herr Schönholzer off my back or from giving me the sack.

But when in 1929 the factory began running short of orders due to what Herr Schönholzer referred to as die Wirtschaftskrise, I sensed my dismissal was near. But thanks to a female acquaintance I landed work in Meersburg at Rothmund's clockworks. I went from churning out home furnishings to working with five others making the housings for table, wall and kitchen cloaks. The premises were situated in the upper town of Meersburg, giving me a steep climb each morning from the harbour pier as I was at that time commuting by ferry from Konstanz. I was reluctant to vacate the room I rented from Mathilde Niedermann's sister as I had just begun my relationship with Hilda Lang. Hilda lived in the centre of Konstanz and worked as a cutter at the company of Pius Wieler and Sons located just over the Swiss border in Kreuzlingen.

I was well and truly into the swing of the temperance meetings and attending the Roman Catholic Church with Hilda when my son was born in 1930. Mathilde took it upon herself to name him Manfred. I have not seen him since he was six months old, though I once thought of taking him home to meet my mother, until I realized she would not be welcoming.

In the same year as the birth Rothmund's clockworks shut down. Herr Rothmund was bankrupt. In lieu of the considerable sum in wages he owed me—175 marks by my estimation—Herr Rothmund presented me with a box containing five clock movements. I had no option other than accept his offer, not having a clue what use they would ever be to me.

Once my affair with Hilda Lang had run its natural course I was ready to leave Konstanz to live on my wits in Meersburg. In that hilly town steeped in history and half-timbered houses, I worked for myself, doing odd handyman jobs, often for frustrated housewives. I tried my hand at rye threshing, while living from hand to mouth, accepting a hot meal from a new friend, camping the night wherever I was offered a bed. The freedom of this lifestyle suited me down to the ground. With no taxable income I avoided paying alimony to Mathilde Niedermann for my son.

I could still be living in Meersburg had I not received a cry for help from my mother in 1932. Her wifely patience with my drunkard father had run dry. Being the dutiful son I dropped everything and rushed home to Königsbronn, bringing my toolboxes and Rothmund's five clock movements with me.

I stop tinkering with two of those five clock movements. Leaving them on the desk, I take my hat and coat from the hook and head out for some fresh air. The time is now 10.30 am, too early for lunch with the master carpenter at Alter Simpl, but an ideal time to walk into the old city and pay a visit to Frau Baumann. With winter coming on she'll be eager for me to flex my muscles splitting her wood. And not only will I receive a small reward for my effort, from past experience she will lay on a free lunch.

13   October 30, 1939
The Hague

BEST is busy upstairs using his new electric razor when his housekeeper opens the front door of his residence on Lange Voorhout to find Stevens outside.

"Morning Maud."

"Come to see Mr. Best have ye?" There is a nip in the air isn't there? You must miss India. Mr. Best will be down shortly. Do you mind waiting in the library?"

"Not at all."

Stevens is left to roam about the room that is both library and office. He stands at the window and draws aside the Dutch lace curtain to peer across Lange Voorhout where market stalls form neat lines under the rows of linden trees. When he comes from the window he runs his eye along the shelves, reading silently some of the authors on the spines: Bunyan, Chaucer, Tolstoy, Joyce, Huxley, Scott, Nietzsche, Bonhoeffer. Dietrich Bonhoeffer? Stevens has never heard of this writer. He takes the book down from the shelf to read the title: *Act and Being.* He flicks through a few pages and is returning the book to the shelf when Best bursts through the door.

"You're early!"

"I came early in case there was something you want to discuss prior to the meeting," replies Stevens.

"I can't think of anything offhand, though you can help me carry the sandwiches to my company office."

"So we meet over there rather than here?"

"I thought that best. Maud is a lovely lady but a terrible gossip. Right now I'm having a fag and a glass of Jack Daniel. Interested?"

"I won't say no to a drop."

"I bought a case in 1920 just before prohibition — turned out to be one of my best investments ever."

Stevens watches Best remove the stopper from a cut-glass decanter and splash the golden liquid into two whisky glasses. With glass in hand, Stevens wanders back to the window from where he makes an observation.

"Having the meeting here will save traipsing all over the countryside, playing cat and mouse with the Dutch police like last time."

"I am glad you approve. Another experience like that and we could be severely compromised. Fischer has pulled off a minor miracle in persuading the Huns to venture this far from the border. Though I am not sure who exactly is coming today. As I mentioned, General Wietersheim was due two days ago, but cancelled at the last moment," explains Best.

"He must have had another army commanders' meeting to attend or some other damn excuse. Is Fischer coming today?"

"No — but I told him I would give him a call if we need him."

"What about Klop?"

"Klop has driven to Dinxperlo to do the pickup. He should be back by midday."

Best props himself on the edge of his desk, enjoying the noxious mix of nicotine and alcohol. Several minutes pass before Stevens has the gall to break the silence.

"You may need to play your fiddle if Klop is late like last time," says Stevens.

"Fiddle?"

"Over there," Stevens says, pointing to the violin case resting on a bookshelf.

"I paid a mint for that. Bought it in Munich in 1913."

"What were you doing in Munich back then?"

"I was studying economics at Munich University and musicology at the Conservatory."

"You must have a soft spot for the Germans having spent that time in Munich."

"Let me say I would be the last to tar them all with the same brush."

"Do you still play?"

"Occasionally, though I miss my weekly afternoons with the Prince."

"The Prince?"

"Prince Henry, the prince consort, husband of Queen Wilhelmina."

"Playing with a Royal is a feather in your cap, Best."

"I simply play for the love of music, old boy."

At 11.45 am the two Englishmen set out for Best's business office, each carrying a silver tray of sandwiches Maud has prepared for the occasion. There is not far to walk, though there is one canal to cross before they reach Nieuwe Uitleg 15. Best's private office on the ground floor is almost a replica of his home library, though the shelves are loaded mainly with commerce, pharmaceutical journals and a good sprinkling of auto magazines.

"Everything going to plan Klop will be coming through the door any minute now," says Best, as he paces up and down the room, dropping ash everywhere.

"I hope you're right," Stevens returns.

"So do I."

"I reread the speech Hitler gave in the Reichstag the day after we declared war on Germany," starts Stevens.

"I can lend you a book if that is all you have to read—but go on," interjects Best.

"Hitler began his diatribe with his usual whine about how the Treaty of Versailles was 'a gun held against the head of the German people'. He then complained how his magnanimous peace offers had been rebuffed by the warmongering British. Towards the end of his speech he turned to denouncing traitors who would dare to plot against him, as if he is paranoid."

"Paranoid? I would think that goes without saying."

"He then moved on to his succession plan, stating either Göring or Rudolf Hess are to take the reins should something dire happen to him."

"So what?"

"So any assassin worth his salt should target the whole leadership of the Nazi Party — otherwise the Nazi stench might linger on."

"Hard to see that happening. I mean the elimination of all the Nazi bigwigs in one hit, though we can only live in hope. Good Lord! It's almost one o'clock. We might need to nibble on the sandwiches if Klop and the Huns don't show soon," concludes Best, swirling the dregs in his glass.

The boredom of waiting is only marginally lessened when Stevens challenges Best to a game of chess. Stevens has been checkmated three times and Best has emptied the ashtray twice when there is a rap on the door at 3.15 pm.

Best springs to his feet, knocking Stevens' queen off the board as he goes to answer. Klop hurries the three visitors inside while Stevens puts on his jacket, straightens his necktie, pats down his black hair and comes from the office to get his first glimpse of the German general. He soon notices only Lieutenant Grosch has survived from the meeting that ended nine days ago in Arnhem. After overcoats, scarves and hats are loaded onto Klop to be hung on the hallstand, Grosch introduces the two newcomers.

"Please meet Colonel Martini of the General Staff."

Stevens steps forward to introduce himself and Best to the fifty-five year old man with beady eyes set in a rubbery face. He responds with an obsequious grin.

"And Captain Schaemmel," announces Grosch.

The two Englishmen shake the hand of the younger man with little enthusiasm.

"Why don't you take our quests to the conference room?" Best asks Stevens, not expecting a reply.

As Stevens leads the three visitors up the stairs to the second floor, Best hangs back to interrogate Klop in the vestibule.

"What was the hold up?"

"Long story. I'll tell you later, Sir," says Klop.

"There'd better be a good explanation. And where is the general?"

All Klop can do is shrug his shoulders.

A long oak table with eight chrome chairs upholstered in tan leather fills half the conference room. The other half is laid with a Moroccan rug over the blackened floorboards. Several antique maps hang from the white washed walls. The three visitors and Stevens are still standing circumspectly by the sandwich trays as Best walks in followed by the Klop.

"You may start on the sandwiches," Best advises as he hurries to switch on the Giso pendant lamps before lowering the Holland blinds hung to the three large double casement windows that overlook the canal.

Holding a cheese and gherkin sandwich Captain Schaemmel lifts his eyes to the antique map hanging over the buffet.

"This map is most unusual in that it shows the North Pole at the centre of the world," he comments as Best draws alongside him.

"Unusual and quite rare. Cartographer, Heinrich Scherer of Munich published this map in the 1770's to illustrate the voyage of the *Victoria*, the only ship to return from the circumnavigation of the world by Ferdinand Magellan. You will recall Magellan never made it back to Seville. The poor fellow was speared to death in the Philippine Islands halfway through the voyage," expounds Best.

"Let us pray our lives do not end as tragically, Captain," remarks Schaemmel.

"You look as if you've already been in a scrap judging by those scars on your face," observes Best.

"They are dueling scars from Bonn University," explains Schaemmel.

"I should have realized. They're your badges of honor, so to speak."

"You could say that, Captain."

"Can you let the others know we will begin our meeting at 3.30 pm. And if you are wondering the loo is at the end of the passage on the left," advises Best.

After a flurry of activity the conference table is populated at 3.35 pm. Klop and Stevens sit on one side facing Grosch and Martini, while Best and Schaemmel sit facing each other at the opposite ends of the table.

"Will you take notes, Major?" Best asks Stevens.

"At your service," replies Stevens, taking his fountain pen from his top pocket.

"Gentlemen, I thank you for coming," Best begins. "What held you up for over three hours is not my business, though I will receive a full report from Captain Coppens later. More to the point we expected a general would be here today. I must be candid and ask the question: where is HE?"

"The general you refer to has expressly asked us to come on his behalf. Colonel Martini is the general's adjutant. Provided we make good progress today the general is eager to come on another day," says Schaemmel.

"So without a general how do you propose we proceed today?" asks Best.

"If you have no objection I will begin by giving a rough outline of the present position in the Reich," answers Schaemmel.

"I've no objection. Do you have any objection, Major Stevens?" asks Best.

"None whatsoever."

"Though you may think or have heard otherwise, the truth is the current situation in Germany is chronic. Since September there have been great losses of men and materiel in the Polish campaign. In the first few days of the invasion the Wehrmacht sustained heavy losses. We are talking about an entire armored division, thousands of soldiers, and 25% of our air strength put out of action. With the Wehrmacht under such extreme pressure it is imperative this war not be allowed to continue. Though I must point out the present military inactivity can only last as long as there remains the possibility of negotiations for an early peace settlement."

"I am surprised to hear of such heavy German losses. Perhaps you underestimated the Poles. But what plans do you have for Herr Hitler?" asks Best.

"He is at the centre of the problem, I concede. Time and again he refuses to take well-reasoned advice from his General Staff. The present difficult situation cannot be allowed to continue. We need to act," offers Schaemmel.

"Assassination?" murmurs Klop.

"We do not believe that drastic step to be the answer to the problem. With Hitler having such incalculable charisma with the German people, his assassination would only lead to chaos. Our intention is to take Hitler prisoner and force him to give orders authorizing a junta of Wehrmacht officers to start negotiations for peace. You will appreciate that we are proud Germans and have to think of the interests of the Fatherland first. But before we can take decisive steps we need to know whether England is willing to grant us peace terms that are both just and honorable."

"Are you proposing Hitler be retained as a figurehead?" asks Best.

"I don't like the sound of that," Stevens adds.

"The Wehrmacht is bound by oath to Hitler, but not to the Nazi Party," Martini chips in.

"I can't see the distinction you are making Colonel," queries Klop.

"We should not get caught up in semantics," warns Best.

"I agree. Our prime object is to return Germany to peaceful relations with the rest of the civilized world and support a pan-European policy with England and France," responds Schaemmel.

"Göring would be the only active Nazi leader we would permit to be part of a Wehrmacht government," adds Colonel Martini.

"Even with his debilitating morphine addition?" quips Klop.

"His morphine addition arose from the bullet he took in the groin in the Beer Hall Putsch in 1923, making him a respected national leader," retorts Martini.

"More importantly Göring is a realist and is in agreement with the Wehrmacht that Germany lacks the means to go to war," Schaemmel adds.

"That is no guarantee he won't change his attitude in the future," remarks Stevens.

"If he becomes a problem we can always put him back into a straight jacket," offers Colonel Martini, with a rubbery grimace.

"What about vital issues such the evacuation of German forces from Poland, Czechoslovakia and Austria, the return to freedom of religion, and the return of all the property confiscated from the Jews," advances Klop.

"I suggest these details can be resolved at a later date," counters Best.

"Is it possible the British would be prepared to enter into negotiations with a representative of the old Royal Houses, other than Hohenzollern or Habsburger, or with a person of a similar noble standing?" inquires Colonel Martini.

"I presume you are thinking a royal personage will give your peace negotiations greater credibility. Frankly I do not have the foggiest idea, but we can ask the question," replies Best.

"We need to put all these points on paper for the British Government to consider," urges Schaemmel.

"I would think Major Stevens has already made sufficient notes to rough something out," concludes Best, just as the telephone rings.

"Shall I get that, Sir?" asks Klop.

"Please do, though I can't think who would be calling," Best replies.

Klop goes to the extension phone hanging on the wall near the buffet to answer.

"Dr. Fischer is on the line wanting to know if he should come over," reports Klop.

"Fischer! Err — what should we tell him?" asks Best.

"If Captain Schaemmel and his colleagues are agreeable I suggest we tell Fischer there is no point in him coming now — he could only confuse matters," suggests Stevens.

Schaemmel nods in agreement.

Two hours later at 6.45 pm, after hot debate and after Stevens has used much ink and paper, there is general agreement on the wording of the communication to be transmitted to the British government.

"I will send this off tonight with a request for an urgent response," enthuses Stevens.

"This has been extremely promising. Do we have need for a further meeting gentlemen?" asks Best.

"I doubt Whitehall will rubberstamp this overnight. I suspect they will not be happy until Hitler is dead and buried," Klop mutters.

"Maybe so, but let us wait and see what transpires," entreats Best.

"To answer your question, Captain, it is imperative we have another meeting in order our general can attend," states Schaemmel.

"I had almost forgotten him," quips Best.

"Before we meet the general might I put forward a suggestion?" asks Stevens.

"By all means," replies Best.

"I believe these negotiations could be expedited if we communicated in the future by use of a wireless receiving and transmitting set."

"Seems a little radical, but what do you think Captain?" Best asks Schaemmel.

"It is crucial we keep our lines of communication open. Meeting here in The Hague is fraught with danger and presents considerable risk for us", states Schaemmel.

"That settles it. I imagine the wireless equipment will take some time to organize, Major," surmises Best.

"Not at all. A set will be ready first thing tomorrow morning."

"On that most decisive note I believe a small celebration is in order. You are all invited to stay for dinner. Tonight my wife is out and I have the run of the house," Best announces with a glint in his monocle.

"But we must depart no later than 9 am tomorrow morning to return safely over the border," bleats Lieutenant Grosch.

"I was not planning the dinner to drag on that long, old boy," Best responds.

"Are you sure about this?" Stevens whispers to Best in English.

"Why not?"

"You told me how your housekeeper gossips."

"Maud? Leave her to me. I will think up some cock and bull story. Besides, how can you have a dinner party without a cook?"

While Klop organizes the transfer of the German contingent to the party venue, Stevens goes into Best's office to make two phone calls. First he makes a call to London to give a verbal report on the negotiations to Lord Halifax, the Foreign Secretary. Stevens then telephones his office in The Hague to dictate the wording of the communication to a member of his staff who will be responsible for transmitting a coded telegram to Whitehall.

Two hours later Alexander Cadogan, the Permanent Under-Secretary for Foreign Affairs in Whitehall has cancelled his dinner appointment to answer the communication that has just landed in his IN tray. Stevens' request for a response by 6 am the next morning is optimistic, to say the least. Nevertheless, Cadogan will make every effort to respond to the message from the Passport Control Officer in The Hague, perhaps due to the pressure Lord Halifax has exerted on him after receiving Steven's earlier phone call. The telegram reads:

MOST SECRET
Following declaration is sent at the request of German representatives. They further promise details of their Party in the future. Am arranging to be in daily wireless communication with them, as frequent visits present great difficulty. Germans must leave here 0900 hours October 31st. Request that any comment in reply should reach me latest 0600 hours October 31st.

        Declaration is as follows:-

A. WEHRMACHT has upper hand and although it is prepared to defend Germany, will not countenance a war of aggression.
B. WEHRMACHT is bound by oath to Hitler but has no similar engagement towards the Nazi Party.
C. WEHRMACHT feels strong enough to take a leading part in the formation of a new government but of the Nazi leaders would like GOERING only to be retained in office.
D. Of this Government Hitler would be the constitutional head but the influence of the WEHRMACHT would be decisive.
E. The object of the Government would be the return of Germany to peaceful friendly tranquil relations with the world and it would be sympathetic to a pan-European policy.
F. The change in Germany from a war to a peace footing is only possible with the full co-operation of all civilized countries and therefore the total peace which allays all religions, nationalist and ideological differences would be guaranteed.
G. Would H. M. Government be prepared in principle to enter into negotiations with the representative of one of the old Royal Houses (other than Hohenzollern or Hapsburg), or a person of similar standing.
H. Present military inactivity claimed by our friends to be due to their influence, which they will continue to exercise pending further negotiations.

Footnote: 'Habsburger is misspelt as 'Hapsburg' in point 'G'.

14 — October 30-31, 1939
The Hague

BACK at his house on Lange Voorhout Best requests Klop to keep the Germans entertained in the front parlour while he deals with a more delicate matter.

"Maud!" he calls as he enters the kitchen.

"Yes, Mr. Best?"

"Look here, I have three Swiss bankers coming to dinner, plus Major Stevens and probably Klop."

"Are you telling me I have to cook for six tonight, when I was only planning on one?"

"Is that a problem?"

"Not if you only want omelettes."

"I had something more than omelettes in mind, Maud."

"Cook it yourself then!" protests Maud, whipping off her apron.

By 9 pm the dinner party is in full swing. Best has already arranged for the three German visitors to stay the night in the house of his business partner. Best is also grateful to Klop for suggesting De Poentjak, the nearby Indonesian restaurant. The Germans have never tasted nasi goreng, chicken satay, and the beef rendang before. The take-away food is an instant success.

Drink is flowing liberally once the hot spicy food has been consumed. While Best is dusting off another case of Bladnoch Scotch whisky from his well-stocked cellar, Stevens has a word to Captain Schaemmel.

"I trust the digs Best has found you are not too makeshift," says Stevens.

"I am sure they will be perfectly satisfactory."

"By the way Captain, where are you based?" asks Stevens, realizing he knows nothing of the man who appears to be in full control of the German contingent, even though Colonel Martini is of higher rank.

"Düsseldorf," Schaemmel replies blankly.

"And your unit?"

"Transport, though I have been recently seconded to the Permanent Secretariat of the German Foreign Office."

"That is some promotion! Do you mind if I ask your age Major?"

"Twenty nine."

"Now I think that's enough interrogation for one night. Let me refill your glass Captain," interjects Best, waving an uncorked bottle in the air.

"I will take these plates to the kitchen," Klop offers.

"Excellent idea. What would we do without Klop?" adds Best once he is out of earshot.

"I thought his name was Coppens," queries Colonel Martini.

"Err—it is. Best and I call him Klop, a nickname that's short for Coppens," counters Stevens.

"I will never learn English," sighs Colonel Martini.

"Don't you worry Colonel. The English will need to learn German if Hitler gets his way," quips Stevens.

Best refills the glasses of his guests as Lieutenant Grosch, keen to contribute something to the conversation, goes off on a tangent.

"Did you hear of the young aristocratic English woman who learnt to speak German just so she could befriend the Führer?"

"No, I can't say I have. And did she fulfill her ambition?" inquires Best.

"She did and met with him on a regular basis from 1935, often lunching with him and others in his inner circle at Osteria Bavaria, an

Italian restaurant in Munich. From what I have heard she spent a good deal of time on her knees before him, pleading he keeps Germany on peaceful terms with Britain."

"How commendable, even though she is a Nazi sympathizer," Best declares.

"There is more of course," offers Grosch.

"Like what?" asks Best.

"On the same day Britain declared war on Germany the woman pedaled her pushbike to the English Garden in Munich and shot herself in the head, using the pearl handed pistol she carried in her handbag."

"What a damn theatrical act! Do you know of this, Major?" Best asks Stevens.

"I think the lieutenant is referring to Unity Mitford of the Mitford family of Oxfordshire. Her father is a Peer, and from the reports I have read she is quite unbalanced and more Nazi than the Nazis," states Stevens.

"Unity Valkyrie Mitford is her full name," adds Grosch.

"Good riddance to her, is all I have to say," mutters Best.

"Unity Mitford is not yet dead, Captain. She is receiving excellent medical treatment in a hospital in Munich," Grosch adds. "She may well recover even with a bullet lodged in her head."

"'Valkyrie' is a most unusual middle name for an English woman," observes Klop, having returned from his errand to the kitchen.

"In Norse mythology 'Valkyrie' is one of a host of females who choose those who will die in battle and those who will live," comments Schaemmel.

"I suspect there is more to this story than a simple case of attempted suicide," remarks Klop.

"There is. Unity Mitford was conceived in a town named Swastika in Canada," Grosch reports with a gleam in his eyes.

"This conversation is getting completely out of hand lieutenant. I cannot imagine our hosts want to hear this scuttlebutt fit only for the SS mess halls—particularly as what I want to do now is propose a toast to Captain Best for this most enjoyable evening," says Schaemmel, standing to his feet.

"Well, thank you Captain. What can I say?" responds Best.

"Perhaps you can play us a tune on your fiddle?" Stevens urges half in jest.

"Perhaps I will. But first I need a decent smoke," replies Best as he jumps up to his feet and advances to the sideboard to break open a box of Hoyo de Monterrey Cuban cigars he purchased on a recent trip to Zurich.

"What a shame Dr. Fischer is not here to join in the party," remarks Klop.

"Give the good doctor of economics a ring on the blower. Tell him if he gets on his bike he will be in time for coffee. He only lives a few kilometers down the road," exclaims Best as he distributes cigars to his captive audience.

Next morning Stevens receives the reply to the communication that was sent the night before to London. While lying in bed suffering from the effects of Best's Bladnoch Scotch whisky and the Cuban cigars he reads:

MOST SECRET

```
    A.  Immediate considered reply impossible, but general
        impression given is that proposals make little
        advance whilst retention of Hitler might prove
        insuperable obstacle to any progress in
        negotiations.
    B.  Does WEHRMACHT plan envisage complete elimination of
        Party control with disappearance of leading figures.
    C.  Proposed Royal contact hardly likely to appeal but
        with W/T facilities more considered reply will be
        sent.
    D.  Your verbal statement that there is difficulty in
        obtaining leave for personal contact appears
        inconsistent with your paragraph H.
```

The reply from Alexander Cadogan in Whitehall is less than Stevens had hoped for, though in the circumstances entirely predictable. The strength of the expression 'insuperable obstacle' attracts his attention, while in point 'D' he sees nothing but nit-picking. The mention of 'W/T facilities' reminds Stevens he needs to send the wireless equipment to Best's office pronto.

Klop is on hand to load the wireless equipment into the boot of the same car he will use to drive the three Germans back to the border. Before the Germans show their faces, Best has time for a few words with Klop in his office.

"I appreciate all your help, Dirk, particularly picking the broken glass out of the carpet."

"All part of the job, Sir."

"Now that we have a chance to talk in private, you can tell me the reason for the delay yesterday?"

"The story is bizarre. When I arrived at the border the Germans were nowhere to be seen. I made discreet enquiries to discover they were being held at the local police station. The trio had for some strange reason wandered off into a wood near the border before the Dutch police arrested them.

"Perhaps they went to see a man about a dog," surmises Best.

"Whatever the reason I had one hell of a time persuading the police to release them into my custody. Though there was one positive aspect to this comedy."

"And what was that?"

"I have had serious doubts about these Germans, wondering whether or not they are imposters. So while they were being body searched by the police, I thoroughly searched through all their clothes and their documents."

"And what did you find?"

"Nothing to support my suspicion they are Gestapo or are from any other Nazi intelligence agency."

"I bloody well hope not Klop! Though a scar-faced blighter, Captain Schaemmel seems a decent sort of fellow."

15
Munich

November 1-2, 1939

I AM not dining at the Bürgerbräukeller tonight. I have come with Brög to Alter Simpl. With only one weekend remaining between today and next Wednesday, November 8, it is vital I install the prime component of my apparatus tonight. But first I must see the master carpenter off the premises. For his sake he must remain ignorant of the deadly nature of my invention.

"What movie will you be seeing tonight?" I ask Brög as we wait to be fed.

"*Uproar in Damascus*, with Brigitte Horney and Joachim Gottschalk."

"I loved Brigitte Horney in *Faded Melody* last year. She's a real honey," I confess.

"You should come with me tonight."

"Nay. I need to work on my invention tonight. But what is *Uproar in Damascus* all about?"

"Err—some heroic tale of German troops battling an Arab uprising led by Lawrence of Arabia and the British Army in the 1914-18 war."

"Sounds enthralling."

"I hope so, my friend. The last movie I saw called, *Shoulder Arms*, was ridiculous."

"How so?"

"How could you ever imagine a German emigrant living in Australia becomes so worried his son is being influenced by the democratic, permissive attitudes of his adopted country, he sends him back to Germany for military service? To cap off the stupid plot, the idiot son, who at first resists his unfamiliar lifestyle back in the Fatherland, is eventually converted to the Nazi cause."

"I see what you mean."

Once we finish licking out our bowls of ochsenschwanzsuppe, we nod knowingly and part company. As the master carpenter waddles off down Türkenstrasse into the twilight, I dash back into his workshop, as the time is already 7 pm. I go to the storeroom where I have kept all the vital components of my apparatus locked inside my wooden trunk. I carefully unpack and lay out everything on the floor arranged in the final configuration. The procurement and the manufacture of every one these components for my deadly apparatus has not happened overnight. Nor has all the work been done here in Brög's workshop. If the truth be told a skilled team of local artisans and purveyors have contributed, suppling parts and or their labour, while being oblivious to the true nature of my venture.

For instance the locksmith named Solleder, introduced to me by Brög, has made the 15 mm thick rectangular iron lid with three holes for the connection to the firing mechanism. Solleder has also soldered wire rope for a connection to the ignition device. From the hardware store on Türkenstrasse, Suckfüll, I purchased iron straps, a spiral spring, two bolts with nuts and a threaded screw for the flat iron frame to hold the explosive containers. When I needed small screws I purchased these in a screw specialty shop near to the Viktualienmarkt. On Rosenheimstrasse in Kustermannpark I had a 'T' shaped iron block cast with one slotted hole. In a tool and machine shop in the vicinity of Baderstrasse I purchased two clock weights that needed to be internally threaded. Also I purchased a solid iron rod that I had left threaded by a hardware supplier in Reichenbachstrasse. If I have left out anyone who contributed I apologize.

Once I am fully satisfied all the components are present and are ready for final assembly, I load them back into my trunk for transport to the Bürgerbräukeller. To haul the trunk 4.5 kilometres I need to put Brög's handcart to good use once more. Though this operation is not without an element of risk as pushing a handcart through the streets of Munich could arouse suspicion at any time, day or night. The police, the brown shirted louts or the Gestapo ghouls could intercept me on the street. With the look of a homeless person I could easily be detained and end up in a labour camp, rendering all my solid work a total loss and waste of time.

In fact I am now homeless without a lodging place in Munich. This morning I vacated my room in Lehmann's apartment. Two weeks ago I informed Alfons of my intention to leave at the end of October. My reason had nothing to do with a squealing newborn baby being brought home. My reason was purely financial. With my work rapidly coming to a climax at the Bürgerbräukeller I can save a few extra marks by sleeping rough.

At 9 pm with the loaded trunk roped onto the handcart I set out on my delivery run. I trundle along Türkenstrasse at a moderate pace before speeding up at Odeonsplatz. Without daring to stop to rest I fly past the evil arches of the Feldherrnhalle like the propeller driven train. Not until I reach the Ludwig Bridge do I slow to a normal pace and start to relax. On the bridge I am hit by the realization I only need to cross the Isar one more time before my work is done. I cannot yet imagine what my joy will be like when my heavy burden is lifted and I have crossed into Switzerland.

But thoughts of future bliss evaporate well before I reach the rear of the Bürgerbräukeller at 10.25 pm. Tonight I am not going through the main entrance. Apart from potential damage to the polished parquetry floors, wheeling a handcart loaded with a wooden trunk would look suspicious even in this establishment. I breathe easier when I find the rear door to the beer equipment room is unlocked. Leaving the handcart and the trunk in a dark corner I check the way is clear ahead. Finding the hall lights extinguished and not a soul in sight, I haul the dead weight of the trunk through the hall and up the gallery staircase. As I stop to regain my breath at the top it occurs to me there is no good reason why I cannot commence my work immediately. The sooner I finish the less chance there will be of interruption by an air raid warden on the loose with his wretched dog. Besides, I have no meaty morsel to share with a canine mutt tonight.

After I have opened the secret door I begin to transfer the contents of the trunk directly into the chamber inside the pillar. Once all the bulky components are positioned and connected I pack all the corners of the cavity with as many cartridges and detonators as I can possibly fit. This delicate operation is made possible by using a pair of long wooden handled tongs I have designed and manufactured specifically for this task.

Within three hours I am finished. With a degree of pride I stand back to view my work, allowing the beam of my dimmed flashlight to roam over the dull gleam of the metallic parts. In my mind's eye I enact how the assembly of cogs, levers and the sled with the three firing pins will be set in motion, resulting in a not insignificant explosion. All that now remains to be done before completion is the installation of the timing device.

As I shut the secret door for the last time tonight I sense the extra weight due to the investment I made a number of nights ago. As I feared there existed a possibility the wooden secret door could be penetrated by a nail or a screw driven by a person putting up decorations in the hall I have sheeted the inside of the door panel with 2mm thick plate steel.

Overkill?

Possibly, but as Murphy's Law reminds all reputable tradesmen: if anything can go wrong, it WILL!

Once my hand tools are either back in my pockets or packed into the trunk with surplus detonators and other leftovers, I roll up my kneeling mat. I have been using an offcut of carpet to avoid any further damage to my knees. Why I did not think of this simple solution earlier, I will never know.

When I retreat to my usual hiding place I am greeted by a surprise. The room is bare! All the cardboard boxes have disappeared. Only my workpants remain folded in the corner where I left them last time I was here. The cardboard boxes were only cardboard boxes. Nevertheless they gave me a sense of security. So rather than sleeping alone in an empty room I haul the trunk back to the beer equipment room where I left Brög's handcart. Totally spent I curl up on the damp floor between the beer kegs. My father should be proud of me tonight.

16

November 4-5, 1939
Munich

LATE this afternoon Brög asked me to help deliver another wardrobe. His request could not come at a worse time with the completion of my work now in the death throes. But how could I refuse the master carpenter? For the last three nights I've been camping like a gypsy in his workshop.

Once I have fulfilled my obligation to the master carpenter I hasten to the Bürgerbräukeller, taking the shortest route possible carrying in my arm a package neatly wrapped in a page of newspaper. The installation of my timing device tonight will be the final act in my long running one man show.

But when I walk into the restaurant for my usual hot meal with one glass of beer I am struck by something I had not reckoned on. Up until now my night work has been performed only on weekdays, as I like to keep my weekends free. I had no reason to take any interest whatsoever in the weekend functions at the Bürgerbräukeller — so I never anticipated a Saturday night dance!

What time this dance will end is what disturbs me most. If this dance ends at the normal closing time I have no fears. But if this dance goes past midnight, as some often do, I am in deep trouble. And when I say 'dance' I am referring to the waltz as 'un-German' dancing — such as the jitterbug and the tango — is now strictly prohibited by a killjoy Nazi decree.

"Finished?" the waitress asks, swooping like an eagle to retrieve my plate.

I shock her by drinking down my beer in one gulp. With my timing device wrapped in newspaper and tucked under my arm I head for the hall. Why wait in the restaurant like a social misfit when I can buy a dance ticket?

Avoiding couples reversing and rotating like clockwork on the dance floor, I weave my way towards the staircase to the gallery, waltzing my regime-changing package in my arms as I go. Reaching the gallery I join the handful of spectators who apparently have nothing better to do on a Saturday night. From a chair beside the candidate pillar I watch the dancers below — men in tuxedoes, women in dazzling dresses, some in colourful traditional costume. At the end of the hall the red velvet curtain has been drawn aside to reveal the small stage where a five-man band is playing the music. The gay scene below reminds me of the other side of my life — my musical side.

My musical talent first came to light during my school days. I learnt to play the flute and the piano accordion while a pupil at the local school in Königsbronn. At the end of my schooling and whenever I was freed from soiling my hands with farm work for my parents, I escaped to the house of my best friend, Eugen Rau. He was a live wire. Eugen owned a gramophone and played Ragtime gramophone records. He was also good on his feet and taught me to dance, while I taught myself to play the harmonica.

After leaving the family home in 1923 to pursue my vocation as a cabinetmaker, I might have never played another note had I not met my clarinet playing fellowworker at the Dornier factory. Leo Dannecker was therefore instrumental in taking me across the Bodensee to Konstanz.

Living in that water kissed city I was destined to discover the mother of all stringed instruments — the zither.

My first zither was the Salzburg concert type characterized by a pregnant bulge on the side opposite the straight of the fret board. The stopping of the many strings is done with the left hand. The melody is played with a plectrum fitted onto the thumb of the right hand. The accompaniment strings are played with three fingers, but never with the little one.

A carpenter named Dassler sold me my first concert zither for 20 marks in 1926. I met the man in Konstanz at the Trachtenverein Upper Rhine Valley Traditional Dance and Dress Club where I had become a member. Every Saturday night we would gather to practise together for our entertainment nights of folk music and dance. I became friends with many of the families who attended, including Dassler's daughter, Rosa. Though my interest was solely in the music and in the playing of the zither.

To improve my playing I took private zither lessons with a music teacher. He charged a hefty 1.50 marks per hour. I must have gone to him for thirty odd hours of lessons before I joined the Zither Club in Konstanz. After joining I was encouraged by other zither players at the club to change to a more experienced teacher. He charged me even more per hour. I ended my lessons when I ran short of funds due to my bout of unemployment.

Making music on the zither in Konstanz was interrupted when I moved to Meersburg after Rothmann's bankruptcy. It was during this period of free living that my dear mother's letter arrived, pleading with me to face the music at home. I returned to a situation far worse than before I departed seven years earlier. Simply to stay sane and escape the daily drudgery of the farm work and the endless abuse meted out by my drunkard father I became a member of the Königsbronn Zither Club in 1933.

I recall there were up to twelve players meeting either on a Friday or a Saturday night in a back room of the local inn, Gasthaus Hecht, in Königsbronn. There was Anton Egetemeier, the tailor; Fritz Huber and his brother Paul; two brothers going by the name Staudelmeier; Georg Elser, a locksmith and a distant relative of mine; and my little brother, Leonhard. There were also three pretty young ladies to make up the numbers. I remember their enthusiasm to be coached in the fingering of the zither. I recall one young lady was named Hartmann. Somehow I have forgotten the names of the others.

But other things are not so readily forgotten. Politics hit a harsh discordant note the same year I joined the zither club in Königsbronn, as 1933 was the year Germany fell into the filthy palms of the criminal dictator.

Early in that ill-fated year the fire in the Reichstag in Berlin was a burning question even for simple Swabians. Some in our zither club foolishly believed the arson attack was the sole work of the half crazed Dutchman, Van der Lubbe. Though the intelligent knew full well the Nazis were the instigators and most likely had hired poor Van der Lubbe to do their dirty work. While everyone had their own opinion, one thing was certain. The Nazi bigwigs, Hitler, Göring and Goebbels, turned the Reichstag fire into a political inferno! Even as the building blazed they claimed the conflagration marked the start of the German Bolshevik Revolution that threatened to turn the Fatherland into 'a blood-soaked expanse of rubble' — to use Goebbels's colourful phrase. Within hours the brown shirted louts of the SA with their evil swastika armbands were howling through the streets of cities and towns. Whoever was thought to be a Communist or a sympathizer was beaten to a pulp or vanished overnight. From that time on I decided to wear the Red Front Fighters badge I had gained in Konstanz on the inside of my coat collar.

As I look down from the gallery at the dancers below gyrating to the Blue Danube waltz, I wonder whether my fellow zither players are at practice tonight. They in turn would be wondering why I have not been to a practice since that stone fell on my foot, putting me out of action. Before leaving for Munich on August 5, I sold my string bass for a good price, while entrusting my concert zither to Georg Schmauder, Maria's father. Perhaps I was acting in gratitude for allowing me to live peacefully with his family in their comfortable house in Schnaitheim. This was after I had been forced out of my family home as if I was an intruder. Though the rift I had with my mother and my little brother, Leonhard, bolstered by his bolshy wife, is another saga entirely and not something to mull over now.

My friendship with the Schmauder family began when I met Maria working at the Waldenmaier factory in Heidenheim towards the end of

1938. Maria had an appealing innocence, something I could not resist. Our friendship soon developed and continued even when I left the Waldenmaier factory to work in Georg Vollmer's quarry in Königsbronn in 1939. Around this time I set up my workshop in Schmauder's basement and moved into their garret. While living in their family house I was able to work on the design of my apparatus in the months before I came to Munich. I spent much time working on the technical details and made numerous sketches. Occasionally I would accidentally leave these sketches lying about and if Maria or her mother asked what they were for I always told them I was working on an invention. My answer always satisfied their curiosity and even Maria's father believed what I said. He has always been pleasant towards me and may still have thoughts of marrying off his daughter. Maria and I have kissed, but nothing else has happened. The only mistake I have made with Maria was leaving my trunk unlocked one day. When I came into my room I caught her on her knees with the lid up. Whether she noticed the double bottom I cannot say.

The last waltz is played well after midnight, eating deep into my time to perform my vital installation. As the band packs away their gear and as a doorman is chasing the last couples from the hall, I disappear into my hiding place unnoticed. Inside I am surprised to find an office chair in place of the vanishing cardboard boxes. I take a seat on the unexpected furnishing and rest the package with the timing device inside on my lap to wait for all the hall lights to be extinguished and all the doors to be locked.

As I wait I am intoxicated by the realization this is the last time I will need to work at the Bürgerbräukeller — unless I am terribly mistaken.

17
November 5-7, 1939
Munich-Stuttgart-Munich

I SIT coiled like a spring, ogling yet another meal of sauerbraten. An unforgivable error has brought me back to Bürgerbräukeller—for one more night.

"Finished?" the waitress squawks.

I wish I were, I muse—downing the last of my beer in one gulp. Who would ever believe a dance could be held on both a Saturday and a Sunday night?

Exactly like the night before I fork out on a dance ticket and make my way up to the gallery to watch the dancers on the floor below. Like a modern day Wilhelm Tell I bide my time, sitting on the same chair by the pillar. Last night I pined away the hours recounting the musical side of my life. Though I was sidetracked by thoughts of my latest girlfriend, Maria Schmauder—by no means have I forgotten the love of my life, Elsa Härlen.

Life was insufferable when I returned home in 1932 after living free of my parents for seven years by the fun soaked shores of the Bodensee.

However, in the summer of 1933 things did change for the better in my hometown. This change was not due to my father or mother undergoing a radical transformation in their belief I should work without payment as in the days of serfdom. This change came when Elsa Härlen walked into my life.

We first laid eyes on each other in the woods west of Königsbronn. Elsa was a proud and active member of the Strength-Through-Joy travel organisation. Despite her affiliation with this body-bending, mind manipulating Nazi organization, we hit it off instantly. I was thirty. She was twenty-two. We were a perfect match — even if Elsa was a married woman.

Hermann, her husband was and still is a deadbeat, a drunkard and wife basher out of the same mould as my father. He was forever giving Elsa trouble, black eyes, bruises and precious little sending money, even to buy shoes for her infant daughter, Iris. Hiking became a weekend passion for us both. Elsa was able to escape from Hermann, while I was able to escape from the parental yoke. Like two desperados we would calculate the location and the moment to separate ourselves from the other hikers in the party. On open hillsides or in deep rocky ravines we made love like ravenous wild animals. Our innocent affair came unstuck with the premature birth of Elsa's second child, as Hermann denied all responsibility.

There was more upheaval in my life during 1935. Due to my father descending even deeper into debt, the family home was sold for a song. I was forced to abandon the home workshop I had set up to make a few marks on the side that I could call my own. When I turned to Elsa for help she persuaded her no-hoper husband to permit me to set up my carpentry workshop in their basement. In no time I was sleeping on the premises, paying for my lodging by making Elsa new kitchen chairs and cabinets.

The cabinets were never finished. Elsa decided she had had enough of Hermann and went back to living with her mother in Jebenhausen. I visited her whenever I could, once taking her an inlaid trinket box I had made as a love gift. But as the months passed our relationship fizzled. My hesitation to commit myself to Elsa was possibly the reason. Even when she had separated from her husband I held back. And by the time she was legally divorced from Hermann I was obsessed by something other than love and marriage — how to avoid a catastrophic war.

My decision to act has not been shared about with others like a loose woman. I have been discrete, as one loose word on such a sensitive subject would consign me to a concentration camp. Though one day when I happened to meet my old school friend, Eugen Rau, in a street in Königsbronn I had a brain explosion. Eugen was out walking with his cute wife Emma. Both were in the hiking group where Elsa and I were members until Elsa dropped her bundle. The day I met Eugen must have been near the day Czechoslovakia was horse-traded by Hitler in Munich, with the Czechs being hung out to dry by Chamberlain. In the main street I lost it and blurted out:

"Eugen, we won't get a better future in Germany until the government gets blown up. And I tell you: I'll do it. I'm going to do IT!"

Eugen turned white and told me to keep my voice down before he and Emma disappeared around the next corner.

Returning to my suspended love affair with Elsa, she has now moved out of her mother's place to live in a company house at Esslingen, where she works in the woollen factory. Twice I have visited her on my way to Stuttgart. It is only natural I still want to stay in touch with her. Just two weeks ago I wrote her a letter saying: 'Things are going well in Munich and I have a lovely landlady'. As yet I have had no reply, but I remain hopeful.

Mercifully the dance ends on the stroke of midnight — not at almost 1 am as on the previous night. Thirty minutes later I come from my hiding place, open up the secret door and install the dual timing device without any trauma. Last night was a total disaster. I found I had fabricated the compartment for the timing device fractionally oversize. I was forced to devote all day yesterday rectifying my inexcusable mistake in Brög's workshop.

The connection of the cables between the firing mechanism and the timing device takes longer than I had anticipated due to the sensitive nature of my creation. Needless to say, sending myself to Kingdom come is not part of my plan! But when I find I need to tinker longer making adjustments to a locking screw on the detonation trigger due to another dimensional error, I start to sweat. Over an hour and a half passes before I get everything in order and aligned the way I conceived the design. But this is not the end of my troubles. As often happens in transportation the movements have stopped working. I need to spend time setting the twin clocks in motion and advancing the hands to the correct time by comparison with my wristwatch.

Once this delicate work is completed I am ready to pack away my tools. But before doing this I spend a few minutes opening and closing the door to the timing device compartment. The good contact being made between the door panel and the sound attenuating material is reassuring. I purchased this material from a local merchant after seeing an advertisement in a trade magazine. I thought the acoustic insulation was essential to avoid the risk of somebody hearing ticking inside the pillar. Discovery of my apparatus prior to November 8 would be fatal to my project.

Not until 6 am do I close the door to the timing device compartment and the secret door to the pillar. I have finished so late I hardly have time to lie in my hiding place, though sleep is out of the question in my pent-up state. Once I hear the doors to the hall being unlocked I leave without delay using the emergency exit to reach the back street. The weather has turned wet and cold, but my broad brimmed hat protects me from the drizzle. After crossing the Isar I hasten at a rapid pace to the kiosk at Isartorplatz where I enjoy not one, but two cups of coffee to celebrate.

I take the most direct route to Türkenstrasse, oblivious to any danger. Reaching Brög's workshop by about 7.45 am I head for the storeroom. I might have changed into my dark blue suit, the same suit I wore on my arrival in Munich exactly three months ago, but realize I packed it into my wooden trunk I have already shipped by rail to Stuttgart. Once I pack any remaining gear into my small case I go to the back room. When I open the door I find the master carpenter stretched out as if laying on his deathbed.

"I am leaving Munich," I call standing by his door.

"What about your invention?" Brög croaks, instantly coming back to life.

"My invention is now finished. You will read all about my success in the newspapers," I boast.

"I will miss you," he replies.

"Here is the key you lent me for your storeroom," I add, stepping forward and placing the key into his outstretched hand.

"Danke, my friend."

Not knowing what else to say to the master carpenter, I take up my case and leave.

I hasten along Türkenstrasse to reach Briennerstrasse then turn into Ottostrasse to reach Karlsplatz. My mind is fixed on leaving Munich as soon as possible. I arrive at Munich's main station in plenty of time to catch the 10 am train to Ulm, with an immediate connection to Stuttgart.

I arrive in Stuttgart in the mid afternoon. After leaving the main station I cross the square to Württemberg Court Hotel to look for my brother-in-law. As I am not sure exactly where to find Karl I ask one of the staff at the hotel desk. I am eventually directed to a butcher's shop down the street. After we greet we walk together back to the railway station to collect the things I had shipped from Munich several days ago. Karl helps me load a three-wheeler before he goes back to his butchery work, while I ride in the back of the serviceman's van to Lerchenstrasse 52. Once I have hauled my trunk and my two toolboxes up the stairs to the landing, I knock on the door of the apartment and wait with a pounding heart.

"Georg! What a surprise!" says my sister Maria, finding me on her doorstep.

"Hi, Sis. Sorry but I didn't have time to let you know I was coming today."

"Come in — but what is all this stuff you have brought?"

"I have spoken with Karl and he is happy I leave it here with you."

"Really? When did you speak to him?"

"Just thirty minutes ago. Karl helped me load the serviceman's van at the station."

"Err — well you can't leave it blocking the landing. You had better bring it inside and I will speak to Karl later."

I do as Maria tells me before she has a change of mind.

"Is your grandfather clock I fixed still working?" I ask when I catch up with her in the kitchen.

"Yes, it's fine. Would you like a cup of coffee?"

"You don't have to wait on me hand and foot, you know," I plead as I sit down at the kitchen table.

"I was about to make one for myself before Franz comes home from school."

Maria gives me a weihnachtsplaetzchen while I wait for the coffee.

"I was wondering if I might stay the night?" I ask once I've finished munching.

"If you are only staying one night I don't mind. But it is really up to Karl to decide."

No sooner has my sister spoken than there is hammering at the door. I wonder if the Gestapo are already on my tail. I need not fear. Franz, my six-year old nephew, is the one making the racket. Wearing his Pimpfen uniform, he insists on singing a raucous song taught to him by Hitler Youth leaders. Maria eventually shuts him up and gets him to do his homework that includes more Nazi nonsense. I evade the child's disturbing attics by disappearing into the bathroom to wash and shave. When Karl comes home from work at 7 pm we all sit down for the evening meal.

Maria brings a cooking pot to the table to serve the sauerbraten she has been simmering on the stove all afternoon. I do not have the heart to mention to her I have eaten this same dish for thirty odd nights at the Bürgerbräukeller. Once young Franz has had his snotty face scrubbed and is put to bed by his mother, there is more time for relaxed family conversation.

"Must you leave all your junk with us Georg?" whines Maria.

"I was hoping I could."

"Is this because you are going into the military? I asked you this same question in my letter to you a month ago, but you did not reply."

"I've been busy. And Karl is welcome to anything he wants."

"Like what?"

"Clothes, underwear, tools, screws, two unfinished clock cases, three clock movements, though two are defective due to cracked springs."

"The underwear might be useful for Karl."

I unlock my trunk and toolboxes to show Karl and Maria what I have on offer inside. Neither seems too excited.

"You didn't answer my question about going into the military," nags Maria.

"I am not going into the military. I'm going to Switzerland."

"Why are you going there?"

"I must," is all I answer, not wanting to divulge too much.

"I don't understand you Georg," says Maria, giving me the look of scorn only a sister can give a brother.

As Maria starts clearing the table I wonder if she is recalling my missed alimony payments to Mathilde Niedermann for the support of my son, Manfred, and this is somehow connected with the reason I am going to Switzerland.

"Will you go to see our father before you leave?" Maria asks as she stacks the dishes.

"I would like to."

"He is in poor health, you know."

"I know. If I did go I would also call on the Schmauder family."

"Are you in love with that young girl, Maria?"

"Maybe I am."

There is a clatter of dishes before my sister finishes what she is doing at the sink. I am happy she still appears to be ignorant of my love affair with the married woman, Elsa Härlen.

"You haven't had much to say for yourself, Karl," remarks Maria, taking off her apron.

"What do you want me to say?" replies Karl.

"For a start you could tell Georg whether he can sleep the night."

"I can easily sleep on the floor," I interject.

"My brother-in-law doesn't have to sleep on the floor when he comes to visit. He can sleep with us."

"I slept with my sisters when we were kids, but I never slept with my brothers," Maria counters.

"There is a first time for everything," Karl chuckles.

I wake alone in the marriage bed after a good night's sleep. Karl has already risen and left for work while my sister is doing battle with Franz before sending him to school. As I eat breakfast Maria tells me she will not be going to the factory today. Whether she is taking sick leave she does not say, nor do I bother to ask. As I slept until 9 am I have risen too late to catch the train to Königsbronn to visit my father or even to visit Maria Schmauder in nearby Schnaitheim. But neither visit is important. What is important is whether I have completed my work correctly. I have been agonizing over the timing device, not sure if the dual clock movements are still running and set to the correct time for detonation. My rushed work after the Sunday night dance has troubled me ever since I left Munich. There is only one way to end my self-doubt. I must return to the Bürgerbräukeller.

As my funds are now in a poor shape I ask my sister to lend me something for a train fare. Maria willing gives me 30 marks and a good length of sausage to eat on the train. I have not mentioned to her I am returning to Munich. We have not discussed my destination since last night. I can only assume Maria thinks I am going to Königsbronn and Schnaitheim or to Switzerland. She would never suspect I am returning to Munich.

I leave wearing the same clothes as I wore yesterday, with a pair of pliers, my pocketknife, flashlight and numerous bits and pieces that I have accumulated over the months in the pockets of my trousers. In the street outside I catch a tram to the main station, arriving in good time for the 4 pm train to Munich. But before boarding I cross the square to visit Karl at his place of employment. As I did not see him this morning I want to thank him for his hospitality. Once we shake hands I head to the station while he returns to his raw meat.

My train reaches Munich shortly before 10 pm. Rather than walk to the Bürgerbräukeller, as I would normally, I go by tram to save time, fearing the doors will be locked before I arrive. The time is already 10.29 pm when I go through the arched portal off Rosenheimerstrasse and pass the cloakroom to reach the hall. I am relieved the doors are not yet locked and I enter the darkened space without being observed. Reaching the top of the staircase I half run, half stumble past the cluster of tables and chairs to reach the pillar. Pressing my ear hard against the secret door I can only hear blood pulsating through my head. But in time, despite the acoustic insulation, I hear what I have come to hear—a faint ticking.

The clocks are still in motion, but are they correctly set? I take my flashlight from my coat pocket and using my pocketknife I prise open the secret door and then open the inner insulated door to the timing device compartment. After using my wristwatch to check the clocks have not gained time or lost time, and after I double check the time of detonation has been correctly set for 9.20 pm tomorrow night, I am satisfied there is nothing more I can do. After I close the inner and outer door I return to my old hiding place. Without any cardboard boxes to lie behind and without my small case to rest my head, I must make do with sleeping in the office chair.

My backside is numb when I wake to leave via the emergency exit after 6.30 am. From the back street I cross the Isar for what must be the very last time and go to the same kiosk in Isartorplatz to drink another two cups of coffee. After the repeat run of my celebration I hasten to Brög's workshop with the rain coming down in buckets. I want to thank the master carpenter for the use of his workshop facilities, his storeroom and his handcart. I also want to say goodbye again as I may have been short on words the day before. But when I call on Brög he is nowhere to be found.

I walk another block in the wet to knock on the door of apartment No.11. As I wait I start to wonder if the Lehmann's have vanished like Brög — and been taken in for interrogation even before the mayhem of my bomb.

But after a long delay Rosa comes to answer the door wearing her nightdress. I know I have called early in the morning, but still she looks a fright with her long brown hair hanging down in what seems a terrible tangle.

"Has any mail come for me?" I ask.

"No — nothing," she answers, as if I'm a total stranger and a person to be feared.

Not giving me a chance to utter another word she shuts the door. For a long minute I stand on the landing in case she has a change of heart, before I turn and go.

With my broad brimmed black hat pulled down and my coat collar turned up I pace along Türkenstrasse, my eyes seeing nothing save my destination. Reaching Munich's main station I buy a 3rd class ticket to Friedrichshafen, via Ulm. The fare costs me 11 marks, but thanks to my sister Maria I still have sufficient funds to see me across the border. There is nothing to hold me in Germany now — though not receiving a letter from Elsa Härlen is annoying.

18

November 7, 1939

Venlo

AFTER a pit stop on the southern outskirts of Eindhoven, Best puts his foot down. He has been on this fast road before with Jan Lemmens back in September to meet Solms. Stevens is sitting beside the driver, while Dirk Klop has the vast expanse of the Lincoln's back seat to share with himself.

"Best tells me you are to blame for the meeting being held in Venlo," says Stevens, turning to Klop.

"I plead guilty, but bringing the Germans to The Hague again would have been too risky. Venlo is an ideal location being near the border without the problems of Dinxperlo," advises Klop.

"Waiting about in Zutphen that day for you and Fischer to return from Dinxperlo was a real bugger. I hope you are right about Venlo," whines Stevens.

"There should be no problem, Sir," replies Klop.

"So where do we meet in Venlo? Stevens asks Best.

"Hotel American."

"Is that where you meet with that fellow Solms?" asks Stevens.

"No. I meet him at Hotel Wilhelmina."

"So why the change?"

"Meeting in the same location three times running is far too risky. Besides, going by *Les Routiers* the conference room at Hotel American has a unique leadlight ceiling and there is an adjoining room for playing skittles," enthuses Best.

"Skittles! I see. If we have to hang around for endless hours we can play skittles," muses Stevens.

Best has no response, apart from planting his foot on the accelerator pedal.

Venlo is reached without further discussion. After the bridge over the river Meuse, Best turns into Keulsepoort and parks opposite the modest three storey Hotel American. A chilling wind swirls the fallen leaves as the three men get out of the car and take a moment to adjust their felt hats and overcoats.

"Feels cold enough to snow," says Best, rubbing his hands together.

"Those black clouds certainly look ominous," adds Stevens.

"I've booked a room but we'll be waiting in the hotel bar," Best tells Klop.

"Very good," replies Klop, before he goes off to find a taxi to take him to the border.

The two Englishmen hurry inside the hotel lobby. After Best makes himself known to the concierge he prowls about looking for the skittles room while Stevens orders drinks in the overheated bar and settles at a table.

"Did you find it?" asks Stevens when Best rejoins him.

"I did. You should take a look."

"I will, later. Here's to Captain Coppens not being too long and the jerries have arrived on time this time," proposes Stevens, raising his glass.

"Klop should be back within half an hour."

"How far is the border?"

"As the crow flies about five miles."

Stevens makes no reply, content to down his beer and let Best pose the next question.

"Has any communication come by way of your wireless equipment?"

"There were technical hitches in the first few days, though these have been ironed out now. A message came asking our opinion on persons acceptable to conduct future negotiations. This however is now of a secondary nature, as only yesterday a full response came through from Cadogan."

"Have I seen that?"

"I assumed you would have, though the tone was noncommittal, as you would expect coming from the War Cabinet."

"The War Cabinet! If something came from the War Cabinet I think I need to be kept informed,"

"Mr. Best!"

"Err—yes."

"There is a phone call for you in the hotel office, Sir," the concierge advises.

"If that's not Klop I'll eat my hat," Best quips as he heads to the hotel office, taking his drink with him.

"Captain Best?"

"Yes."

"Klop here, Sir."

"What is it?"

"Grosch and Captain Schaemmel have arrived but they refuse point blank to go into Venlo."

"That's ridiculous! What's their problem?"

"They fear for their safety if they stray too far from the border."

"But I can vouchsafe for their safety."

"Can you?"

"Well—within limits."

"There is a café here in no-man's land with a private room which is ideal for our purposes," replies Klop.

"This is a bloody spanner in the works, Klop!"

"I don't think anything you or I say will change their minds. They have dug in their heels."

"Bloody Huns! Hold the line, will you, while I ask Major Stevens what he thinks about this. Err—no I won't. What's the name of this café?"

"Backus. You can't miss it Sir, provided you take the road called, Herungerberg."

Five minutes later Stevens has his *Michelin* map open on his knees as he guides Best out of Venlo, going in a northwest direction towards the border.

"I'm surprised you agreed so readily to the German demands simply on **Klop's say-so**. We need to think of our own safety first, rather than the safety of the Germans," lectures Stevens.

"I'll turn back if you want."

"No—keep going, we are almost there," replies Stevens. "Besides, we have been instructed by our masters in Whitehall to pursue this matter with *energy*."

"I only hope Klop knows what he is doing by leading us out here," mutters Best.

A long straight section of tree lined road stretches ahead. Best grips the steering wheel tighter than normal, even though the speedometer is not budging over 30 mph. Several buildings appear in the distance on both sides of the road. Steven's attention is soon drawn to the red brick building with a red tiled roof standing close to the road on the left hand side.

"This looks like it," he informs Best.

"Positive?"

"Positive. The border boom gate is dead ahead. If we go any further we'll be in Germany."

Best steps on the footbrake, bringing the Lincoln to a stop directly opposite café Backus. He has to back up so he can nose into the parking space on the Venlo side of café. Once Best is out of the car he looks towards the roof terrace where umbrellas are closed due to the inclement weather. The big windows are complete with flower boxes and canvas awnings.

Klop comes to the front door to greet the Englishmen. He then leads them through the public dining room to reach a private room where the Germans are waiting.

"Good afternoon gentlemen," says Best as he enters, removing his felt hat.

Klop closes the door and Lieutenant Grosch and Captain Schaemmel rise to their feet to shake hands.

"I see Colonel Martini is not with us," remarks Best.

"He had another appointment today," Schaemmel explains.

"Pity. I thought the Colonel's contribution was invaluable at our last meeting. Though I must pick a bone with you Captain. I am exceedingly disappointed you were not willing to go a few extra miles to the agreed rendezvous," complains Best.

"We are safer here in no-mans land, Captain," replies Schaemmel.

"Maybe. But I had a luncheon booked at Venlo's premier venue, the Hotel American," explains Best.

"I've arranged with the manager to provide a light meal at 1 pm Sir," interjects Klop.

"I only hope I can last out till then," mutters Best.

"I am sure you will, Captain," says Schaemmel.

"Shall we sit down?" Stevens suggests.

"Cigarette anyone?" asks Best, waving his pack of Pall Malls.

All accept the offer.

"I will leave it to Major Stevens to provide you with a resumé of our government's position. He is more au fait with the intricacies of the negotiations than I happen to be at this juncture," explains Best, flicking open his lighter.

Best leans back in his chair to study the ceiling and puff on his cigarette as Stevens leans forward to deliver his message.

"Yesterday I received His Majesty's Government's response, apropos our communication of October 30th. The main gist of our government's position is unequivocal—there must be a restoration of the confidence that has been destroyed by the Nazi regime and this can only be achieved by a change of both the regime and the spirit behind it. The new German government must inspire confidence if our negotiations are to continue."

"Is this code for Hitler must go?" Klop interjects.

"Quite possibly. Our government also requests further details of the Wehrmacht's proposals to return Germany to peaceful relations with the rest of the world, with the object being—I quote, 'total peace'. And the final point in the communication is that the French must be consulted first."

"The French! We would prefer to negotiate only with the civilized English," snaps Schaemmel.

"Maybe, but the simple fact is Britain and France are in lockstep," Stevens explains. "And our Prime Minister has stated, though neither country has any desire to carry on a vindictive war with Germany, there remains the determination to prevent Germany making life in Europe unbearable."

"Unbearable? Life in Europe will be more than unbearable. Life will be horrific if this war proceeds!" counters Schaemmel.

"That maybe so, but as far as Whitehall is concerned the next move in the negotiations is entirely with the representatives of the Wehrmacht," concludes Stevens.

"Which brings me to ask — where is the general?" Best asks, returning his monocle to eye level.

"He could not come today. However I will come with the general tomorrow. And if necessary we will fly to London together in order to complete the peace negotiations with the British government," advises Schaemmel.

"I can arrange to have an aircraft at Schiphol airport at any time, day or night," offers Stevens.

"Forget the aircraft for now. We need to take one step at a time. Bring your general tomorrow to show you mean business," counters Best.

"Believe me Captain," starts Schaemmel, "the general is just as anxious to meet with you as you are to meet with him. He also wishes to entrust secret papers into your hands. The plot in which he is involved may fail, as plots often do. He would not want the record of his work and that of his friends to be lost, and there are other important points he can only discuss with you."

"I see. Then at what time can your general come tomorrow?" Best inquires.

"Midday. You can meet him here in this room," Schaemmel confirms.

"I would prefer to meet at a hotel in Venlo, rather than here," retorts Best.

"The general would not agree to that."

"No?"

"No, Captain."

"Well — I guess we meet here then. But if you do not produce a general tomorrow I will have you for dinner!" warns Best.

19   November 8, 1939
Venlo

BEST is getting more open road driving than he had bargained on. Stevens and Klop are again his travel companions. After a pit stop on the southern outskirts of Eindhoven he drives on to Venlo. With the Lincoln guzzling the fuel on a straight stretch of road Stevens has something to offer.

"If Schaemmel turns up with a general today we could be on the threshold of genuine peace negotiations."

"Looking for a knighthood are you?" quips Best.

"Who knows? On the other hand we could be writing our own death warrants by agreeing to meet at the same location," mutters Stevens.

"The Gestapo could have Schaemmel under surveillance and as the meeting place is only metres from the German border they could catch us all red handed?" Klop chips in from the back seat.

"Only yesterday you pooh-poohed the idea there was any danger. Now you suddenly come out with this most unpleasant scenario," Best complains.

"If you stop in Venlo at police headquarters I will arrange armed protection for us, Sir," proposes Klop.

"Now you are talking sense!" enthuses Best.

The two Englishmen remain seated in the parked Lincoln while Klop makes the arrangements inside Venlo police station. The time is already 11.55 am, far too late to go for a drink with the meeting scheduled for midday.

"All done," is all Klop says as he returns to the back seat of the Lincoln.

At 12.15 pm Best parks the Lincoln beside café Backus exactly as he had parked the day before. In the same private dining room they find Schaemmel standing alone by the window.

"Sorry to be late Captain, but we had to change a flat tyre," Best lies needlessly.

"Is Lieutenant Grosch coming today?" asks Stevens.

"No, not today," replies Schaemmel, as he moves from the window to the table.

"And is the general on his way? I expect he would have his own transport," Best surmises.

"The general is not coming," announces Schaemmel as he grinds the butt of his cigarette into the glass ashtray.

"That's a body blow," bleats Best.

"Sit down and I'll explain," says Schaemmel.

"Anyone need a fag? I know I do," mutters Best, going for his coat pocket.

"Have one of mine — Turkish," offers Schaemmel, waving his pack of Fatima cigarettes in the air. Best and Stevens accept. Klop declines the offer.

"General von Wietersheim was intent on coming today in order to form his personal opinion of your bona fides and to give further details. Unfortunately he was called away at the last minute by Hitler to attend an urgent conference in Munich. The purpose of the conference being to consider an appeal for peace by the Queen of the Netherlands and the King of Belgium."

"That sounds a worthwhile meeting," Stevens concedes.

"If Queen Wilhelmina can't twist Hitler's arm, nobody can, just ask my wife," quips Best.

"What has your wife got to do with it?" asks Schaemmel.

"She is painting Wilhelmina's portrait, but that is a private matter, something I should not have mentioned," concedes Best.

"What chance is there Hitler will be swayed by this Royal overture, Captain," asks Stevens.

"I expect zilch, as the Americans would say. That is why there will still be an attempt against the Führer this coming Saturday," advises Schaemmel.

"That sounds promising. So we sit on our hands until then," suggests Stevens.

"No way. Tomorrow is the last chance you have to meet with the general," advises Schaemmel.

"Are you flagging another friggin' meeting?" groans Stevens.

"I am. Many lives are at stake. It is encumbered on us to do all we can in the cause of peace—even if we suffer a little personal discomfort," replies Schaemmel.

"Noble words," quips Best.

"So do you agree to meet the general here tomorrow?" Schaemmel inquires.

Best turns to Stevens to gauge his reaction.

"Coming again will be a bugger but Whitehall is expecting us to meet the big man," offers Stevens.

"In that case expect to see us tomorrow," Best confirms.

"You have made a wise decision, gentlemen," remarks Schaemmel.

"Midday would suit us," says Stevens.

"Sorry, but midday is quite impossible for the general. He'll be still returning from Munich and cannot possibly be here until 4 pm," advises Schaemmel.

"4 pm is far too late in the day!" Best protests.

"What is your concern Captain? Afterwards you can dine at that hotel in Venlo you were itching to patronize," suggests Schaemmel.

"The American?"

"I have not been there myself, though I once enjoyed a drink at the nearby bar named after the American writer, Hemingway," Schaemmel confesses.

"I found *A Farwell to Arms* by Ernest Hemingway a most moving novel, Klop chips in, unable to contain his enthusiasm.

"Maybe, but to my mind that book was nowhere as moving as the book by Erich Maria Remarque, *All Quiet on the Western Front*," interjects Stevens.

"The less said about Remarque's book the better," snaps Schaemmel.

"Why so, Captain?" asks Klop.

"A book that polarizes the German people and denigrates the ethos of the German soldier must be suppressed. I have no regrets that copies were first burnt in public in Kaiserlautern back in 1933," Schaemmel states.

"You have an exceptional memory, Captain," observes Stevens."

"Some things stick in your mind, particularly as Kaiserlautern is not so far from my hometown of Saarbrücken," admits Schaemmel.

"Did you take part," probes Klop.

"I took no part in book burnings in Berlin, Munich or anywhere else though a few university students I knew did take an part," Schaemmel retorts.

"To my mind the Nazis did Remarque a favour by sending him into exile in Switzerland. Now he must live off his huge book royalties in Hollywood, while being totally besotted with Marlene Dietrich," jokes Stevens.

"I don't want to sound an illiterate or be boorish, but can we get back to the matter at hand," intervenes Best, giving Stevens a glance of utter disgust.

"Not before time," says Schaemmel, looking a little inflamed. "So is it settled?"

"Is what settled?" asks Best.

"Will you be here at 4 pm tomorrow to meet with the general? If you are in agreement there exists the real possibility this war can be ended quickly — saving the world from a catastrophic conflict that could last five years with casualties in the millions."

Best stubs his cigarette in the ashtray on the table and stands tall before he offers his answer.

"We will be here, Captain. I just pray to God your general can work a miracle."

20

November 8, 1939

Friedrichshafen-Konstanz

MY train terminates at Friedrichshafen at 5.55 pm. With a handful of other passengers I hurry across to the pier to find the next steamer to Konstanz departs in forty-five minutes time. I have not shaved since staying with my sister Maria so rather than stand about in public with the dark shadow of a criminal I take a walk along the main street to find a barber.

There are two youths ahead of me, but I take a seat, hoping the ferry will not leave without me. As I wait my turn I browse the pretty faces in *Wiener Magazin,* saving me from my dark thoughts of malfunction in Munich.

"What you like, Signore? I give you smart haircut?" the Italian barber threatens once he has me in his chair.

"Nay! I only have time for shave." I plead, fearing a fascist shearing. As a musician I have always had long wavy hair rather than short back and sides.

The cologne is still stinging as I hurry back to the pier. Tonight the

Bodensee is wrapped in a black shroud in stark contrast to the day I first made this same trip with Leo Dannecker in the summer of 1925. With the sun blazing high in the sky we basked on the deck chairs, toasting our chests, not having a clue what lay ahead of us. Though, I can recall my mother once saying—if we knew the future living would become unbearable.

Tonight I join a well-coated bunch of comatose passengers huddled in the saloon by the hissing engine. A moment after I board the boat is moving out into the darkness. When we reach Meersburg my mind returns to the box of five clock movements given to me in lieu of wages. Old man Rothmund could never imagine where two of those five movements are now installed, or the unique purpose they have been assigned.

After blasting its horn several times the steamer passes the green light on the harbour wall, leaving Meersburg behind. Seeing ahead the flicker of lights in the blackness I know my destination is near. I also note the time is 8.30 pm—the starting time of the Nazi rally at the Bürgerbräukeller tonight. My mind sizzles on these two thoughts until we dock at Konstanz.

With my feet on dry land my mind switches to the task of crossing the border. Though I have not eaten a sausage all day I have no thought of stopping to fill my stomach. My only thought is on how to cross into Switzerland. When I lived here I had a permit that allowed me to cross the border daily, going to and from my workplace by bicycle. I lost that permit long ago. Though after eight years I would expect the permit would have expired by now. So without a permit what are my options? Attempting to talk my way past the border police would be unwise. Jumping the boom gate hoping to catch the border police off guard would be idiotic. I could easily end up with a bullet hole in my back. The only way to go appears to be through the fence. I recall the fence is about two metres high, made of chain-wire with two strands of barbed wire at the top. With a pair of pliers in my pocket I have the means to cut my way to freedom. All I need do is find a location out of sight of the border police.

From the harbour my feet are guided more by instinct than by anything else. I walk along darkened streets I know and others I have never trod. After ten or twelve minutes I come to the entrance to the Wessenberg gardens. I stop. Ahead I can see the dull glint of chain wire beneath a streetlamp. Further to the right the fence is in darkness. I set off again, heading in that direction. After twenty paces I stop and stand perfectly still. Hearing nothing and seeing nothing I start across open ground as if out on an evening stroll, passing the corner of Wessenberg house.

"Hello!" a voice calls.

I stop and look about. Seeing no one I continue towards the dark length of fence. The voice I heard call out must have been inside my head.

"Where are you going?" the same voice calls a moment later.

Again I stop. Screwing my head to the right I see a man coming from the shadows beside Wessenberg house. It seems the voice was not my imagination.

"What are you doing here?" he asks.

Now that he is standing more in the light I see by the uniform he is wearing he is attached to the border police. I also notice he is not alone as another man has stepped out from the deep shadows cast by the house.

"I'm looking for a friend," I reply.

"What is your friend's name?" the man asks as he comes a few steps closer.

"Feuchtelhuber. He's an old friend from the Konstanz Folk Dress and Dance Club."

"Sorry, I cannot help you but I know someone who may be able help you find your friend," he says as if he has a genuine concern for my welfare.

Not wanting to act in a suspicious manner, I have no option other than accept the help of the officer. I wait as he speaks in confidence to his silent partner, apparently telling him to return to standing in the shadows. When the officer joins me we walk together to the border control office. Once inside I am asked to empty my pockets onto a table. I assume the reason for this is to discover whether I have a concealed weapon, such as a gun. Without thinking I pull out the pliers and all the metallic bits and pieces that have accumulated in my pockets over the past few months. As I look down at these objects, that include detonator parts and igniters I took from the Waldenmaier factory in Heidenheim, I am hit by my stupidity. While in Munich this morning I thought of throwing all this stuff into the Isar, but I forgot. Before boarding the steamer tonight I thought of throwing everything into the Bodensee, but I forgot.

As I stand at the table with my pockets turned inside out my last gram of energy drains from my body. My knees go weak. I feel terribly weary. I need to lie down. On the floor would do. I could fall asleep anywhere — instantly. But I am not allowed to lie down — not here.

But it turns out the border police are not so interested in the contents of my pockets when one of them discovers something pinned inside my coat collar.

"What is this?" asks the officer as if he has struck gold.

"A keepsake."

"So you are a member of a banned organization, the RFB!" he snaps.

"I was never an active member."

My feeble claim is ignored. I am put in handcuffs and two border policemen walk me to a building located somewhere in a backstreet of Konstanz. They take me into an upper room where I am told to wait. When I am allowed to sit on one of the chairs I lay my head down on the table, hoping to fall asleep. Sleep has almost overtaken me when I am poked in the back and told to wake up. A young man in a uniform I recognise to be Gestapo, sits down opposite me. He offers me a cigarette from the pack he waves in front of my nose. I accept his offer even though I gave up smoking years ago. After he lights my cigarette his questions begin.

I maintain my story I have come to Konstanz to look for my fictitious friend, Feuchtelhuber, and the pliers and the other odds and sods in my pockets are my tools of trade as a cabinetmaker and a quarryman. When I mention my recent employment at Vollmer's quarry in Königsbronn he appears impressed by my plausible story. If not for the RFB badge I had pinned inside my collar years before, the young Gestapo officer might have kicked me out the door.

Just as he is nearing the end of his tedious paperwork, punching the keys on his Adler Standard typewriter, and well after I have smoked the cigarette, he is called away by another officer. When I start thinking he is never coming back, he returns with both good and bad news.

"We have just received a message of an explosion in Munich. All borders are now closed. All suspicious characters are to be detained until the perpetrators are caught."

"I understand — but have you a room with a comfortable bed?"

21

November 9, 1939

The Hague–Venlo

AT 10.15 am on another dismal day Best steers his red Ford Lincoln Zephyr into the gravel driveway of the mansion at Nieuwe Parklaan 57. Stevens has the front door open even before Best can reach for the doorbell.

"Saw me coming, did you?" jibes Best.

"I heard the crunch of your tyres on the gravel," responds Stevens.

"So why have you dragged me here this early?"

"Follow me."

Best trails his colleague along the hallway before entering a spacious room opening onto a garden.

"What do you think?" asks Stevens as he waves his hand over the two pistols lying on the billiard table.

"I thought we had ironed out our differences?" says Best.

"This is no time to jest—Best!"

"I almost shot myself in the foot with one of those," Best confesses.

Stevens looks incredulous before offering an explanation.

"You were probably using your Webley service revolver. These little beauties are the latest thing and hold thirteen rounds, not six."

"So you think we should pack a gun today?" asks Best.

"I do—just in case."

Best lifts a pistol off the baize and aims at the cuckoo clock over the mantelpiece.

"If you want to shoot somebody release the safety catch and squeeze the trigger. You can kill a man at fifty metres with a Browning HP-35," enthuses Stevens.

"You seem to have an unhealthy knowledge of firearms, but in our business I guess we need to bite the bullet."

"Cut the wisecracks. Just load it and stick the flaming thing in your pocket."

Best does as he is told under supervision. Stevens then diverts to a different matter.

"I expect you saw the report from Munich in the *De Telegraaf* this morning?"

"Since early this morning I've been frightfully busy catching up with private paperwork, but I presume you are referring Hitler's narrow squeak last night."

"I am. Regrettably it seems he and his entourage left the beer hall a few minutes too early."

"Do you think Schaemmel and his general had anything to do with this?" asks Best.

"I doubt it. One report from Paris Radio suggests Himmler and Hitler orchestrated the bombing for propaganda purposes," remarks Stevens.

"If that is the case Herr Hitler is madder than we thought," surmises Best.

A ring on the doorbell causes Stevens to leave the room, allowing Best to make himself comfortable on the Chesterfield. He barely has time to pull a pack of Pall Malls from his coat pocket when Stevens returns with Klop.

"Sorry to be late but I was held up due to a report the German invasion is on the cards any moment. Nevertheless good morning, Sir," Klop greets Best.

"With the Hun at the door what is *good* about it?" Best groans.

"I doubt the German invasion will happen today or tomorrow from the information I have," Stevens responds with confidence.

After a good deal of brainstorming by the three on whether General von Wietersheim may be using today's meeting as an escape route from the Nazis, and how such an eventuality can be handled diplomatically, the phone rings. Stevens hurries to answer. Two minutes later he returns mystified.

"We could be off the hook."

"Has Schaemmel cancelled?" asks Klop.

"Not sure. We'll know when the message is decoded in thirty or forty minutes."

"You two had better play billiards or pool while we wait," suggests Best.

Klop takes a stick from the rack and instantly pockets the red ball. Stevens is not interested in playing.

"If the meeting takes place today I can only hope Schaemmel brings the big man," grinds Stevens. "All this shilly-shallying is driving me up the wall."

"Maybe we should wash our hands of the whole infernal business and leave it to the Huns to run their own regime-changing rigmarole," muses Best, blowing smoke rings across the billiard table.

After a long period of contemplative silence deepened by the sudden click of colliding billiard balls, Best comes up with something important to say.

"I told Lemmens we would pick him up at midday."

"Is he driving today?" asks Stevens.

"No, but as his wife has now had the kid I asked him to come along. If we decide to return from Venlo by train, he can drive the Lincoln back alone," Best explains.

"I don't mind returning by train. Driving at night is the pits," admits Stevens.

"May hates me driving day or night. She says I drive too fast, the silly woman. But knowing I'll not be driving at night will be of some comfort to her, though she did tell me not to come home until after her bridge party."

"Sounds like you are living in a marital minefield and a meeting on the German border will be a cakewalk."

Best makes no response. Klop pockets the black and returns the stick to the rack. When the telephone rings a minute later Stevens rushes to his office.

"Has he cancelled?" Best inquires, as Stevens returns looking less perplexed.

"The message had nothing to do with our meeting today in Venlo. It *was* from Schaemmel or from one of his crew, but was innocuous, being simply a request for a change of hours of wireless transmission," reports Stevens.

"So the matter is settled. We go. Do you mind ringing Lemmens? Tell him we will pick him up outside his garage in ten minutes," says Best.

"You're calling the shots, Captain," mutters Stevens, heading back to his office.

Venlo is over a three-hour drive from The Hague, excluding stops. After crossing the Lek, the Waal and the Meuse rivers, a roadside café in the northern fringes of Den Bosch is as good as anywhere to stop for a quick lunch. The weather is as bleak as ever when the four climb from the red Ford Lincoln Zephyr and enter the steamy café. At this time of the day truck drivers are freewheeling with the gypsy ladies working the tables. Who the new arrivals are or where they are going is of no interest to them. Even if their meeting today saves the lives of fifty million people, what would they care? All that matters is the new arrivals have the guilders in their pockets to pay for the spicy meatballs and the hot cocoa they order.

While the four are still in a huddle at a table, Lemmens does some lateral thinking.

"I don't mind if you drop me off in Venlo before you go to your meeting, Mr. Best."

"I presume this is so you can drink at the Hemingway bar like we did after meeting Solms," replies Best.

"Anything wrong with that?"

"No—but I would have to drive back to Venlo railway station. There could be a hitch and you never know what might happen. So I think it best we stick together."

"Whatever you say, Mr Best," concedes Jan Lemmens, even if the logic escapes him.

Before the journey of the four is resumed there is a change in the seating arrangement inside the left-hand drive Ford Lincoln Zephyr. Stevens moves from the back seat to sit in the front, while Lemmens moves from the front seat to join Dirk Klop in the back directly behind Best, the driver. By some strange coincidence this is the first time all Best's covert companions are on the road together—apart from the illusive Dr. Franz Fischer.

After the gasoline tank has been topped up at a filling station, Jan Lemmens offers to take the wheel. But Best insists on driving, in spite of his lack of sleep last night. Stevens is equally intent on staying on the job. With a notebook and a fountain pen in hand, he is busy compiling a list of personnel to be evacuated from The Netherlands in the event of a German invasion.

As on the previous day a stop is made at the Venlo police station where Klop arranges for an armed police squad to be deployed to the frontier. Once Klop returns to the back seat and Best has the Lincoln Zephyr accelerating out of town, Stevens comes up with a very good question.

"How long will it take the armed police squad to reach the border?"

"Depends on how fast they peddle," Klop replies.

"Peddle!" exclaims Best.

"Peddle their bicycles," Klop clarifies.

"So they may take half an hour to reach the border while we'll be there in ten minutes," observes Stevens.

"I would say so, Sir."

"Should we wait a bit?" Stevens asks Best.

"The time is already 3.50 pm. I'll be damned if I'm going to arrive late again," exclaims Best.

"Not after your carry on over the 4 pm start time," Stevens murmurs.

Best ignores Steven's sarcasm, while Klop makes his contribution to the situation.

"Sunset is at 4.55 pm today, so the sooner we start and finish the better. But that's only my humble opinion, Sir."

"Good thinking," concedes Stevens.

Best refrains from commenting on Klop's prognosis. He is too busy working his way through the gears as if he is leaning to drive all over again.

On the outskirts of the town and immediately after a right-hand turn a man steps onto the roadway waving a red flag.

"What tha___!!" exclaims Best, slamming on the brakes.

"What's up?" Best asks the soldier as he winds down his window.

"You cannot proceed past this point. This is a militarised zone," the Dutch soldier replies.

"Should we turn back?" Best asks hopefully.

"You must."

"Let me speak to your commander as we are on important official business," Klop pipes up from the back seat.

"In that case, come with me," agrees the Dutch soldier.

Best and Stevens watch through the windscreen as Klop walks down the road towards a Dutch military command post.

"This is a bugger," groans Stevens.

"I'm hoping Klop has met his match so we can all go home for dinner," says Best.

"Nice thought—but what if the general comes and we are not there?" reasons Stevens.

"True—and while I think of it—I noticed the list you were making earlier. Do you think it is wise to be carrying that sort of information in your pocket?"

"You're right. I will dump the list the first opportunity I get, but here comes Klop. We will know our fate soon enough."

Upon reaching the Lincoln, an effervescent Klop leans through the open window to report.

"Good news. We can proceed with caution."

With sullen face, Best restarts the engine. The car moves off down the deserted road, the whitewall tyres spinning like prayer wheels in the failing light. Reaching the next fork in the road, the last before the long straight stretch to the border, another Dutch soldier is sighted making hand signals by the side of the road. But this time there is no signal to stop.

Halfway along the last straight stretch of tree lined road the three buildings in the distance become more distinct to those inside the Lincoln. The small Dutch customs house set back on the right hand side of the road is visible. Café Backus is directly opposite with the awnings over the large windows retracted. Also on the left-hand side of the road, though almost obscured by Café Backus, stands the two storey German border house.

Stevens is first to notice something different from yesterday and the day before that.

"The border is open without another vehicle in sight. How odd," he remarks.

Best makes no response. His eye is caught by something else—a girl playing with a ball and a black dog on the right-hand side of the road. Fearing the girl might run into the path of the car he slows to a crawl, as a man standing at the front corner of the café veranda raises his hand in the air.

"That's Schaemmel. He must be indicating the big man is already inside," says Stevens.

Best stops the Lincoln in the centre of the road directly opposite Café Backus. When he finds reverse gear he backs the car in beside the building—unlike the way he drove in nose first on the two previous days, perhaps so the Lincoln is facing in the right direction for a quick get-away.

Stevens opens his door on the right hand side of the car and gets out. Best pulls on the handbrake and cuts the engine. He is about to remove the ignition key when a big open car rounds the corner of the café at speed.

The car skids to a stop an inch from the bumper of the Lincoln. Best freezes behind the wheel. Men in the garb of bandits jump from the running boards, waving guns, shouting and gesturing to Best to get out of the car. He complies in a trance of disbelief—to join the stupefied Stevens.

K—pang!!

The windscreen of the open car has been holed. The Dutchman has fired his pistol from behind the rear door of the Lincoln. He leaps into the open. With his arm outstretched he fires as he bounds towards the road.

A moment later a burst of gunfire leaves him a crumpled heap on the ground.

ACT 2

22

November 9, 1939
Konstanz-Munich

THERE is no point in praying this is all a bad dream, as everything is real enough. I am shown to a room in the basement that is little more than a floor, four walls and a bad smell. The young Gestapo officer throws me a blanket and bucket. I must have fallen asleep as the next thing I know the same young officer is kicking me in the rump. He gives me time to pee in the bucket before I am walked to the street and pushed into the back of a limousine.

The good people of Konstanz are still sleeping soundly in bed as we drive by the end of the street where I shared the back room with Fiebig, the Communist who coaxed me into joining the RFB.

Once we cross the Rhine we head west, passing other streets that bring back fond memories of my years living in this city. The warm glow of streetlights soon ends and the darkness begins. With the bitumen unravelling before the glare of the headlights, my eyes grow heavy and close. I snooze until I wake to see the Bodensee glowing like mercury in the predawn light. When I come to my senses I realise we are passing through the upper town of Meersburg, reminding me again of old man Rothmund and his payment in kind. And more to the point two of those clock movements would be now scattered like shrapnel in the hall of the Bürgerbräukeller—unless perchance they are embedded in the Führer's head!

When the driver turns inland on the road to Ravensburg, I wonder if I am being driven home to Königsbronn, though my instinct tells me I am being returned to Munich, the scene of the crime. When I am hit by another wave of inertia, I slump low in the seat to drop off to sleep.

I am woken by the thump of tyres on a tramline in the western parts of Munich. The time is 9.15 am. My wristwatch has been confiscated but Munich has more clocks on buildings than old man Rothmund ever had in his stockpile. I sit a little straighter in the seat when we are slowed by the morning traffic in Bayerstrasse. We pass Munich's main railway station, a familiar landmark for me, as is Karlsplatz. When the driver turns into Briennerstrasse we pass the end of Türkenstrasse. One glance down that straight narrow street returns my mind to my time living peaceably with the Lehmann couple. As you would expect the master carpenter also looms large in my mind. I recall the Sunday I meet him in Alter Simpl and how he spoke of Maurice Bavaud captured on a Paris bound train with a gun in his pocket. I knew there was a lesson in there somewhere.

When we reach Königsplatz I start to wonder if I am being taken on a private tour of the Nazi sights of Munich. Or the driver has lost his way, being born and breed in Konstanz. When he makes a U turn at the twin honour temples for the sixteen 'blood martyrs', I have a sweet thought. These fascist fantasies will soon be flattened to the ground now that the Führer is finished!

On the corner of Briennerstrasse and Türkenstrasse the driver stops in front of a palatial pile set back from the street. I am dumbfounded, as I must have walked past this gothic edifice dozens of times and thought no evil of it. Two thugs assist me inside and after minimal paperwork I am locked in a basement cell with a guard hovering outside the grille. For the next few hours the place is a circus with clowns like myself being hauled in off the street for sneezing out of tune or for wearing the wrong coloured skirt. I barely have time to rerun my alibi through my mind before two guards escort me to a room at the end of the passage where two men are waiting. One holds a clipboard and pen while the other is in uniform of high rank, but not Gestapo. He has a nose as big as I have seen and tells me to take a seat on the bentwood chair. Apart from dripping water coming from the adjoining washroom the only thing I hear are his footsteps on the concrete floor. He keeps me waiting as he paces up and down with his nose stuck inside a brown folder. I presume he is reading the report the young Gestapo officer took an age to type in Konstanz last night. When he has finished reading he stops and turns towards me.

"My name is Nebe, the commander of Kripo, the Criminal Police. What is your name?"

"Johann Georg Elser"

"Date of birth?"

"4th January, 1903."

"Place of birth?"

"Hermaringen, Baden-Württemberg."

"Occupation?"

"Cabinetmaker."

"Place of residence?"

I think before answering as since leaving home I have lived in a number of places. I could give Maria Schmauder's address, or my sister Maria's, but I give Lehmann's address. Where I live seems irrelevant.

"Where do your parents live?"

"Königsbronn, a smallish Swabian town in the Brenz valley."

"We will find them."

"Is that all?"

"No. I have one more question, Herr Elser. Did you have anything to do with the bombing of the Bürgerbräukeller last night?"

"Last night I was in Konstanz, so how could I?"

"So what are these?" he asks holding up a plastic packet containing the stupid metallic pieces I had in my pockets.

"All work related items. I explained everything to the young officer who interviewed me last night in Konstanz. Is that information not in his report?" I ask.

The man from Kripo makes no reply. Instead he keeps his big nose down while making a few extra pencil marks inside the brown folder.

"Call in the next one," he tells the clipboard man.

I am then returned to the cell to await my early release.

23
November 9-10, 1939
Venlo-Düsseldorf

SEEING the Dutchman shot down like a wild animal only reinforced the Englishmen's eagerness to raise their hands in the air. With the muzzles of submachine guns pressed against their heads Best and Stevens are marched on the double past the veranda and the front door of Café Backus. Inside the terrified customers are still hiding beneath the dining tables.

Beyond the raised border boom gate the two captives are herded into the German customs house to be stood against a wall and searched. Relieved of their Browning semi-automatics, they are handcuffed and marched to the open car that has been driven alongside. As two bandits use the butts of their submachine guns to smash the remaining glass from the open car's windscreen, Stevens is pushed into the back seat. Best follows close behind. The next man into the back seat is the bandit leader, Major Alfred Naujocks of the SD. Like all his men he is dressed in rough peasant clothes. Another two bandits occupy the rear facing fold-down seats in the back of the open car. Surplus submachine guns are chucked onto the floor at the feet of the prisoners. Lemmens is then thrown in, landing awkwardly on his back. What to do with Klop poses a bigger problem. Blood is trickling down a loose arm and is oozing from his head as he is carried to the open car by two SD men. When it is realized he will not fit he is carried back to the Lincoln. Stevens is told to shut his trap when he makes a pessimistic remark about Klop, while Best would like to express his regrets to Lemmens for getting him into this mess.

The engine of the open car is being revved when another bandit runs from the Lincoln as if he has won first prize in the lottery. "The other one is Dutch!" he informs the man in command, handing him some papers.

When the convoy rolls a fierce breeze blows through the open car due to the lack of a windscreen. Fearing he might freeze to death Best has a quiet word with the bandit in command, causing a trench coat to be thrown over him. Encouraged by this small victory Best fosters more conversation.

"I suppose you think you have made a great catch?"

"I don't care about you, I am just so happy to have caught those German swine betraying their country! I would kill them with my bare hands — the pig-dogs!" Naujocks barks back at a bewildered Best.

The time is near 7 pm when the open car, minus a windscreen, crosses the Rhine in the city of Düsseldorf. The Lincoln with the wounded Dutchman is nowhere in sight when the three captives are bundled into the basement of a grey stone building. Best receives the same treatment as Stevens and Lemmens, being stripped naked and searched in every orifice.

Handcuffs are returned to his wrists once Best is in a blue tracksuit. His possessions are then scrutinized, with every cigarette being broken into tiny bits. His passport, money and all other belongings, including his monocle are put into a large brown envelope to be held in trust by his captors. To be doubly sure he does not attempt suicide overnight Best must share a cell with a young SD man who took part in the action. He can stomach half the stale sandwich offered to him but baulks at the ersatz coffee.

"What is this drink? Tar!" explodes Best, spitting a mouthful onto the floor.

"Did you expect rum as we serve in the Kriegsmarine?"

"So you are in the navy?" Best answers, keen to get whatever he can out of the young man.

"Yes. From Bremen."

"I would give my right arm for a cigarette right now," Best moans, causing the young SD man to lob him his pack from his bunk.

"So how did you get this job?" probes Best, helping himself to two cigarettes before returning the pack.

"I foolishly volunteered. They told us we were going to Holland to capture Germans plotting against the Führer and responsible for the bombing in Munich last night. They said nothing about Englishmen. The only German we found at the frontier returned with us as a free man and he seems to be a friend of our chief. Now I don't know who or what to believe."

"While you pontificate, could you give me a light?"

"Of course."

Sleep under the rough army blanket is near impossible for Best, with the events of the day racing through his mind. Now his failure to return home at a reasonable hour will have May worried sick should she notice his absence. His mind snaps back into his present predicament when he is told to get dressed. Handcuffed, he is escorted up the stairs to a comfortable office. Sitting behind a large desk are two neatly dressed young men. At a smaller desk with typewriter sits a young woman in a tight grey dress.

"Please sit on the chair," the first man says.

"We are so sorry to disturb your sleep at this early hour but we need to complete our paperwork before your departure," confides the second man.

"And when will that be?" asks Best.

"Soon, as far as we are aware," replies the second man.

"Care for a cigarette?" asks the first man as he leans across the desk with a cigarette protruding from the pack.

"I would."

Best leans forward to catch the cigarette between his lips. The second man comes from behind the desk to strike a match.

"Shall we start with your full name?" asks the first man.

"Sigismund Payne Best."

The typist stops filing her nails and starts depressing the keys on her typewriter.

"Date of birth?"

"April 14, 1885."

"Place of birth?"

"Cheltenham, Gloucestershire, England."

"So you are an Englishman?" asks the first man.

"Yes, I am."

"We thought you were Dutch as you speak German with a Dutch accent," says the second man.

"I am definitely English."

"Then your German is excellent for an Englishman," the first man says."

"Danke. Are there any more questions?"

"Yes, several. What is your occupation?" asks the second man.

"Businessman."

"Married or single?"

"Married."

"Wife's name?"

"Maria Margaretha Payne Best Van Rees. I call her May. And it may be of some interest to you to know my wife is the daughter of a Dutch Admiral, and is herself a painter of royal personages, most notably Queen Wilhelmina of the Netherlands."

"Really. No need to record that, Silvia," the first man tells the typist.

"Religion?" asks the second man.

"Church of England."

"That's it. There are no more questions," says the first man.

"We hope you are being treated well by our military?" the second man asks.

"Not too bad. My biggest gripe is these handcuffs. See how they are cutting my skin."

"Oh yes. Nasty."

"Can you take them off?"

"Sorry, but handcuffs are outside our jurisdiction," replies the first man.

"Typical public servants," Best mutters as he is returned down the stairs, passing a bleary eyed Stevens on the way up.

At dawn Best is escorted to the courtyard where a car with an intact windscreen, roof and side panels, is waiting. Best is invited to sit in the back seat beside Major Naujocks, who is no longer dressed in tatters, but as an impeccably attired officer of the Third Reich.

Best is still simmering over there being no shaving and washing facilities or even a breakfast when he tackles Naujocks on another matter of concern.

"Major, a man was shot yesterday at Venlo by your men. Please tell me what has become of him?"

"Do you mean the Dutchman?"

"He is Captain Coppens, an Englishman."

"Crap! You know as well as I do his name is Klop, a lieutenant in the Dutch Intelligence Service."

"You are mistaken."

"No, you are mistaken. I have his papers in my pocket. My chief in Berlin will find them extremely interesting."

"My reason for asking is simply to know if the man is alive or dead."

"He was taken to hospital in Düsseldorf last night and was admitted unconscious, knocked out by a bullet that grazed his head. He should pull through."

"I pray he does. He is an outstanding officer and a gentleman."

24
Munich
November 10-11, 1939

NOTHING has happened since my interview with Nebe, the nosy man from Kripo. There have been no follow up interviews. No release. Nothing. All that has happened is my idleness is wearing me down. For over a year I have been preoccupied with planning, designing, testing, procuring, assembling and onsite installation. Now I am like a stopped clock. But I must be patient. I must keep my nerve. Soon I will hear the good people singing in the streets when the word is spread — the Führer is dead!

The next day starts no better. No one wants an interview. It seems the world has lost all interest in me. I have no idea what is going on. Then sometime before midday while I am wondering whether my drunkard father will be proud of his son for what he has done, a booming sound comes through the grille in the door. You don't have to be Einstein to figure out the origin of the racket. A Volksempfänger has been placed in the passageway with the speaker turned full volume.

Over the airwaves I hear the announcer saying:

Flanked by the deputy Führer and Gauleiter Wagner, Adolf Hitler himself now returns to his fallen comrades. The Führer is here!

The Führer is here? How can this be? This must be a repeat broadcast of a previous Nazi rally — I try to believe. But in the next minute I hear the announcer repeating a similar sickening line:

Adolf Hitler stands before the victims torn from our midst by a cowardly act of murder.

Tears steam down my face as the orchestra plays *Aase's Death* by Edvard Grieg. Next comes the raving oration of Rudolph Hess:

At this time the German people take their sad leave of the victims of a gruesome crime, a crime almost unparalleled in history . . . a ruthless act of murder . . . All of Germany is mourning . . . Eternal is the river of blood that flows for Germany, eternal the commitment of German men to their people, thus, to, Germany will be eternal — this Germany for which you gave your lives.

The deaths of these seven victims have served to fully arouse the bitterness and the passion of the German people . . . The perpetrators of this crime have succeeded in teaching the German people to hate. They have heightened immeasurably the commitment of the German people to this battle that has been forced upon them . . .

What the death of our husbands means to us can be felt only by those who have lost their closest loved ones. But more important than the lives of our husbands is knowing that the Führer is alive. With the miracle of his salvation, our faith has become unshakable: Providence has protected our Führer, and Providence will continue to protect our Führer, for it is Providence that sent him to us.

I am of the rock-solid conviction that this enormous crime, this war which was forced upon us, will turn out in favor of the Führer, in favor of Germany — in favor of the entire world!

But to our enemies, the perpetrators of this crime, we call out: You attempted to take our Führer from us, but you brought him closer to us than ever. You wanted to make us weaker, but you have made us only stronger than ever. You hoped you could rob us of our belief in the future, but you have only strengthened our belief in a Providence which is on the side of Germany. You hoped you could take away our confidence in victory . . . and if you put the forces of Hell itself into motion, victory will still be ours. For victory will be our thanks to the dead.

O God!
    The Führer has survived!
    A miracle?
    I am immobilized by this agonizing thought.

My immobilization is still in action when two men come to pick my carcass.
    "Herr Elser—sit up and pay attention," says Nebe.
    I do as I am told.
    "Did you hear the broadcast from the Feldherrnhalle?" he asks.
    I nod.
    "Do you know the circumstances of the broadcast?"
    I shake my head.
    "It was the memorial ceremony for the seven killed by a bomb at the Bürgerbräukeller."
    I say nothing.
    "What did you feel when you heard it—Elser?"
    "Sad."
    "Why did you feel sad—Elser?"
    "Because those seven people died."
    "More may die yet."
    Nebe looks towards the other man as if a cue for him to speak.
    "Sit up straight and roll up your pants," orders the other man.
    "Why?"
    "Don't ask why!"
    "Do as you are told. Roll up your pants," repeats Nebe.
    I do as I am told and roll the legs of my suit pants to just below my knees."

"Higher," orders the other man.

I roll them higher and the other man points his finger at my gnarled knees.

They look at each other like two oracles and leave.

25
November 10-17, 1939
Berlin

THE eerie emptiness of the autobahn greets Best when he wakes. The great bands of white concrete carved into the landscape seem wasted effort with so few vehicles on the road. Though when he looks through the rear window he sees five cars following. One is a red Ford Lincoln Zephyr.

As the odometer ticks over another kilometre, Best groans inwardly. Being a prisoner is starting to hit home. This time yesterday he was at the wheel of his own car, in control of his destination, the master of his own fate. At fifty-five he was cruising, savouring the good life, enjoying a round of golf, playing classical music with a Dutch Royal. Now he is going deep into enemy territory. He could be in for some bruising.

After passing a windswept airfield the convoy pulls off the autobahn to refuel. Best's head aches from eyestrain he blames on the confiscation of his monocle, but his mood lifts a fraction when he sees the filling station has a restaurant attached.

Naujocks gets out, telling Best, "Wait here."

With two SD men still on guard in the car Best has little option. When Naujocks returns he tells the two SD men to go for their meal. Alone with Best Naujocks feeds his handcuffed prisoner chucks of apple cut with his Swiss army knife. Once the last chunk has been deposited into the Englishman's mouth the time is ripe for the German to make his farewell speech.

"Up till now you have been in my care. Soon I must hand you over to the Gestapo. If you have unpleasant experiences with them do not blame me, as I have only obeyed orders and done my duty."

Best remains silent, lost for words, doing his utmost not to choke.

When the Potsdam turnoff appears Best knows the road trip is nearing an end. He has visited Berlin on business trips and recognizes the great triumphal avenue through the dense forest of the Tiergarten. After the circle at the Victory Column the broad avenue goes straight to the Brandenburg Gate. One street beyond the monumental city portal the convoy turns right into Wilhelmstrasse, a thoroughfare flanked by the ministries of the Third Reich: the new Reich Chancellery, the mammoth Air Ministry of Göring and the Ministry of Propaganda of Goebells. Best's car comes to a stop in the shadow of a ponderous stone edifice in Prinz-Albrecht-Strasse.

The prisoner is hooded and dragged from the car. His treatment is so well orchestrated he is dazed and disoriented by the time he reaches a room on an upper floor. A welcoming committee is waiting led by a little man who introduces himself as Dr. Max. Naturally Best resents the roughhouse tactics, and drawing on his past experience of doing business in Germany, he takes on the little man in a shouting match. His handcuffs are soon removed and he scores a cigarette. But his plea to have a wash, a shave and dinner before answering any questions falls on deaf ears. With Best refusing to cooperate Dr. Max belatedly enlists the help of his workaholic boss, the Head of Gestapo, Heinrich Müller. The man who once had the nerve to refer to his employer as 'an Austrian draft-dodger' and 'an immigrant unemployed house painter', comes in screaming:

"The Führer is invincible! He will liberate the people of England from Jews and plutocrats! We are at war! Germany is fighting for her existence! You are in the greatest danger! If you want to live another day you must be extremely careful!"

Müller's rant is impressive for someone who only joined the Nazi Party in 1938 after being pressed into membership by his boss, Heinrich Himmler.

Müller follows up his bombast with serious eye contact. Best suspects the rapid flicker he detects in Müller's irises is designed to strike terror into the prisoner. He puts an end to the eyeballing session by saying he *also* has an eyesight problem, principally due to the confiscation of his monocle.

"Monocle! You'll probably be dead before morning! You won't need your monocle then! Don't you know you are at the headquarters of the Gestapo! Don't you know what that means? We can do anything we like with you! ANYTHING!"

When Müller runs out of words Best decides the time has come to empathize.

"To be honest I refuse to read English newspapers that slander the German people. Journalists tell all sorts of lies about what is happening in Germany. Take for example the bombing in Munich last night. Some foreign reports had the temerity to suggest that Herr Hitler and Herr Himmler were responsible for this horrific act. I think that is a load of bull dust!"

Müller's eyes melt. He turns to Dr. Max. "Give Mr. Best whatever he wants."

Best is escorted through the adjoining clerical office to the washroom. When he returns refreshed to the makeshift interrogation room a plate of sandwiches and a bottle of Bitburger beer wait on a folding table. To embellish his supper Dr. Max produces a full packet of Roth-Händles.

"I must say these German cigarettes put a fire in your belly," Best coughs.

"So? Now we must start the interview," Dr. Max announces.

"But I was looking forward to going to bed after my smoke," Best protests.

Dr. Max makes no reply as two men come into the room carrying a table and a typewriter. A stout woman with grey hair tied back in a bun follows. Though midnight is close, Best realizes the inevitable cannot be delayed.

Dr. Max begins by explaining to Best his present situation in succinct legal terms.

"You are in most serious trouble as a result of your actions in meeting and negotiating with traitors determined to overthrow the German government. Even though you are a foreigner and your actions took place outside Germany, you are guilty under a new law of high treason. The penalty for your crime is death by beheading. But should you be willing to help the German people bring the loathsome traitors to justice it is possible the Führer will be merciful and treat you only as a prisoner of war."

Once Best gets another coughing fit under control Dr. Max begins his interrogation. His questions centre on the covert meetings Best has had with the German traitors, namely: Dr. Franz Fischer, the man called Solms, Captain von Seidlitz, Lieutenant Grosch, Colonel Martini and Captain Schaemmel. After the initial meetings are addressed by Best, the meeting held on October 30 in The Hague is of special interest to Dr. Max.

"Was this the same meeting where you had a dinner party in your house and you generously supplied the traitors with a wireless receiver and transmitter?"

"In fact it was, though the party was devoted solely to the music of Beethoven."

The role of the Lieutenant Klop at the meetings is more difficult to explain.

"Why do you insist Captain Coppens is an English officer when there is indisputable proof he is Dutch and an officer of the Dutch Intelligence Service? On top of this deceit you have said nothing about your plans to kill the Führer! There are more holes in your story than in Swiss cheese. I am extremely disappointed with you Mr. Best. You must tell everything again."

"Again?"

"Ja—start from scratch."

Best does his honest best to describe every detail of every meeting a second time, hoping his memory will match that of Stevens, who in some other place at some other time, will be asked to give his version of the meetings.

But by 2 am Best has had enough, refusing to answer another question. Dr. Max relents and a folding bed is wheeled into the room.

Best is woken at 7 am so he can use the washroom before the clerks arrive to start work in the adjoining office. Following a light breakfast, with the same ersatz coffee, Best is taken upstairs to be photographed, fingerprinted, weighed, measured and medically examined.

Dr. Max arrives later with Frau Roland, his typist, to resume the interrogation. He has had a Jekyll and Hyde transformation overnight and is happy to joke and exchange humorous yarns with Best from their experiences during the 1914-18 war. But after lunch the direction of the interrogation is radically altered. Dr. Max wants details of every visit Best has made to Germany and other countries in the preceding six years. As Best has made numerous business visits to Germany, France, Switzerland and Belgium in recent times he struggles to recall exact dates, destinations and other irrelevant details. Best is let off the hook with the arrival of a man of considerable influence, coming from the Führer's inner circle.

"Heil Hitler, Herr Reichsleiter!" the flunkies shout, raising their arms in the Nazi salute as the ox-headed Martin Bormann storms into the room to inspect the English prisoner at close quarters. The Führer's financial adviser and private secretary who once wisely observed, 'every educated person is a future enemy', has an equally profound message today.

"Germany is a dead set certainty to win this war," says Bormann looking up into Best's unflinching face.

When Best begs to differ Bormann leaves faster than he arrived, not wanting any discussion on the matter. With the rare appearance of Bormann on an upper floor of the building, Dr. Max feels a minion by comparison and ends the interrogation session earlier than he planned.

The next morning Dr. Max arrives bright and early and informs Best the interrogation is only now beginning. But before he can even begin, Müller comes in quaking, ripping apart the pages typed by Frau Roland, while informing Dr. Max he is a stupid little man. As for Best he is given one more chance by Müller to confess everything—otherwise it will be the END!

With this ultimatum and with the apparent axing of Dr. Max, Best finds he has the rest of the day to himself and spends the afternoon sitting in the sun by the window on an upper floor of the Reich Security

Main Office. Looking south he recognises the roof of Anhalter railway station, helping him position himself in the city.

Next morning a young lawyer with an even younger assistant arrive with an attractive brunette. Müller follows the trio into the room to get things underway.

"I want EVERYTHING from the beginning! When you have finished I want to know more about the prisoner than he knows HIMSELF!" Müller shrieks.

The young lawyer not only starts at the beginning, he probes into Best's ancestry, checking for evidence of his Aryan or Jewish origins. In the first two days of the rejuvenated interrogation Fräulein Blumental has typed the first thirty years of Best's autobiography. He is in the middle of a long and fulsome description of the 1914 Henley Regatta, when Müller reappears to intervene. Best never sees the two legal men again.

While Best is being bemused in Berlin, in Whitehall Alexander Cadogan is being befuddled by the continuance of wireless messages from the 'German Opposition'. In order to fully brief the British and French governments on the perplexing situation arising from the recent border incident at Venlo, he sets down in writing the sequence of events. The following is an extract:

There followed a pause, which lasted till November 13th. Late in the evening of that day the operator in The Hague picked up a message from the [German] Generals which read as follows: *"Two of our agents disappeared, presumably arrested, work rendered very difficult. When may we expect proposals of which you notified us? What news of you?"*

To this 'C' replied (on November 14th-10 am) *"One of our representatives was foully murdered and the other kidnapped on the Dutch side of the frontier on Thursday evening. Have you any explanation? What happened to your delegates?"*

In the evening of the same day the Germans replied as follows: *"We must take into account the possibility of arrest. No special measures have been observed as yet. It appears doubly necessary to enter into negotiations for which we still lack the agenda which it was stated would be sent. Nothing has been heard as yet of the kidnapping which was announced from there. We request further instructions without delay. We may come to an understanding".*

26

November 12-14, 1939

Munich

AFTER Nebe left with the knee specialist I stayed immobilized on the bunk for endless hours. I might have never moved again had I not needed to use the bucket. All night I have been expecting the third degree but nothing has eventuated. Ending up looking like Karl's raw meat is the least of my worries. How the Nazi leaders managed to escape unscathed is the question burning inside my brain. Have they really got the blessing and the backing of the Almighty, as they like to claim?

If they have there is only one conclusion. God must be INSANE!

My blasphemous brooding is still blackening my soul when I hear jackboots in the passageway. And when I hear someone passing my cell remark, "This is taking too fucking long Nebe. I'll kick the shit out of the prick," I wonder if these crude words refer specifically to me. But the jackboots pass, going further down the passageway, causing me to relax a tack. But a minute later the jackboots return. The cell door is flung open. Two guards enter and drag me out backwards. They drag me on the double to the room at the end of the passage. Nebe is there. There is a second man with a look of horror on his face. The third man is only a short-arse like me, but of considerable rank. With spectacles pinching his nose stopping his eyeballs dropping out, he is the spitting image of Heinrich Himmler.

"Remove the skunk's clothes. I don't want to soil them," Short-arse directs.

A guard pushes me backwards so my head bounces off the concrete floor like a lead ball. Once I am stark naked Short-arse attacks me with his jackboots.

"Are you the turd that set off the bomb?" he squeals.

"Nay. Not me Sir."

"Teach him a lesson for lying."

Two guards drag me to the washroom. One places his boot on my neck as the other whips me with a leather strap. Not even my father did that. When they drag me back outside the jackboots start to lash out again.

"Now answer me properly," requests Short-arse when he stops for breath.

"I did," I murmur.

He starts kicking again — really laying into me.

"Give the runt a swim after a double dose with the strap," orders the prick now wheezing like a weasel.

The two goons drag me back to the washroom. This time one goes hell for leather with the strap as if he has gone berserk. When I start to howl like a wolf they lift me up and bash my head into the toilet bowl. As they hold me under to drown me — I taste blood. When they drag me back to Short-arse I leave a red trail smeared across the floor.

"What mongrel put you up to it?" Short-arse squeals expecting an answer.

My bottom lip has split wide open. With blood flowing like a river my jaw locks up like a vice. A grim faced Nebe looks down on me. The man with the look of horror is about to vomit. Short-arse starts attacking my groin with his jackboots. When I straighten out he aims for my vital parts. By the time he has me writhing in agony like a headless snake I am in no state to confess to anything.

I must have passed out and the guards hauled me back to my cell. It was nice of them not to leave me lying in my pool of blood. Someone has even taken the trouble to throw a blanket over my nakedness. But why do they bother? To make life easier for everyone they should simply kill me.

Every part of my mauled body is still on fire when Nebe calls in to see me at some time either in the day or night. He has come alone and looks down on me like a father who has come to say 'good night' to his son. My father never did that either. When he tucks the blanket up to my chin I notice he is wearing an impressive Omega Laco Aviator Swiss wristwatch.

"What is the time?" I whisper to him, looking straight up into his big conk.

"9.15 am, Monday morning. You have slept for twenty-two hours. I will send an orderly with some broth. You must be hungry."

"Danke," I say with great difficulty as my lip has swollen to be like a Zeppelin. At least the blood flow has been stemmed with a wad of sticky tape.

"I am sorry this has happened. But it could not be helped. I will do my best to protect you. But there is no guarantee I will be able to. Do you understand?" asks Nebe.

I nod and lay my throbbing head back on a blanket that has been folded as a pillow.

"At 2 pm today you will be taken to the interview room. I tried to have your case delayed till tomorrow to give you more time to recover. But that was not possible due to the priority your case has in high places. So get dressed and be ready. Hans Lobbes, my assistant, will come to collect you."

"Will the man who smashed me be there?" I ask with some difficulty.

"No. Himmler has another engagement. Herr Huber will be there."

"Huber?"

"You met Huber the other day. He is head of Vienna Gestapo."

As Nebe leaves he looks as grim and as burdened as ever, causing me to wonder what misdemeanors he is carrying in his baggage.

As Nebe promised Lobbes comes to collect me. The guards chortle like hyenas as I creep along the passage. My racked body is an assemblage of **dysfunctional transplants** like in the horror movie I saw with Brunhilde in 1925. When I reach the interview room unaided, I find a square of red carpet has been laid over where I spilt blood yesterday. Centered on the carpet is a square wooden table. Nebe is sitting on one side. Huber is seated on another. Lobbes shares the third side with a plumpish woman of indefinable age. I have the fourth side to myself and I ease into the chair.

The woman has two bottles of seltzer beside her typewriter. I would do anything for seltzer right now. She must have read my mind as she slides one my way.

"Have you finished typing the confession, Frau Krantz," Huber asks the woman.

She nods and pulls a page from the typewriter.

"We have prepared a confession for you to sign. Do you want to read it first?" asks Nebe.

This opening line by Nebe comes as something of a shock to my system. If I sign my confession now this meeting will be over in thirty seconds and all that will be left for me to do is crawl back to my cell. Having come all this way in total agony I plan to make it worth the effort.

"Nay. You have no evidence," I assert, sounding as confident as my inflated lip permits.

"We have the evidence," Huber assures me.

"Do you?" I say with casual insolence as I lift the bottle of seltzer to the corner of my mouth.

"The crime scene has been thoroughly combed. In the great heap of rubble two back plates from two clocks have been found with the name of the manufacturer clearly labeled on both. It may take us some time to follow the paper trail to the purchaser, but rest assured we will," says Huber.

"Is that all you have?"

"We are only at the start. All staff at the Bürgerbräukeller have been interviewed. A waitress recalls serving a man with a Swabian accent who ordered the same meal every night over a period of three months. Her suspicion was aroused when he never drank more than one glass of beer," reports Nebe.

"Wise fellow," I remark.

"If you were not so disfigured by your swollen lip I would bring the waitress here to make a positive identification," claims Nebe.

"You know who to blame for my disfigurement," I say with too much cheek for my own good.

"That is something we must not mention," whispers Nebe.

"Is there any other evidence?" I ask.

"There is," says Huber.

"A Munich merchant has come forward and stated he sold acoustic insulation to a man with a Swabian accent. He said the man told him he wanted to stop a ticking clock keeping him awake at night," explains Nebe.

"I would not be the only Swabian man with some sort of phobia," I quip.

"This is no joking matter," retorts Huber.

"And there is a young woman living with her parents in Schnaitheim who has been willing to come forward. When visited early this morning she was eager to inform our investigators a man fitting your description slept in the attic and had his workshop in the basement. The young woman said this same man told her he was working on an invention," says Nebe.

"Do you know this young woman?" Huber asks in a hopeful tone of voice.

"I have known a number of young women in my life," I admit, causing Frau Krantz to blink.

"Then turn your head towards the door as Herr Lobbes opens it," Nebe requests.

I find it strange Nebe wants me to face the door during the interview. Nevertheless I do as I am told and look towards the door as Lobbes rises from his chair. When he opens the door I see a young woman in her best blue and white lace dress. She clasps her hands against her cheeks as if horrified by my grizzly appearance.

"Do you know that person?" asks Nebe as Lobbes closes the door.

"I do — her name is Maria Schmauder."

Nebe looks at Huber as Lobbes returns to the table, having played his minor role in this melodrama. I finish off the first bottle of seltzer and as I look towards a second bottle I decide to bring this playacting to an end.

"Well — it was me."

"What did you say?" asks Huber.

"I am responsible. I am the one to blame," I reply, keeping my words as simple as possible.

"Do you know what you are saying?" asks Nebe, looking into my damaged face.

"I am not insane, if that is what you are suggesting. But I am still very thirsty."

Frau Kranz slides the second bottle of seltzer my way and I instantly start drinking.

"Were any waitresses hurt?" I ask in a casual manner when I return the bottle to the table.

"One was killed outright. Another had a miraculous escape," Huber replies.

"The luck of the draw?" I say without thinking.

"Sadly—yes," replies Nebe.

A long silence follows apart from Frau Kranz exercising her fingers on the keys of the typewriter. I take the opportunity to guzzle on the seltzer.

"How soon will I be shot?" I ask to keep the conversation alive.

"Your confession will not be the end of the matter. Those in high places are convinced you did not act alone in planting the bomb in the Bürgerbräukeller. And to be perfectly honest with you I still have an open mind on that matter," answers Nebe, looking more worried than ever.

"You think I had accomplices?" I inquire.

"Did you?" asks Huber.

"Nay. The whole idea was mine!"

"But were you aided financially by someone abroad?" asks Nebe.

"Nay. I used my hard earned savings. I was the sole instigator from A to Z."

"Think carefully about this Elser. If you are prepared to reveal your accomplices you might save your life, though there is no guarantee of this," says Nebe.

"When you were apprehended at the Swiss border you told the border officer you where looking for a friend. What was your friend's name?" asks Huber.

"I can't remember."

"Did you intend to cross the border into Switzerland?"

"I did."

"And what did you intent to do once you had crossed?"

"Live a quiet life."

"Did you plan to meet someone in Switzerland?"

"Nay."

"Was your plan to meet someone from the British Intelligence to receive your reward," Huber asks.

"As I told you before, I worked alone. It was all my doing. It would have been nice to have been paid, taking into account all the overtime I worked."

"Overtime?" Huber repeats as if he has never heard the word before.

"I only worked at night at the Bürgerbräukeller, after the lights were extinguished."

"Tell us precisely how, where and when you placed the bomb?" asks Nebe.

As I have drunk all the seltzer I wish I could lie down to die now that I have confessed. But hearing Nebe's question I wonder where and how I should start to explain my decision to act. Huber is tapping a pencil on the table and Frau Kranz is falling asleep waiting. I try to be as concise as I possibly can, but I still need three to four hours to give a rough outline. Even at the finish, after telling how I returned to the Bürgerbräukeller to check if the clocks were set correctly, Nebe wants to squeeze more out of me.

"Can you make a sketch to show how everything worked?" he asks.

"I can if Herr Huber will lend me his pencil and Frau Kranz will give me some paper."

Once I have spent an hour or more making several detailed sketches at both large and small scale, Nebe and Huber and even Frau Kranz have a rough idea of the design and complexity of my apparatus and overview of the whole operation.

"Tomorrow morning we should return to the scene of the crime and inspect the damage so Herr Elser can confirm what he has set down on paper," says Huber.

"Nay! I do not like that idea. What would be the point? What would it prove? I have confessed, drawn pictures a child can understand and besides — whenever I stand I feel dizzy," I plead.

"And there is the strong possibility Elser would be ripped apart in the street by someone incensed by his act. The whole population is aghast at this attack. Those in high places would not be pleased should Elser be killed in such circumstances as he is more valuable alive than dead," says Nebe.

"I had not considered that aspect," Huber sighs, sitting back in his chair.

After a prolonged moment of hesitation Nebe leans towards me to ask, "Why did you do it — Elser?"

Deathly silence follows as I search for my answer to this fundamental question. I brood on my motive of pure hate for the Führer, only to raise the tone and utter, "For the masses in all countries war means hunger, misery, and the death of millions. Hitler means war. If he goes, there will be peace."

Nebe sits digesting my answer until Huber brings him back to the present.

"We need to end this interview now otherwise we will be here for ever. I suggest Frau Kranz retypes the confession for the failed assassin to sign."

It takes many hours to fashion the wording of my confession. Nebe is such a stickler for neatness and accuracy every time he thinks a word or phrase is vague, incorrect or might cause an explosion in high places he has Frau Kranz tear up what she had typed and start with a clean sheet of paper. Lobbes is sent out for something to eat at some stage during the night. The extra large plate of schupfnudel he brings back meets with a mixed reception. However his selection sustains us until I have signed my life away at 2 am.

27   November 19–20, 1939
Berlin

THE pain of my confession is nothing compared with the pain of my rejection. Maria Schmauder's enthusiasm to share me with the world is far worse than any busted lip. Whether she was hoping for financial reward or was paying me back for not writing her a letter, I do not know. All I know is one kick in the guts from Maria hurt more than a hundred jackboots in the groin from Himmler. At least I know she will not grieve too deeply over my departure from this world.

Yesterday I came by limousine from Munich to Berlin with Nebe. It appears my grilling in Munich was only foreplay. Nebe was his usual serious self when telling me I'm to come before a Special Commission to get to the bottom of the Bürgerbräukeller bombing. To my mind this is a total waste of time and money. What else can I add to what I have already said in my confession? I've drawn detailed diagrams of all aspects of my installation. Do they now want a full-size re-construction of my apparatus?

Being billeted in Berlin has not been without benefits however. Rations are edible and regular. My quarters are quiet and comfortable with high ceilings and a decent window. And when I look through the window from an upper floor of this labyrinth of a building I not only see the sky, I can see the arched roof of a railway station.

My appointment with the Special Commission is at 10 am today. Ten minutes before the scheduled start my live-in guards escort me via a tortuous passage to a large airy room that has gives me the impression this building was once an art school. I am invited to sit at a table facing a bench where three men are already seated like three monkeys. I observe their nameplates read from left to right—Schmidt, Kappler and Seibold. A not unattractive typist with grey hair tied back in a bun sits to one side at her own table. Everything is formal and impersonal. This must be the way things are done in Berlin.

As I wait wondering whether to put my hands on the table or under, a high ranked Gestapo officer struts into the room like a cock on heat. He is of my age and would be a handsome hombre had his hair not been shaved to the skull back and sides, leaving only an inane mop on top. This hairstyle might be the latest fashion in Berlin, but I hate the look. His eyes are also weird—looking like they could be used to burn holes in armour-plate steel. I feel less under the blowtorch when he decides to leave me be.

Kappler, the monkey sitting in the centre with steely blue eyes and a disappearing hairline, is the first to speak. I fix my attention on him, not wanting to be left behind by any fast talk. After he identifies me as the person under investigation, noting my full name, date and place of birth, just as Nebe had in Munich, he goes straight to a question regarding my parentage.

"The confessed assassin will state the names of the parents."

"Maria Müller and Ludwig Elser."

"Were they in wedlock when you were born?" Seibold asks as if he has been primed.

"My mother married my father one year after I was born."

"Record the following: 'I was born the illegitimate son of Maria Müller'," Kappler dictates to the typist.

It seems they are out to get me on every technicality right from the start.

"What is your father's occupation?" asks Schmidt.

"We owned some farm land and my father earned his living logging and selling lumber and by doing other agricultural work in and around Königsbronn."

"What about your grandparents?" asks Seibold.

"What about them?"

"Did you know of them?" Kappler clarifies.

"My maternal grandparents lived in Hermaringen and once a year I visited them with my parents. And from the age of four I visited my paternal grandparents alone as they lived nearby in Königsbronn."

"What are the names and dates of birth of your siblings?" Schmidt asks, causing my brain to work overtime.

"I have four siblings. My sister Friederike was born in 1904, the exact date I do not recall. Maria was born about three years after me in 1906. Sister Anna came next, maybe in 1908. The last child born was my little brother Leonhard. I think he came in 1913."

"How would you describe your family life?" asks Kappler.

"As long as I can recall my father has had a problem with alcohol, habitually coming home late after drinking in the pub, giving him a tendency to terrorise my mother and his children. Other than that our family life was normal."

"Did you sleep with your sisters?" asks Seibold.

What a question to ask!

"I never slept with my sisters or with my brother. I always had my own bed."

"Is there anything else you wish to say about your family life?" asks Kappler.

"With my father having his timber business to run, the brunt of the agricultural work fell on my mother's shoulders, though my siblings and I helped her in the field and the house. As the eldest child I was always the nursemaid for my siblings though at some stage I remember we had a maid."

"Now tell us about your schooling," asks Kappler.

I sit up straight and fold my arms on my chest as I think back to my school days. I tell how I started at Königsbronn elementary school when I was six; how the classes were mixed with both boys and girls and I can even recall my teachers' names.

"But what about your grades?" asks Schmidt.

"Generally I was a mediocre student, but in drawing, penmanship and arithmetic I always had good grades and once received 10 pfennig as a commendation from a teacher. In dictation, composition and other subjects I was not so bright, while in religion I had only satisfactory results."

"Did you get many beatings?" asks Seibold.

"Only when it was necessary. I got no more than others did, and only when I had not done my homework."

"Did you ever skip school?" asks Schmidt.

"I never skipped school except when I was sick."

"Ever been on detention?" asks Seibold.

"I recall only one detention for not doing my scripture homework. The penalty was given to me by Pastor Hauser who gave me religious instruction throughout my schooling."

"Now tell us what you did after leaving school," Kappler asks.

Unfolding my arms I lay my hands on the table as I think back almost twenty years.

"After my schooling I helped my father with his work, carting and woodcutting, and helping my mother in agriculture, doing field work and feeding the cows in the barn. For this work I was not paid nor given any pocket money by my parents. All I received was my meals and lodging."

"How well off was your family?" asks Schmidt.

"Our family always had plenty to eat except during the wartime emergency when we went hungry at the end of the year mainly because we were only allowed to keep a small percentage of our potato crop."

"Did your parents ever leave home?" asks Seibold.

"I recall my father once took his horses and wagon to Ulm for fort construction during wartime. My mother left for a week after she had been beaten by my father."

"Now tell us everything about your four siblings." says Kappler.

And so it goes on—question after question. What my siblings have to do with planting a bomb to save my country from ultimate humiliation I do not know. Nevertheless I begin with my sister Friederike, telling how she worked in the local cigar factory before her marriage in 1926 to a welder, Willi Kraft of Schnaitheim. I include my dispute with Friederike over the ownership of a cabinet we once bought together for the family home.

Concerning my sister Maria I tell how I made three or four trips to Stuttgart after she married Karl Hirth two or three years ago. I mention that my nephew, Franz, was seven when his mother married, and that Karl is the natural father. When I happen to mention I once fixed a gong rod in a grandfather clock for Maria, Kappler wants me to remember the name and the address of the welder I used in Stuttgart to do the work. And when I happen to mention how I slept in the same bed with Maria and Karl in their Stuttgart apartment more recently, Seibold wants to snigger.

Seibold gets something else to snigger about when I say more than I need.

"Once when going to Stuttgart I stopped at Esslingen on the way to see a married woman with whom I had a relationship. I have concealed this from my sister Maria and her husband Karl. Even now they do not know of my affair with this woman."

"What is the woman's name?" asks Seibold.

"Elsa Härlen."

While this revelation is light entertainment for Schmidt and Seibold, Kappler keeps his surly face intact, though he wants to know everything about my last visit to Stuttgart. By the time every detail of my overnight stay is scrutinized Kappler says it is time for lunch. As Fritz escorts me back to my room to enjoy my tinned rations, I wonder how long this interrogation will take. If Kappler wants to crawl into every crevice of my life we could be here till Christmas.

After the meal break my two other siblings, Anna and Leonhard, raise little interest.

"My sister Anna is married to a locksmith named Fritz — his other name I cannot remember. They live in Zuffenhausen and the last time I saw Anna was in the autumn of last year when she visited my parents in Königsbronn. My brother Leonhard lives in Königsbronn in the parental home, being registered as a co-owner. He is a journeyman carpenter at the foundry in Königsbronn and is married with one child. I was on good terms with him until he and his wife forced their way into the family home. Now we never speak to each other."

Kappler is not so interested in family conflict and moves rapidly to my friendships. I recall two classmates, Eugen Rau and Hans Scheerer, stating I still see Rau occasionally as he lives in Königsbronn, however Scheerer has been missing for many years since he migrated to America.

With my friends accounted for on two fingers Kappler moves on to a new topic.

"Now give a full account of your employment history."

Answering this question could take forever. After cracking a knuckle, I get started.

"After I worked some months with my father in his timber trade, I made the decision to become an iron turner. My father wanted me to support him in his profession, and though he did not beat me or make much noise, he tried darn hard to dissuade me from my decision. As my mother sided with me I won the argument and started at the foundry in 1917."

"Why were you so determined to go against your father's wishes?" asks Seibold.

"Working in agriculture brought me no joy. As a boy I made fretwork and did other handicrafts. Even during my apprenticeship I still liked to tinker at home, building a rabbit hutch and a small gasoline engine using a manual I had purchased. I guess I was also influenced by Eugen Rau who had started his training to be a lathe operator at the foundry in Königsbronn."

"Did you complete your foundry training?" asks Kappler.

"Nay. I left in March 1919 as the noxious environment of the foundry sometimes gave me headaches, though I had progressed to work on the big lathe."

"How much were you paid?" asks Schmidt.

"I forget exactly but I know any pay was taken by my parents."

"After then, what?" asks Kappler.

"I turned to woodwork as near our home were carpentry workshops where I would go for sawdust and wood shavings for my parents. The sawdust and short shavings we used for stable litter, while we used the long shavings to light fires. My parents agreed for once and I was apprenticed to Robert Sapper and started a course in carpentry at the Heidenheim trade school. Early on I made simple boxes, stools and the like, that required no special skills to cut, plane and assemble the wood. At the end of my apprenticeship I customized large and heavy pieces of furniture. I had a great interest in this type of work. My parents and my master were pleased when I came top of the trade school in December 1922. Nevertheless I quit with Sapper as I wanted to work in the Rieder furniture factory in Aalen."

"To make more money?" asks Schmidt.

"Sapper paid one mark a week in the first year of training, 2 marks in the second year, and 3-4 marks in the third year. The wage paid by Rieder was considerably higher."

"Did you live in Aalen when working for Rieder?" asks Kappler.

"Nay. I continued to live at home and commuted by train to Aalen. After the autumn of 1923 when money had loss all value due to the hyperinflation, I left Rieder and returned home to help my mother and father as before. I received neither salary nor pocket money from my parents for my labour. My only compensation was to visit my friend Eugen Rau in my free time. He owned a gramophone and he taught me to dance."

"Dance! What sort of dance?" exclaims Seibold.

"Any sort of dance."

"Shall we move on?" urges Kappler.

"In the summer of 1924 I took a position as an apprentice carpenter at Matthias Müller's works in Heidenheim. There I made kitchens and wardrobes and was trusted to work independently. Müller found no fault in my work, nevertheless I resigned my position in January or February of 1925."

"Why did you do that?" asks Schmidt.

"I wanted to travel to further my training in my chosen vocation. Müller was reluctant to let me go for some unknown reason. When I happened to meet a carpenter from nearby Oberkochen, he suggested I write to a master turner he had once worked for by the name of Wachter. Upon receiving an acceptance I took the train to Tettnang and walked for about 2 hours to Bernried, a remote place with a few farmhouses by a lake. At night I slept in the roof of his house and made furniture in the workshop below during the day. Wachter's homemade circular saw was a dinosaur, while the isolation and loneliness depressed me totally. I left after six weeks to wander further south looking for employment nearer to the Bodensee."

"We will now take a short break," interjects Kappler, interrupting me just as I was warming to the task. Perhaps he was becoming bored by my employment history. After the break I pick up from where I left off.

"For weeks I was sleeping rough as I searched for work without any success. But when I reached Friedrichshafen I made enquiries at the employment office to be told Dornier needed skilled carpenters. I was signed up the very next day to work with a few others in the propeller department."

"Dornier! You were lucky to land a job there," says Schmidt.

"What year was this?" asks Seibold.

"1925."

Who did you associate with when you worked at Dornier?" Kappler asks.

"The only worker I can now recall is Leo Dannecker. He also worked in the propeller department. I think I only liked him because he played the clarinet."

"Did you meet with any others in the vicinity of the Dornier aircraft factory?" asks Kappler.

"Nay. Sometimes I went for walks on Sunday along the shore by the Zeppelin factory or into Friedrichshafen, but I never met with anyone there."

"Where did you live?" asks Schmidt.

"I rented a room in nearby Markdorf and came by train each day to the Dornier plant at Manzell."

"How long did your employment at Dornier last?" asks Kappler.

"Six months, from memory."

"Were you sacked?" asks Seibold.

I think back to the day the master carpenter asked me the exact same question in his workshop. That day now seems like a lifetime ago.

"I left because Dannecker persuaded me to go with him to Konstanz to join a music club."

"A music club! What sort of degenerate are we dealing with?" sneers Seibold.

"Depends on the music," counters Kappler, unmoved by Seibold's discord.

As the time is now exactly 5 pm, according to the Swiss Zenith clock high on the wall, I wonder whether Kappler will end the day. But he tells me to continue with my employment history on the other side of the Bodensee.

I search my memory for every detail of my employment, from the fire in the Konstanz clock factory, to my employment across the border in

Bottighofen, Switzerland, to my time at Herr Rothmund's clockworks in Meersburg. Kappler wants to know everything about the company I kept during these seven years of my life—their names, addresses, what they ate for dinner, while Schmidt is more interested in my means of transport.

"So how did you get across the border to Bottighofen?"

"I rode a brand new bike I bought in 1927. From memory it cost me about 140 marks."

"How could someone like you afford 140 marks for a new bike?" asks Schmidt.

"I saved up. I sold the bike in November or December last year to a work colleague in Heidenheim and I received only 16 marks."

"You could not expect much more for a twelve year old bike," says Schmidt.

With time on 9.30 pm Kappler calls a halt to the proceedings. Schmidt and Seibold hurry away, leaving Kappler to gather up the pages that have been typed by the grey haired typist. He places them into his attaché case before he leaves. Those pages will make riveting bedtime reading—I don't think.

The second day of the Commission begins at 10 am. Kappler returns to my time of employment at Rothmund's clockworks in Meersburg. With Seibolt and Schmidt looking disinterested I tell how I cut the boards and assembled the cases for table and kitchen clocks; how every day I took the ferry from Konstanz to Meersburg and back; where I took lunch; the hours I worked, and how my limited free time was monopolized by Hilda Lang.

"Were the clock movements purchased from abroad?" Kappler asks, perhaps only to confirm what he and everyone else already know.

"They were, but from where exactly they came I do not know. The fitting of the clock movements was done by Herr Rothmund and his brother."

"So how long did your work for Rothmund," asks Kappler.

"I was let go with four others in the spring of 1932. Two others had already been released some time before for some unknown reason. But I suspect that it was due to bad business. I know nothing more about the activities of Rothmund."

My recollection of how a carpenter named Zimmermann gave me four or five weeks work and how I lived off the smell of an oily rag during the next six months in Meersburg pads out the session to lunch.

Upon the resumption my return home to Königsbronn in August 1932 is the focus of Kappler's questions. With the warm sun shafting through the windows Schmidt and Seibold are quietly losing all interest and drifting off as I recount the misery my father wrought on his poor wife and children.

"My mother said in her letter my father was more on the booze than ever. Upon my arrival home she expected an improvement in his behaviour, but he took my return with indifference. I soon realized my parents were heavily in debt due to the timber trade of my father. Through my uncle, Eugen Elser, I learnt my father always stood at the back of the wood auctions under the influence of alcohol and this was the reason he paid such high prices. He would drink almost every day in the Königsbronn area having endless business lunches overflowing with beer and wine — the exact quantities of which I cannot estimate. Neither my mother nor my brother could exert any influence over him. I repeatedly tried to influence him in a favourable sense, but without success. My father would not listen, consistently coming home drunk, making a terrible racket, and using abusive language with my mother, my brother and with me. He always said we were the 'guilty' ones before he wrecked the place."

"How heavily in debt was your father?" asks Kappler, still wide-awake.

"By the end of 1935 the debt had become so great my father had to sell the property, which in my estimation was worth 10,000 to 11,000 marks. But the property was sold for only 6,500 marks to the cattle dealer, Maurer, in Königsbronn. Maurer just happened to be one of my father's frequent drinking partners. From the proceeds my mother demanded and received 2,000 marks. The remainder was used to pay off my father's debts. A condition of sale was that my father be allowed to live in a shed on a portion of the land. My mother moved to Schnaitheim to live with my sister Friederike, while my little brother Leonhard went into the Reich Labour Service. I was left to rent a room from the married woman, Frau Härlen, after I had relocated my home workshop into her basement."

No one is too interested in my drunkard father or his debts, but when I mention how I moved into the house of the married woman, Frau Härlen, Seibold and Schmidt stir with renewed interest. But their interest is short lived as I go on to describe my job with the master carpenter Grupp, my musical ability, my membership of the Königsbronn Zither Club and the Trachtenverein traditional Dress and Dance Club. By the time I get to tell how I learnt to play the zither, Schmidt and Seibold are fast asleep.

But Kappler sees his fellow commissars are not pulling their weight, and cleverly devises a question to re-arouse their interest.

"Now go back to the relationship you had with this married woman, Frau Härlen."

"First I made a dolls' house for her. She paid me five marks and gave me the order for the kitchen cabinets and chairs when I was still working for Grupp. The material and labour cost of the chairs covered my rent. But the cabinets were never completed as her husband objected for some unknown reason."

"There must have been some good reason?" says Kappler, not one to miss a beat.

"Since the spring of 1936 I entertained a love affair with Frau Härlen. Whether her husband had knowledge of this, I do not know — though it is possible their marriage ended in divorce in the fall of 1938 for this reason."

"You cocky little bastard!" sneers Seibold.

With this reaction I'm glad I did not confess our affair in fact began in 1933.

The unflappable Kappler carries on unruffled, sensibly changing the discussion to my productive period of employment at the Waldenmaier factory in Heidenheim. Schmidt comes out firing.

"How could a guy as crooked as you get a job in this factory?"

"It was not so difficult. In mid-December 1936 I happened to meet a foreman, Wilhelm Hermann, in the Rössl restaurant in Königsbronn. When I told him of my work situation he suggested I try the factory. A day or so later I went by train or by bike to Heidenheim and was hired."

"Doing what?"

"I started work in the fettling shop where Hermann worked. For six months I did the dirty plaster cast work."

"Did you move from Königsbronn to Heidenheim?" asks Schmidt.

"Nay. I continued living in Königsbronn."

"With the married woman?" interjects Seibold.

"Nay. When her husband learnt how I felt about his wife I returned to live with my parents."

"But you said your parents sold the family house and went their separate ways," Kappler retorts.

"Later they bought half of a double house, though smaller than our previous house. I lived in the garret until May 1939, until I moved to Schnaitheim."

Schmidt then wants to know the people I talked with commuting to and from the factory.

"When I rode my bike I had no companions. When I took the train I saw the same faces every day, but had no link with any of them. Nor did I talk at work. I had no close workmates in the factory and was known as a 'quiet' person."

Next Schmidt wants to know my wage as a labourer, probably still wondering why I accepted a labouring job in a factory.

"I was paid 0.58 to 0.62 marks per hour in the fettling shop. I admit I could earn more as a skilled carpenter, but I would have to pay alimony if I was to earn more than 24 marks per week."

Schmidt has no follow-up question about paying alimony for my son, Manfred. Instead Seibold digs into my social life, wanting to know what I did in my spare time.

"I played music as a member of the Königsbronn Zither Club. And I was busy in my workshop making things, like the wooden box I made for Maria Schmauder from Schnaitheim who I had met at the factory."

"Tell us more about this Maria," asks Seibold.

"Our relationship was not especially close, though we got on well together."

"Have you had sex with her?" asks Seibold.

"We have kissed — but I have not had sexual intercourse with her."

"Too bad!" Seibold snipes.

Unlike the pervert Seibold, Kappler shows no interest in my innocent relationship with my ex-girlfriend. Instead, he wants to know where and with whom I took my meals when not taken at home. In my detailed reply I put in a favourable recommendation for the King Karl tavern in Heidenheim. Should by some miracle I survive all this I expect at least one free lunch.

At last Kappler comes to the business end of my act—giving me the opportunity to explain my pivotal promotion into a responsible position in the shipping department at the Waldenmaier factory. After covering my sometimes-quarrelsome interaction with other supervisors and my excursions into the 'special department' where I discovered explosive devices, namely detonators, were being manufactured, I give a detailed and exhaustive explanation of the input and output work procedures I managed in the shipping department. By using a boxful of technical terms like: banded springs, cellulose lacquer, detonators, igniters, needle pieces, needle guns, projectile fuses, pressed grains of powder, slotted nuts and wooden pestles, the three wise monkeys seem bamboozled by the time I finish. Kappler has the good sense to then ask a fundamental question.

"When did you decide to place a bomb in the Bürgerbräukeller?"

Kappler's use of the word 'bomb' catches me off-balance, as this is the first time this word has been used in this room, but I am able to come up with an answer.

"I made the decision to act in the fall of 1938."

"So you must have worked at the Waldenmaier factory for eighteen months before you made your decision to act," suggests Kappler.

"As far as I can remember."

When Schmidt asks if I got the idea for my bomb from something I read in a book I answer, "I have never read that much. I once read half of a short story in a newspaper but thought it stupid. As a rule I only read builders' and cabinetmakers' magazines."

As the time is now 5.55 pm, I wonder whether Kappler will quit at 6 pm. My backside is burning and the wounds inflicted by Herr Himmler and his strappers are still almost as raw as Karl's meat. But Kappler has no thought of stopping.

"HEALTH is next. The prisoner will now itemise all the ailments he has ever suffered in his thirty six years," announces Kappler.

Responding to the challenge, I mention measles and the possibility of scarlet fever as an infant and frequent headaches at school, though Seibold is not worried about my headaches, as he says this is a common ailment.

"Have you had a sexually transmitted disease," Seibold asks in hope.

I answer in the negative and return to my injuries. I tell how my little finger was almost minced when I put it between the gears of my father's whetstone and how I fell from a tree when pruning for my father, breaking a rib in the process, causing me to go to hospital. I also mention the stone that fell on my foot while I was working in a quarry. But Seibold has no interest in my foot or the quarry judging by his next question.

"Has anyone in your family committed suicide?"

"I do not know whether some relative has died by suicide. If they have I have heard nothing about it yet."

Questions about my drinking and my smoking habits follow. Not wanting to appear too inhibited I claim to never drinking more than six beers in a row. I add I smoked like a chimney for two years during my mid-twenties, but now I do not smoke as a rule.

Kappler then turns the flashlight on my SEX LIFE, giving Seibold open slather.

"Where did you first learn about sex?"

"The generation processes were told to me by a schoolmate."

"Do you masturbate?" asks Seibold.

"I know of the term 'masturbation' only in theory. I never do it."

"When did you first have intercourse with the opposite sex?" asks Seibold.

"My first time was with a girl named Brunhilde during my time in Konstanz. I only knew her by her first name."

"So what other sexual relationships have you enjoyed?" asks Seibold.

"After Brunhilde came Anna, then Mathilde Niedermann and Hilda Lang. When I returned to Königsbronn there was the married woman, Elsa Härlen, who now lives in Esslingen."

"Anyone else?" asks Seibold.

"With other girls I had an occasional relationship I have not had sex."

"Have you produced any offspring from your enviable love life?" asks Schmidt.

I was hoping this area of my private life would not be investigated and my failed attempt to deal effectively with the pregnancy of Mathilde Niedermann would go undiscovered. But it is not to be. I must go through all the traumatic details surrounding the unwanted birth of my son, Manfred.

I have barely come to the end before Seibold has thought up another highly relevant question for a confessed assassin.

"Do you practise perverse forms of sexual intercourse?"

"They are not even theoretically known to me."

Seibold sniggers, but has no follow up question. A long pause follows as if the three monkeys have drained the bucket of intelligent questions.

But I am wrong. Kappler has come up with a new topic — RELIGION.

Schmidt is the first to test the water, asking me questions about the religion of my parents.

"My mother is very religious, though my father is less so. Both are Protestant as are my siblings."

"Do you pray?" asks Seibold.

"My mother always prayed with me as a child. When I was older I continued on my own, praying the Lord's Prayer before going to sleep at night, though not always."

"Do you ever pray your own prayers?"

"I have never prayed for a deed or a wish to be fulfilled, if that is your question."

"Do you go to church?" asks Schmidt.

"As a child I was taken to church by my parents. Later I went many times alone, but less and less".

"Have you been to church recently?" asked Schmidt.

"During this last year I have gone to church more often, probably thirty times. Lately I have gone during the week to a Roman Catholic Church when no Protestant church is open where I can pray the Lord's Prayer. It does not matter where I go as I always become calmer after praying."

"Do you consider the act you committed a sin?" asks Schmidt.

"According to the Protestant doctrine, I would like to say in a deeper sense — NAY!"

"Do you believe in Heaven and Hell?" asks Seibold.

I glance out the window at the inky black sky before answering.

"I believe the soul lives on after death."

"And where are you going — to Heaven or to Hell?" sneers Seibold.

"I would go to Heaven if I had an opportunity to prove by my future life that I wanted good. I wanted to prevent even greater bloodshed through my deed."

A long silence follows. Kappler passes the time making notes in his book, though he could be playing noughts and crosses for all I know. Schmidt is the monkey who comes up with the next stream of questions on religion, ending by asking if I mix with other sects and if my mother has any contact with people of strange persuasion. I answer in the negative, as I know the Nazis have banned the Jehovah's Witnesses.

With the time having moved on to 8 pm and with all questions on religion put to bed I pray Kappler will give me an early mark, but he introduces a new topic entirely—the POLITICAL views of my parents and myself.

"My parents are apolitical as neither parent belongs to any political organisation—and besides they do not bother to read newspapers."

"Do you read newspapers?' asks Schmidt.

"I only read furniture and joinery journals as I have stated, unless I happen to pick up a newspaper in a guesthouse or on board a train—but I never pick up Socialist or Communist papers."

"What exactly are the political views of the confessed assassin?" asks Kappler, looking more perplexed than ever.

"I am not politically minded. Though after attaining the voting age, I always chose the German Communist Party."

"Why would you ever do that?" asks Schmidt.

"I thought the KPD is a workers' party that fights for the workers' rights."

"Did you not know the goal of the KPD was to establish a Soviet dictatorship of the proletariat in Germany by a violent overthrow?" asks Schmidt.

"It is possible I have heard something about this, but I have never heard about the violent overthrow of National Socialism at the meetings I attended," I assert.

"You were caught wearing the Red Front-Fighters badge at the Swiss border. When did you join this banned organisation?" asks Kappler.

"From memory it was either in 1928 or 1929 while I was still living in Konstanz."

"Why did you join?"

"I joined after frequent coaxing by a fellow worker called Fiebig who worked with me in the clock industry in Konstanz. We lived together for some time in Inselgasse."

"How active were you in the RFB?" Kappler continues.

"I paid my dues but never had a uniform or held an official post. I was only ever three times in a political meeting and was not involved in leaflet distribution, demonstrations or the painting of graffiti on trains."

There are no follow up questions. My FINANCIAL situation is next. I stuff my hands into my empty pockets to answer.

"My financial situation is in order. For most of my life I have worked to pay my way. I have no assets and expect none, as the property of my parents is heavily covered with debt. Personally I have no debt, though from the District Court of Konstanz I was ordered to pay 45 Reich marks per month for the maintenance of my son, Manfred. I have not been able to afford this payment to this day, so thereby I assume a considerable debt has accumulated. How much the debt is today, I prefer not to know."

No one is even slightly interested in my answer, perhaps due to the lateness of the hour. Still, the persistent Schmidt wants to know if I have a police record.

"I am not a criminal. A criminal case has never been brought against me," I plead.

With the time now on 10 pm Kappler decides to quit. He fills his attaché case and bolts for the door with Schmidt and Seibold close behind. As I wait for my lazy guards, the typist lets out a bored yawn. She has already produced a wad of paper. How many more pages and days will there be I wonder if in two long days there has been only one mention of the Bürgerbräukeller.

28 November 17–December 8, 1939
Berlin

IN the days following the disappearance of the young lawyer and his assistant there is a complete lull in proceedings. Best is left in limbo to enjoy the sunny Berlin weather and his view from room No.315.

But with no news of the war and not knowing whether Holland has been invaded by Germany his thoughts inevitably turn to his wife, May, and her safety. Though these thoughts are incidental to his memory of Klop being shot down in full flight. Best recalls the pistols he and Stevens had packed. Why had they not put up a fight, he wonders ad nauseam. Visions of shooting down the dozen SD men one by one follow. Between him and Stevens they had twenty-six slugs in their Browning semi-automatics so numerically it would have been possible, even by missing every second shot. Dying in a shootout at Café Backus would be far better that being a prisoner hibernating on a couch in the sun in Berlin.

Best's thoughts of a heroic death do not last long. Being a prisoner takes a turn for the better when a factotum named Grothe takes him under his wing. Almost every day he comes with sandwiches, apples and cigarettes. One day Grothe brings a parcel with pyjamas, socks, handkerchiefs, a safety razor and other toiletries. Though Frau Roland and Fräulein Blimental are not to be outdone. In the evenings they come to his room bringing tea and biscuits. His pleasure is complete when once a week he is taken down to the basement of the building for a hot bath.

Still Best remains mindful of his colleague, Richard Stevens. The last time he saw him was going up the stairs in Düsseldorf to be interviewed by the two neat young men. He wonders whether he is in the same building as Stevens. This is answered one day when being taken by his guards to have a bath he sees Stevens stepping from the lift. Best smiles in recognition but receives no reaction from Stevens. He has a vague, distant look on his face — the look of a man who has just coughed up every secret of the SIS.

Best has another odd moment when a man with a suitcase opens his door and looks alarmed to find the room is occupied. Next day Best is moved to room No.238, a move he finds degrading. Sunless and modest in dimensions make the room fit only for a junior clerk, in his own estimation.

A day after his relocation, Best is taken upstairs to the attic for more photos. When he is returned to his room Heinrich Müller is waiting to intercept him.

"Settling into your new room okay?" enquires Müller.

"Do you call this a room?"

"One of our basement cells might suit you better?"

"This will do for now."

"Is your health good? Are you feeling the strain?" continues Müller as if he hopes Best will complain.

"I'm as well as can be expected under the circumstances."

"Then follow me."

This is ominous, thinks Best, as Müller leads him into his suite of rooms opposite. The first room Best enters is filled with SS officers lounging about in dress uniform like extras in a war movie. In the second room Best enters he is told to stand at a certain spot. When the door ahead is opened three men dressed in black SS uniforms come out goosestepping. Clicking their heels, they come to a halt facing Best.

"We bet you did not suspect you were entertaining officers of the SS?" Colonel Martini, Lieutenant Grosch and Captain Schaemmel squeal in unison.

More impudent questions are flung in the face of the dumbfounded Best. When they have run out of gags the Vaudeville act about faces and goosesteps off stage. Surrounded by a chorus of chortling SS officers, Best looks for the door. Before he can escape an officer of resplendent rank springs to his feet to scream in his face, demanding he cooperates or be handed over to 'those who know how to extract the truth'. As Best has noticed portraits of this long-nosed, fair-headed man in numerous rooms he has a premonition this prima donna has some status in the Nazi organization.

"Who is this excitable young officer?" Best asks Müller, causing the Chief of Security Police and the SD, Reinhard Heydrich, to hiss and spray him with spit.

"Your impudence is bound to have consequences, but don't take the matter too seriously—soup is never eaten as hot as it is cooked," Müller reassures Best once he is returned to his room.

In the afternoon of the same day Captain Schaemmel pays Best a visit. He has not come to apologize for the cheeky goose-stepping act in the morning, but to introduce a short, middle-aged man with a hint of unkempt hair.

"Dr. Schäfer will continue your interrogation. Your life now depends on your cooperation with him," warns Schaemmel.

"Is that so. You played a dirty trick on me and Stevens," Best carps.

"I sympathize with you being in the unfortunate position you find yourself, Captain."

"I don't need your sympathy for my error of judgment," Best retorts.

"Don't compound your mistakes. We refuse to believe you are as ignorant as you pretend to be. And by the way Captain, my real name is Schellenberg."

"Schellenberg! And I suppose you will tell me Colonel Martini and Lieutenant Grosch are phoney names as well."

"Of course. Do you think we are so stupid as to use real names?"

Next morning, after a night of having his ankles strapped due to his impudence, Best is taken to Dr. Schäfer. After he dismisses the guards, sends his typist to buy cigars, and gets rid of the fetter, Schäfer has some reassuring words.

"Don't you worry about what Schellenberg said to you yesterday. You are under the Führer's personal protection. I have the task of preparing a report to the Reichstag who will decide if you are to be put on trial for treason. Though having looked at your file I don't think you have much to worry about. So look upon me as a friend."

In the next week identity parades are interspersed with interviews. Since images of Best have appeared in the German press, many civic-minded people have written to the Gestapo claiming to have seen Best. As the men who are paraded with Best are always obvious Germans, Best is picked out every time. Dr. Schäfer has no qualms in dismissing the claims.

The interrogation lasts for almost ten days before petering out. On December 7 Best is relocated from the third floor to a corridor-like room on the first floor. His downgrading is accompanied by the removal of all his privileges and possessions. He is fettered and handcuffed at night and when his cigarettes are confiscated, he realizes his situation is dire.

In Whitehall the situation has also gone down hill. Alexander Cadogan must reveal in his report to the British and French governments that the German Opposition has broken off wireless communication. He records:

In the evening of November 17th a final message was received from the Germans:

"Corresponding with conceited and foolish people becomes boring in the long run. You will understand our breaking off relations. Best wishes from your good friends, the German Opposition".

A week later Lord Halifax records his opinion on the nature of the covert meetings between the SIS and the German Opposition in these terms:

The interesting point about this is at what point the Gestapo chipped in. It may have been that we were being had for a mug from the start, but I don't think so, and our Secret Service people are very positive that to begin with it was what they call a 'genuine contact'.

29

November 21, 1939
Berlin

THE third day of the inquisition commences at 8.30 am. This earlier than normal start time is obviously due to the spectators already seated for the freak show. Kappler looks on edge due to the presence of the gang who have come armed with pencils, pens and notebooks. But after he coughs into his hand and blows his nose, Kappler is ready to deliver his opening blow.

"The Special Commission will continue with the examination of the thirty-six year old criminal, Georg Elser, who has already confessed to his horrific act in Munich, the attempted assassination of the Führer."

Kappler waits for the press gang to hush before he continues with his spiel.

"The greatest task of every German is to serve his community at all times and in every way, giving his life for its greatness and its eternal life, while a person without honor has lost not only the respect of his community, but also his rights within that community. The Führer is the great role model toward whom each individual German can strive and imitate. And everything, whether in politics, the economy, culture, or the private life of the individual must be examined, seen, and fulfilled according to the fundamental concepts of National Socialism. With these National Socialism values in our minds the confessed criminal will now state what monstrous ideas led him to commit his murderous act against our Führer."

It sounds like someone had been up all night writing Kappler's lines. But now with everyone's eyes fixed on me I pause before I come up with my reply to his heavy question. I need time to gather together my facts and figures.

"Since the National Socialists gained power the economic conditions for the workers have deteriorated in several respects. For example, I have found that wages are lower and deductions are higher. While I earned an average 50 marks weekly in 1929 at the clock factory located in Konstanz, the deductions at this time for tax, health insurance, unemployment benefits and disability benefits were only about 5 marks. Today the deductions are already as high as 25 marks a week. The hourly wage of a joiner in 1929 amounted to 1.0 mark. Today the hourly wage has dropped to 0.68 marks. Also from the conversations I have had with various workers even lower wages are paid to workers in other occupations."

The three monkeys look like they've been euthanized—struck dumb by my answer. The silence ends when Kappler asks a foolish follow up question.

"Do you wish to add anything?"

"I do. In my opinion the working class is under more pressure since the National Socialists came into power. For example the worker can no longer change his employment as he pleases, and the worker is no longer the master over his own children because of the Hitler Youth Movement, while in religion the worker can no longer worship as he pleases."

"Where did you get this nonsense?" asks Schmidt.

"I have observed these things wherever I've worked, in places where I've stayed, and by talking to people on trains."

"Can you name the people you talk to?" asks Kappler.

"Whenever I have had conversations the names of the persons who agree with me are unknown to me. Likewise the names of persons who disagree with me are equally unknown to me."

I am not surprised Kappler goes in a new direction after my last ham fisted answer.

"What is your opinion of the war Germany has been forced to fight?" asks Kappler.

"Amongst the working classes there is great unrest about this war. There is even outrage. Last year I came to the conviction the Munich Agreement would not result in peace because Germany would only make more demands and invade more countries. Therefore this war has become inevitable."

"Who told you this rot?" growls Kappler.

"This is solely my own opinion, though I do admit to hearing foreign broadcasts."

"Foreign broadcasts! Where did you hear these broadcasts?" squeals Schmidt.

"I heard these broadcasts at home. A music shop in Heidenheim was offering wireless sets on a free trial basis. I think it was a Philips costing over 200 marks. But when I took the set home my mother said she did not need entertainment. So I returned the set to the store at the end of the 14 days' free trial period."

"What did you listen to when you had the set in your possession?" asks Schmidt.

"The set was in my room connected with an extension cord from my electric lamp. When I searched the stations I tuned to Moscow, though I did not seek to listen to a Moscow station. Only when listening to the talk show did I realize it came from Moscow."

More questions follow related to my unforgivable sin of listening to banned radio stations from Moscow to London. I deny knowledge of Freedom Station 29.8, which Seibold refers to as a dumb fishing boat that has run out of steam. When I happen to mention I also listened to the Schmauder's family wireless set, Schmidt jumps up like his pants are on fire.

"What did the Schmauder family talk about?"

"I can no longer remember their exact conversations. Though I do recall they rejected the messages that were obviously wrong, while they wondered whether others could be correct."

I trust my answer will keep the Schmauders out of trouble.

After a break for lunch and after the press gang have resumed their seats and flipped open a new page in their notebooks, Kappler has a new topic—MOTIVE.

This session might never end if Kappler lets me have my head, I muse as I begin.

"In the autumn of 1938 I came to my decision on how to improve the conditions of the workers and to avoid a war. I was encouraged or influenced by no one. I had never heard from anyone, including Radio Moscow, that the Nazi regime must be overthrown. I simply believed in the removal of the current leaders, the men in high places: Hitler, Göring and Goebbels."

When the hissing amongst the press ends, Schmidt has the next question.

"Was your intention to eliminate the National Socialist Party?"

"I did not necessarily want to entirely eliminate National Socialism. I was merely of the opinion a moderation in policy would occur by the elimination of these three leaders."

The press are still in the middle of digesting my words as Kappler diverts to a different matter, though only by returning to the same old question.

"Who told you to bomb the Bürgerbräukeller?"

"I spoke with nobody. I was the sole perpetrator as I have repeated time and again."

Kappler goes back into his bomb shelter as Schmidt changes the point of attack.

"What was your strategy to achieve your foul ends?"

"I thought to myself that the elimination of these three men is only possible if they are together at a rally. From the daily press I learnt the next time these leaders would be together was on November 8, at the Bürgerbräukeller in Munich."

For the next two hours or more I must rack my brains for Kappler on my movements in November 1938, telling of my first visit to Munich. I include my train journey, my frustration in finding suitable lodging, waiting behind the police barriers with the onlookers, seeing the Führer and his cronies speed off in a convoy of Mercedes, how I entered the hall and walked about to assess the assassination potential, how I ate in the restaurant afterwards and how I met a slaughterhouse manager from Aalen.

"From Aalen! Who was this man—this slaughterhouse manager from

Aalen?" Kappler exclaims, his voice high pitched with expectation.

"I never meet this man before in my life nor have I seen him since."

"Can you give a description of this man?"

"Err — yes. He was about 1.74 m tall and about thirty-seven to thirty-eight years old. A more detailed description of this man I cannot give to you," I confess.

Kappler instructs the typist to record my description word for word, perhaps to impress the press gang of his meticulous attention to detail. He then calls a meal break and we do not meet again until 6.15 pm.

Kappler's opening words at the start of the next session do not sound good for an early night.

"The confessed assassin will now state when he conceived his evil plan and the means by which he carried out his satanic act."

This double bung question could take an eon to answer, but I come straight to the point.

"In the weeks following my return from Munich in November 1938, I concocted my idea to pack explosives into the pillar behind the speaker's podium and to detonate those explosives at an exact moment in time. I chose the position in the pillar so that the flying projectiles from an explosion would hit only those persons sitting near to the speaker's lectern."

"Did you plan for the whole bloody ceiling to collapse as well?" sneers Seibold.

"I wondered if it might."

"How did you know who would be sitting near to the lectern?" asks Schmidt.

"I did not know exactly. I only knew that Hitler speaks at the lectern and I assumed the other leaders would sit next to him."

"Where did the assassin receive his training to build a bomb?" asks Schmidt.

Obviously this is the question fascinating the boys from the press. They would like to believe I had foreign backers as Nebe and Huber had hinted.

"I have never had theoretical or practical training in the constructing of an apparatus for the timed ignition of explosives, or for the making of drawings or models for an infernal machine."

"That beggars belief! The assassin is lying!" explodes Seibold.

The imperturbable Kappler ignores Seibold's impulsive outburst. He wisely prefers to move on to an unexplored, yet highly important area of the inquiry.

"The confessed assassin will now tell how he acquired his stockpile of explosives."

With my hands deep in my pockets, remembering the metallic bits and pieces I emptied onto the table at the Swiss border, I explain my method of acquisition.

"After my return from my first visit to Munich I continued to work in the Waldenmaier factory in Heidenheim. Before I had a specific plan of execution, I gained a supply of explosives when working in the shipping department."

"Where did you hoard this highly explosive stuff," asks Seibold.

"While I was still living at home I wrapped the cartridges in paper, put the packages into the bottom of my wardrobe and covered them with underwear. My family never discovered anything as I always kept my room tidy."

"What caused you to go off to Munich again in April this year?" asks Kappler.

"As I thought about the construction of the apparatus in my head or by the making sketches on sheets of paper, I realized I needed to know the exact dimensions of the pillar into which I planned to install my apparatus."

My second visit to Munich at Easter, April 4-12, 1939, is then put under the microscope. Kappler wants to hear of every move I made. With a tale better than the Brothers Grimm could conjure, I begin by telling how I went from one unsatisfactory lodging to the next. Schmidt is so moved by my story he wants to know the tariff I paid in each defective lodging. As for Seibold I must explain my measuring methods so he can understand.

"I measured the dimensions of the candidate pillar with a folding metre stick and entered the measured dimensions into my notebook, that is to say, I made a small sketch in my notebook and noted the dimensions on this sketch."

Next Kappler wants to know the persons I spoke with. This innocent question opens the possibility my answer will drive Kappler to drink.

"On my first or second day in Munich a Bürgerbräukeller houseboy, whose name I no longer remember, sat by chance at my table to take a meal or to drink a beer. We got into conversation and he told me, among other things, that he was probably going into the military. It occurred to me that it would be very helpful for the preparation of my intended act if I could become a houseboy. I therefore asked him if I could take his place. He promised me he would ask the manager. The next few days I kept reminding him of his promise as he kept saying he had not yet had the opportunity. In the end I spoke to the manager myself about the matter. He was surprised to hear that one of his houseboys was leaving, as he had not said anything to him. The houseboy told me afterwards he was upset I had asked the manager without telling him first. Later the manager came to my table to tell me he would probably not employ me as he hoped his houseboy would stay. I talked with another houseboy on this question, buying him a glass of beer. I promised him 50 marks to let me know if he was going into the military."

"Did you meet any other persons?" asks Kappler, desperate these questions will lead somewhere with the press chewing like beavers on their pencils.

"I went with another houseboy to drink a glass of beer. A third boy I met in the restaurant came as well. His name I cannot remember nor can I recall what he looked like. On another occasion I went with the same houseboy to a tavern. His name I cannot remember, though I remember I paid for all his beers as well as my own."

"Did you have any further contact with these houseboys?" asks Kappler.

"Before I left Munich I arranged with the houseboy to write me a letter if he intended to enlist. If I got the job at the Bürgerbräukeller I would pay him 50 marks. I made this commitment in writing. When the houseboy asked why the job was so important to me I told him it was the only way I could live in Munich. He believed my story and asked no more questions as the money was more important than my reasons. Besides, he liked to drink."

"How could you afford to pay the houseboy the princely sum of 50 marks?" asks Schmidt.

"I could have paid out of my savings which were already about 70 marks. Also I could increase my saving by the sale of wood from my workshop and by selling my double bass and other possessions. I could have accumulated 350-400 marks by August."

"And what else did you do in Munich when you were not drinking with houseboys?" asks Seibold.

"Most of the time I went walking in the city streets—but wait! I have just remembered I met and talked with three young waitresses at the Bürgerbräukeller. They noticed I had a camera and asked me to take a photo of them in the beer garden."

"Where did you get the camera?" asks Schmidt.

"It was a Christmas present from Maria Schmauder."

"Did you photograph anything else in Munich besides pretty young girls?" asks Seibold.

"I took some shots inside the hall of the Bürgerbräukeller, including some of the pillar which I blew up later."

Much time is then wasted on questions about my camera and my photographs, including where I had them developed and printed. As far as I can remember I used a photographic agent in Heidenheim whose name was Schuster. As for my camera, it is now with the rest of my stuff in Stuttgart with Maria, my sister.

After a short break Kappler wants to know why I left home for a second time. This takes a while to explain as the details cut close to the heart. The essence of my answer is: although I lived in my parents' new house until May 1939, according to my mother and my little brother I was meant to have cleared out of the house in December 1938. Leonhard and his bolshy wife wanted my room for themselves and my mother wanted a whole lower floor of the house to herself. When my father was the only one to stand up for me I decided it was time to leave anyway. And besides, living with the Schmauder family looked a better proposition to me.

With my domestic dustup off my chest, Kappler returns to my most recent place of employment—the limestone quarry of Georg Vollmer in Königsbronn. I tell how at the end of April 1939 I left the Waldenmaier factory after a dispute with a supervisor named Kastler. As I was keen to add to my stockpile I applied for a job at the local quarry where I had an interview with the quarry foreman, named Kolb. He was a local man and he employed me as a labourer to load stones into a trolley in the quarry. Kappler then asks me for the names of every employee. I can only recall about half, but this is good enough. I then start to describe the blasting operations.

"The cartridges used for the blasting was stored in a concrete bunker located in the quarry."

"What is this 'bunker'?" interjects Kappler.

"It was about 1.5 m long and 1.0 m wide, with a sheet-iron door with an ordinary door lock. Inside there was a lockable gate as well."

"And you stole explosive stuff out of there?" asks Seibold, jumping ahead.

"Not in my first week. The first time I took explosives illegally was when blasting was being carried out near where I was working. Kolb would bring more explosives out of the bunker than he needed and left cartridges lying about unattended. I often put the cartridge in my pocket when no one was looking. I did this about eight times, always during the working hours. Nothing was noticed and Kolb never said anything was missing."

"Did Kolb keep records for the explosives he used?" asks Schmidt.

"Not that I can recall."

"Sounds like slack management to me," Schmidt remarks, stating the obvious.

"Does the confessed assassin have anything to add?" Kappler asks again.

"Only to say in the last weeks I was working in the quarry I stole blasting cartridges at night. I still had a set of keys from my parents' property and I tried opening the bunker with these keys. The third key unlocked the door and I found the inner gate was unlocked anyway. Using my flashlight I saw two wooden boxes on the shelf, about 80 cm long and 25-30 cm wide and about 35 cm high. Both boxes were open with the lid alongside. They were half-filled with cartons of explosive cartridges. The first night I took a package with about twenty cartridges inside, locked the door with the same key and took my loot home in a backpack."

"Which home are you talking about now?" asks Kappler, as if he has lost the plot.

"I was then living happily with the Schmauder family."

Kappler looks at his watch. I look towards the wall clock. The time is 11.20 pm. A few minutes later the room is deserted apart from the typist. The press left long ago. They must have a deadline.

30   November 22, 1939
In the Press

NEWSPAPERS from Berlin to Heidenheim carry the story of the Munich assassin and his co-conspirators. The following translation is from, *Der Grenzbote*, Heidenheim, Germany, Nov. 22, 1939, page 1. This text is believed to be the same or similar to the text on the front page of *Deutsche Allgemereine Zeitung*, Berlin, shown on the next page.

MUNICH ASSASSIN ARRESTED

Ceaseless investigation of the Bürgerbräukeller crime. The culprit: The 36-year old Georg Elser. His Client: The British Intelligence Service. Organiser: Emigrant Otto Strasser. The criminal confessed fully.

Two English secret agents caught at the border crossing

Berlin, November 21. The Reichsführer SS and Chief of the German Police announced: Immediately after the infamous attack in the Bürgerbräukeller on November 8, 1939 measures were taken which were suitable for the investigation of the crime and make possible the arrest of the offender or the offenders. As part of this investigation was a momentary suspension of all German borders in conjunction with a stricter border control. Among those arrested that night was a man who had tried to illegally cross the German border into Switzerland. Namely the 36-year-old Georg Elser, last residing in Munich.

Deutsche Allgemereine Zeitung, Berlin, Nov 22, 1939, page 1
From left to right: Elser, and the British agents, Stevens and Best.

The findings of the interim measures taken by the security police, sent to the Munich Special Commission, revealed numerous references to the preparation and execution of the deed. The offender seemed to be a person whose detailed description was already published on November 12. Further findings strengthened the suspicion that Georg Elser had at least some connection to the assassination.

Infernal machine set to 6 days

As a result of the evidence obtained by the Special Commission at the scene of the crime and at the place where he had taken refuge and after several confrontations and obstinate denials, Elser made a full confession on 14 November 1939.

As in a detective story, he had built through weeks of painstaking work in one of the supporting pillars of the Bürgerbräukeller a time bomb set to explode in six days or 144 hours. The planning of the crime goes back to the September and October 1938. In August 1939 the installation of the explosive chamber took place. The explosive charge was brought in on the seventh day before the rally in Bürgerbräukeller. Six days earlier Elser had attempted to set the blasting machine in the explosive chamber. This failed. The fifth night before was suitable and led him back to the task set by the organiser. However on the night of the third day before 8 November Elser was able to incorporate his blasting machine into the prepared explosive chamber.

Criminal returns to the scene of the crime

The offender then left immediately to go to Switzerland via Stuttgart where those who had set the task were waiting for him. For certain reasons Elser went in the afternoon of the seventh back to Munich. He managed to stay the night of the 7th to the 8th in the Bürgerbräukeller to convince himself once more by personally listening to the ticking of the clock movement. The criminal had not forgotten to provide for attenuation of the noise. He repeated this test several times on the night of the 7th to the 8th. At 8am the criminal then had breakfast at a Munich pub near the Isartor in the valley and then went by train via Ulm to the border. On the night of the 8th to the 9th he tried to cross the border to Switzerland near Konstanz. However the general alarm, which had been raised made this impossible and led to his arrest.

The British Intelligence Service had ordered and funded the operation. The organizer of the crime was Otto Strasser. The investigation to establish the operatives, those who had set the task and his accomplices, has not been made available. Now material dealing with the arrest can be disclosed.

To further elucidate, the following questions are addressed to the public:
1. Who still knows Elser?
2. Who can provide information about his dealings?
3. Who can give clues with whom Elser associated?

4. Where has Elser appeared in the last few years?
5. Where or from whom has he made purchases or placed orders?
6. Who else knows where Elser was dealing with inventions, technical drawings, designs, construction plans, etc.?
7. Anyone who has seen other people with drawings and plans of the Bürgerbräukeller?
8. Who has seen Elser in restaurants, train stations, trains, buses, alone or with others?
9. Anyone who has even seen Elser abroad? When, where and with whom?

The culprit is encircled

On the evidence gathered about the perpetrators from the crime scene and by the wide-ranging inquiry by officials of the secret police whose interviews have resulted in thousands and thousands of pieces of information coming from the entire German people, the results are being researched and organised by the Commission of the Security Police.

As the circle around the criminal became tighter and tighter it was possible to separate the essential from the inessential, from the related to the non-related. All work could therefore focus primarily on the alleged perpetrators, then systematically on the offender, the criminal himself, and then to track the connecting lines of evidence to him.

Due to the results of the first investigation of the Special Commission of all people under suspicion transferred to Munich on instructions from the Reichsführer SS from all over the Reich from border to border the circle has been tightened after extensive hearings. Anyone who understands the term "cross-bearing" in radio or in navigation will clearly understand the logic of the compelling intersection of the results the crime scene Commission has singled out the real perpetrators from amongst the arrested suspects. After the interrogation of each criminal, testing his psychological state, the suspicion fell on Elser. His personal ties, his way of life, his circle of friends were established accurately to the second. After multiple interrogations and confrontations, the real perpetrators were established.

A Satanic Beast

The weight of the evidence, the certain proof of his flight and the criminal's confession, only confirmed the findings of the investigation. We have seen this man. He is the murderer; the dead are the victims of his terrible plan. This is the man whose intended target was the Führer, and with him the leadership of the Reich. One has to keep all of these things in mind, because this man does not have the obvious physiognomy of a criminal, but has intelligent eyes, and expresses himself in a cautious way, carefully deliberating, he considers every word, thinking long and hard before he responds, and when one watches him, one forgets for a moment what a satanic monster this is and what guilt and ghastly burden his conscience is apparently capable of bearing with ease.

The criminal history knows no parallel case for this meanest and most cunning of crimes. To demonstrate how precisely and systematically this criminal worked, the following detail emerged during the interrogation. After his actual confession Elser was requested to go to the crime scene in the Bürgerbräukeller in Munich to clarify certain matters. Elser explained that this was unnecessary and gave the evidence in the interrogation room by making a freehand sketch of the crime scene, totally off the top of his head, going into every last detail of the entire technically complicated murder plot, exactly and truthfully.

A puzzle solved
A mystery remained for the police in the course of the criminal investigation, which the criminal was able to solve. Why had the offender returned on his way abroad to reset the clock in view of the long duration of the clock inside his infernal machine?

The first public announcement of the cancellation of the ceremony in the Bürgerbräukeller and the subsequent postponement of the Führer's speech on the evening of November 8th had induced the offender to return to the crime scene. The happy coincidence that saved the Führer and thus all of us from a horrific disaster was the criminal's undoing. He could be captured before he was able to escape to where Germans had no access.

We all have to be doubly thankful for this action, because the arrest of this man is meaningful in all its consequences, the scope of which cannot be underestimated. Amongst the background of this shameful crime, the German public has collected an infinite number of clues and details in conjunction with the Security Police, thus all the facts are known, detailed down to the last chain of evidence that will prove fatal for those concerned.

They went blindly into the trap of our Gestapo. The British agents are believed to have negotiated with German revolutionaries
Berlin, November 21. Officially acknowledged to be located in The Hague, the headquarters of the British Intelligence service for Western Europe has long tried to foment plots in Germany and organize attacks namely to get in touch with suspected revolutionary organizations. Criminal German emigrants foolishly led the British government intelligence service to the opinion there existed in the Wehrmacht an opposition with the aim of bringing about a revolution.

Under these circumstances, officers of the Security Service of the SS were instructed to liaise with the British Terror and Revolution Headquarters at The Hague. In the belief that they were actually negotiating with the revolutionary German officers representatives the British Intelligence service revealed to the German officials their intentions and in order to maintain a permanent connection with these alleged German officers, they gave them an English radio transmission and receiving device, by which the German Secret State Police was able to maintain the connection with the British government to this day.

On November 9, the head of the British Intelligence Service for Western Europe, M. Best and Captain Stevens, tried to cross the Dutch border into Germany at Venlo. They were monitored and arrested by a German squad and taken as prisoners of the State Police. The conflicting statements about their arrest, whether on Dutch or German soil have been examined.

How the criminal was found

From the detection of the assassination attack in Munich the German police provide the following details:

Immediately following the terrible crime on the evening of November 8th at the Bürgerbräukeller in Munich, upon the orders of the Reichsführer SS all parts of the German police were put on high alert. The alert began within an hour of the crime to quickly capture the offender. All open border crossings were closed and monitored and no suspicious persons were allowed to cross without the special permission of the Chief of the Security Police (Reich Security Main Office). In an extremely short time period the doors to the Reich were hermetically sealed.

At the same time a criminal Special Commission (Crime Scene Commission), with special experts and specialists from the Security Police went to Munich. Immediately after the removal of the dead and wounded, the actual crime scene was completely sealed off. During the night of November 9th, with particularly arduous work, the whole explosive debris was carefully sifted and systematically screened and sorted. After long days and nights of methodical searching, while observing the nature of this terrible explosion, the security police came into the possession of individual, sometimes slightly translucent silver, small screws and spring pieces, which were collected and preserved for the first reconstruction of the objective proof to make the necessary conclusion. There was now a clear image of the movement that triggered the explosion, about the nature of the explosive and the approximate amount of explosive material required for this crime as well as the mounting location of the alleged infernal machine as well as the actual type of construction. Parts of a special timepiece led to important conclusions about the possible manufacturers and therefore gave especially valuable clues in the search for the culprit.

Footnote: This article refers to 'Major' Best and 'Captain' Stevens. This is an error made by the German press or Dr. Goebbels.

31

November 22-23, 1939

Berlin

THERE are no pressmen hanging about today to gawk like there were yesterday. Could this be the last time I must sit here on my burning arse all day? With things starting promptly at 9.10 am I may be in with a chance. Kappler allows me to get into my element right from the start, describing my night raids on the concrete bunker at Georg Vollmer's quarry.

"After I made five visits I had accumulated an arsenal of 105 blasting cartridges and 125 detonators," I boldly confess without showing a gram of remorse.

"Why so many detonators?" asks Schmidt.

"Good question. I knew two or three detonators would be sufficient for my purposes, but I thought the surplus would increase the explosive effect."

"They sure did you arsehole! The brick wall opposite the speaker's podium collapsed on innocent people," sneers Seibold.

After this hurtful remark I explain how I hid everything in my trunk.

"Did your girlfriend Maria Schmauder once take a look inside your trunk?" asks Kappler, indicating he is really on my case.

"She did."

Kappler follows up with questions regarding the markings on the explosive cartridges, the construction of my double bottomed trunk and where I kept things hidden in the Schmauder's house, before he returns me to the blasting operations at Vollmer's quarry. A question coming from Schmidt presents the opportunity to vent my knowledge on the cracking of rock.

"First a series of boreholes are drilled to the right depth, explosive cartridges are inserted, blasting caps added and a fuse attached. I did not perform this work myself, but I learnt how to do these things simply by observing."

"Is this the same quarry where you injured your foot?" asks Seibold.

This question comes as something of a shock. Seibold is not the total fool I assumed him to be.

"Yes, this is where a large stone fell on my foot, causing me to take sick leave. I was forced to lie on Schmauder's sofa for several weeks to recover."

"Did you seek medical help?" asks Schmidt.

"I did. I rode a bike to Heidenheim to visit Dr. Freund for treatment."

"But how on earth could you ride a pushbike with a busted foot?" inquires Seibold, obviously thinking he has found a big loophole in my story.

"I only kicked the pedals with my good foot."

Seibolt is silenced.

More random questions lead me to expound on my neat idea to use rifle ammunition to trigger the detonators. Kappler wants the name and the address of the supplier.

"I cannot recall the name, but the store repaired pushbikes and sold sewing machines, guns and ammunition. I recall the shop was located in Heidenheim near the crossroad with Adolf-Hitler-Strasse."

"Can you give a description of the man who served you?" Kappler asks.

"The man was short and stocky. He might have been the owner and asked whether I wanted 6 mm or 9 mm calibre. I chose 9 mm."

"Did he ask why you wanted the ammunition?"

"Nay. He did not even ask to see a hunting licence or a gun licence."
Kappler grimaces.

Next I describe the explosive tests I conducted in the orchard still belonging to my parents. Though I only used mock-ups comprised of wood blocks, springs and wires to perform these tests, Kappler seems impressed. I add that my father at the time was relegated to living in a shed on the property. In his inebriated state I doubt he ever heard the blasts.

Part way through describing the many sketches I made, sometimes in my workshop, sometimes in the Schmauder's kitchen, Kappler throws rolls of paper in my face.

"Do you mean these?"

"Where did you find them?"

"When our investigators called they were scattered about the house."

After the break for lunch I am given the opportunity by Kappler to describe in considerable detail the unique technical features of my apparatus.

"The most difficult problem in the construction of my apparatus was to trigger the ignition at an appointed time. It was clear to me from the outset I would need to use clockwork and couple the movement of two clocks in conjunction with a standard car winker mechanism____"

This is only the beginning of my lengthy explanation. As the three monkeys look puzzled by the end, I remind them this is only clockwork, not rocket science.

Kappler moves to my arrival in Munich on August 5. After I explain why my departure was delayed by being struck down with fever and being in recovery mode with Maria Schmauder and her mother tending me, Schmidt has a question.

"Did you inform the Schmauder family of your reason for going to Munich?"

"I told them I had landed a job as a cabinetmaker with Deutsche Werkstätten. This was a name I saw on a sign while walking around the city in April."

"That was devious," sneers Seibold.

"Would you expect me to tell them the truth and get them into trouble?"

Seibold has no answer.

"The assassin will now make a complete list of all the materials and devices he took to Munich," demands Kappler, testing my memory and my stamina.

Kappler revels in this nitty gritty, even if the exercise takes me well over an hour to complete. I explain how I stowed my explosives and rifle ammunition under the double-bottom of my wooden trunk while gear such as the 6-volt batteries, car winkers—both from a Heidenheim auto dealer—Rothmund's five clock movements and design sketches were intermingled with spare clothing and clean underwear. My final list includes 250 pressings of explosives, each 19 mm in diameter by 9 mm thick, 150 Donarit and gelatine explosive cartridges and 122 detonators. When Seibold complains I previously testified to having 125 detonators I remind him three detonators were needed for my model tests in the orchard at Königsbronn. The almost full box of 9 mm rifle ammunition is listed last as I am unsure of the exact number of rounds.

Next Kappler turns to the tools I packed into my toolboxes. I list following:

1 set plane;
2 pliers;
1 wood rasp;
1 angle tool;
1 fish hoop;
various wood drills from 3-18 mm;
1 tube winch;
1-2 chisel;
3 hammers;
2 biters;
various files;
2 angles;
1 marking pen;
1 skew view;
various iron drill bits 2-8 mm;
1 foxtail.

The list is by no means complete, but how would Kappler know? Besides he is smart enough to move forward to the more critical question of how, when and where I managed to find affordable accommodation in Munich.

My stays with the Baumanns and the Lehmanns are given a healthy airing, with some comparisons made of cost, amenity and catering. I avoid saying too much regarding my host's idiosyncratic behaviour though I divulge how I explained my nocturnal lifestyle. When Kappler drops that Herr Baumann is a public servant, this comes as no great surprise.

After a short break Kappler returns to my friends and acquaintances, quizzing me on whether I have been in contact with Eugen Rau, the houseboys, or the waitresses at the Bürgerbräukeller. I admit I met Rau and his wife Emma in the street in Königsbronn this year, but have not encountered the houseboy I promised to pay 50 marks. I also admit to sending a letter, enclosing the group photograph I took of the three waitresses, to one of the waitresses, though I have not received a reply from her as yet.

Kappler seems satisfied with my answers and jumps ahead to ask what I intended to do in Switzerland.

"Once I had crossed the border I intended to write from Switzerland to the German police to explain I was the sole culprit and I had no accomplices. Also I would send an accurate drawing of my apparatus, and a description of the execution of the deed so my claim could be verified. I wanted to ensure innocent people would not be arrested."

"Are we meant to believe this?" asks Seibold.

"This is the truth," I reply, as Seibold laughs into the air like a clown at Kircus Krone.

To end the day on a cheerless note, Kappler asks what I hoped to gain by going over the border to Switzerland. I tell him I just wanted steady work and a resident's permit. He concludes by saying had I succeeded in going to Switzerland I would have been deported to France where German refugees are automatically sent to concentration camps.

The fifth day of this circus has arrived. After four days of going around in circles, Kappler at last comes to the crux of my regime changing activity — the thirty, perhaps thirty-five nights I worked alone in the Bürgerbräukeller. The session begins at 9 am. Who knows what time it will end?

I must relive every second, minute and hour, telling how I took my meals in the Bürgerbräukeller restaurant, drank only one glass of beer, waited in my hiding place, dimmed my flashlight, installed my secret door, hollowed out the pillar brick by brick, disposed of the debris by the river, cleaned up at the end of each night's work, culminating in the installation of my deadly apparatus. I make mention of the man who came early one morning for a cardboard box and the black dog incident. To my amazement I have no interruption from Seibold, though when I think I have covered every minute detail Schmidt wants to know the colour and style of the clothes I wore. Some people are never satisfied!

Kappler returns from lunch looking more motivated than ever. Perhaps he has caught a sniff of the end. Though before then he wants to get down to the nuts and bolts. He wants a full technical description of my apparatus, as if he wants to build an infernal machine for himself. He tosses me a roll of butcher's paper and I spend two to three hours preparing large-scale diagrams, labelling everything from A to Z. Once I have taken the time to explain everything to him thrice he appears to have a basic understanding of my apparatus, at least adequate for him to use the technical terms and dictate several typed pages to the frazzled typist.

I think the exercise is over but Kappler wants the price I paid and the names of the suppliers of all the components, whether off-the-shelf or an item I had specially made or modified.

"Did you have anyone assist you in this undertaking?" Kappler asks as an afterthought.

In four days I have not mentioned the master carpenter, and was hoping not to, but before I know what I am saying I am blurting out his name.

"Err — I did happen to meet a master carpenter named Jörg Brög. He is a good man and he allowed me use of his workshop without any charge."

"Without charge!" shrieks Schmidt.

"Did this man Brög know what evil you were planning?" Kappler asks coldly.

"Nay! I only told him I was working on an invention."

"A likely story," scoffs Seibold.

As the three wise monkeys mutter amongst themselves I hope I have not put the master carpenter in the ochsenschwanzsuppe.

As Kappler folds my diagrams he intends to append to the final report of the Commission, I mention the errors that crept into my work due to the interruption of the weekend dance nights and my shameful mismeasurement. But Kappler is not interested my personal problems. He is more interested in my private correspondence. At the rate he asks questions I suspect those in high places have given him a deadline to end tonight.

Once he is satisfied with my explanation of my use of a private postal box in Heidenheim for billings, lottery winnings and love letters from Elsa Härlen, Kappler is primed to return to the last forty-eight hours of my freedom. I must recount my overnight stay in Stuttgart with my sister, my compulsion to return to the Bürgerbräukeller, my desire to thank the master carpenter, my need to call on Frau Lehmann to ask about my mail, my journey by train to Friedrichshafen, my visit to the barber, my crossing of the Bodensee to Konstanz, and my fatal walk to the Swiss border.

When I think I have told all that can ever be told Kappler wants to torment me further. He wants to know the exact route I took to reach the border fence. I have total loss of memory. But Kappler has a town map in his attaché case. Between us we determine the route I took was via: Marktstatte, Rosgartenstrasse, Hüetlingstrasse, Kreuzlingerstrasse, and Schwedenschanze. At the Wessenberg Gardens I went like a lamb to the slaughter.

But Kappler is not done yet. This commission of inquiry could last forever.

"What was your first thought when you were caught," he asks as if he wants to psychoanalyse my stupidity.

"I was annoyed by my carelessness," I confess.

"Do you think of escape?"

"I have not thought of escape."

"Suicide?"

"I have no suicidal thoughts."

Why does he ask about suicide? Can't he see I am dead on my feet?

With the time now at some unearthly hour I imagine Kappler will have the decency to let everyone go to bed. Instead he announces the sleazy Seibold will ask me a specially prepared list of questions to bring the proceedings to an end. Displaying unnatural energy, Seibold springs up like a Jack in the box. He must be on a double dose of Pervitin, I think as he reads from his page.

"What were you thinking when on the night of November 7-8 you looked at your work for the last time and locked the doors?"

"I can no longer remember."

"Did you consider the consequences of your attack?"

"I did wonder about this several times."

"Did you consider a number of people could be killed?"

"I did."

"Did you want this? And who was it you wanted to kill?"

"I wanted to kill the political leaders."

"Did you have this desire during the entire task, or did you at any time have doubts about your actions?"

"I do not remember any longer if I ever began to have doubts, but I think I had no doubts."

"How do you feel now about what you have done? You killed eight people and your plan failed."

"I would never do it again."

"That is no answer to my question."

"Then the aim has not been achieved."

"Is it of no consequence to you that you have taken the lives of eight people?"

"Nay, for me this is not a matter of indifference."

"What would you do if for some reason you were released?"

"I would try to make amends for the bad things I've done."

"How and by what means?"

"I would do my best to cooperate and to become part of the people's community."

"Could you do that?"

"I have changed my intentions."

"Is this only because you were arrested?"

"Nay, I believe that my plan would have succeeded if my plan had been right. I am convinced that as my plan did not succeed it should not have succeeded and my intentions were wrong."

My answers are as tortured as the way I feel.

ACT 3

32

November 25, 1939

Berlin

I WAKE with Fritz prodding my ribs. My execution must be at hand! Nay. Kappler and the high ranked officer with the bad haircut look hell bent on performing some grotesque Gestapo torture on me first. But when Kappler hands me his Artus fountain pen and takes a big bundle of typed paper from his black hide attaché case I realise the pair have only come to extract my signature. With Kappler's attaché case resting on my tell-tale knees I sign above where Schmidt, Seibold and Kappler have already signed.

Once the two have left to hand in their homework I turn to one of my two guards.

"Who was the high-ranked officer with the bad haircut?" I inquire.

"Err—him Müller," Fritz mumbles.

I must have spoken out of turn as less than an hour later a barber comes into my room. Fritz thinks it a great joke as he sits me on a chair to watch my locks fall to the floor and my ugly skull appear.

After this atrocity I am taken up to the attic for more mug shots. When my meal of boiled tinned turnips comes at midday, I wonder how many more meals I will eat. There must be more worthy mouths to feed than the mouth of a failed assassin. With the interrogation over there seems no reason for my continued existence. Waiting to die is killing me. Like the Swiss guy caught with his gun in his pocket, I'll probably just disappear.

The tinned turnips are still talking inside my tummy as I curl up on the folding bed. I face the wall to whimper over the loss of my wavy hair that has served me well as a pillow.

"Get up!"

"Heh?" I turn to see Müller has come to visit.

"Shut Up!"

This must be the END.

Fritz rucks me off the bed with the heel of his boot. Once upright I am handcuffed and pushed into the passage. I am dead certain we will take the lift to the basement prison where unspeakable things are said to happen. But we pass without my escorts pressing the down button to arrive at the same room where I entertained the three monkeys for five long, tedious days.

The tables have been reorganized to form a neat rectangle. At the head table sits a fair-headed fellow with a nose as long as Nebe's but tapered to a fine point. Müller takes a seat beside him. At the adjacent table Kappler, Schmidt, Seibold and Nebe sit like four chimps. With this line-up I realize the purpose of this gathering is my sentencing. The means of execution is probably the only item on the agenda. Whether they hang me, behead me, poison me, gas me or shoot me in the neck makes no difference. I'm happy to go. Hell would be better than hanging about here.

Though as I wait with the shame of my freshly shaved head, I start to wonder who will be sitting at the remaining table in the rectangle. This question is answered when two guards escort a woman into the room. Her matted grey hair is parted with severe precision in the centre of her head and pulled back into a tight bun. Her wrinkled weathered skin is testament to her many years of toiling in the potato plots. This will be a tough day for her, like no other — though this woman has had many years to practise endurance through the punishment meted out by her husband — my drunkard father.

"Frau Elser, do you know the confessed assassin sitting to your left?" asks Müller.

"Yes."

"Who is he?"

"Georg—my eldest son."

My mother has not yet looked anywhere near me. She seems more intent on wringing her hands.

"Did your son tell you he intended to commit his heinous crime?"

"Nay."

"Do you know who conspired with your son to plant the bomb in the Bürgerbräukeller?"

"Nay. I do not know that person. I only know my son could never have done such a terrible thing unless he was influenced by some other person."

Hearing this from my mother's lips causes my heart to ache. My stoic suffering ends. I start to sob. This is the last thing I wanted to happen in front of Nebe and the others. I should be feeling anger towards my mother for not believing in me—for not believing I acted alone. But I feel only sadness.

Only as she is lead out of the room does she glance in my direction. Though her deep brown eyes do not offer a smile there is still a bond between us. As Kappler emphasised five days ago—I will forever be my mother's illegitimate son.

While my sister and my brother-in-law are being brought into the room I remain consumed by my mother. When she wrote pleading I come home from Meersburg to help her manage my father, I stopped my life and came. But there was no fattened calf killed for the return of the prodigal son. The only reward I received was to be cheated out of my rightful inheritance by my little brother Leonhard and his bolshy wife, in collusion with my mother. As I chew over this I begin to wonder if my vendetta against Adolf Hitler was my unique way of proving my worth to my mother. Or was my obsession to kill simply a way to punish my mother? I am released from these shocking thoughts when I tune into Kappler.

"The confessed assassin has testified that he slept the night in your apartment on November 7. Is this correct?"

Maria looks terrified. Her swollen red eyes suggest she has been in tears ever since she heard of my arrest, though she is still able to answer.

"That is correct. My brother had come unexpectedly to Stuttgart from Munich that day."

"What did you talk to your brother about that night?"

"Only family matters. Georg said he wanted to go to see his sick father before going to Switzerland."

"And did he go?" continues Kappler.

"I don't think he did."

"Did he say why he intended to go to Switzerland?"

"He just said, 'he must'."

"He must! Nothing else?" interjects Müller.

"No, nothing else."

Kappler then looks towards Müller to check whether he is allowed to continue.

"Did your brother tell you he was meeting someone across the border in Switzerland?"

"No, he said nothing of the sort," replies Maria, wiping away her tears.

"Did he tell your husband anything of that nature when you were not all together?"

"Karl must answer for himself," replies Maria.

"My brother-in-law said nothing to me about going to Switzerland or who he might be meeting there."

"If your testimony is proven to be false and has misled this special council in any way whatsoever both of you will be dealt with severely. Do you understand?" threatens Müller.

"Yes—we do," Maria says, breaking down completely.

"Take the woman and her husband away and bring in the last witness—Frau Härlen," orders Müller.

Frau Härlen! I shudder at the thought of Elsa seeing me with watery eyes and my ugly head shaven like a common criminal. But there is a delay. Elsa does not enter. Instead a sabre-scarred officer comes through the door to whisper a word in the ear of the man with the long pointed nose. He in turn whispers into Müller's ear. Müller then announces to the gathering the special council is ended for today.

It appears the non-appearance of Elsa Härlen has given me a stay of execution.

33

December 1–6, 1939
Berlin

MY brain has for a long time been monopolized with working through technical details to construct an apparatus to detonate at an exact moment in time. Now my brain is working overtime on matters that have never entered my head until now. I am thinking of the grief I have brought my dear sister Maria, and her husband Karl, as well as the look of horror in the brown eyes of my dear mother.

But what is going on with Elsa Härlen? Why did she not appear before the so-called 'special council'? Did she have stage fright or is she sick?

I am still thinking upon Elsa's nonappearance when the door is flung open.

Müller's eyes are phosphorus.

"You were the one who fucked UP! So why should I suffer for a gutless wonder like YOU!" he screams.

Müller hands his wad of papers to Fritz so he can strangle me with his bare hands.

"Uurrggh!"

He has almost choked the life out of me when the officer with the facial scars rushes in.

"Hey! Cool down. Come and talk things over with Heydrich," the young officer urges, arriving not a moment too soon.

Müller relaxes his grip after thumping my head into the floor like he is cracking a nut. He then takes back the bound papers from Fritz and vanishes with scar face.

Once the airway reopens in my throat I have a question for Fritz.

"What was that all about?"

"Beats me, unless the green scrawl over the cover of them papers upset Müller."

"Did you see what the scrawl said?"

"Something like, 'what idiot wrote this', followed by three question marks."

This is worrying. If someone in high places has rejected Kappler's report I could be condemned to another five days of interrogation by another Special Commission. Now that would be Hell.

Two hours later a different Hell begins.

"Get up!" yells Fritz.

I do as I am told and get off the folding bed. But once I am on my feet I am slammed to the floor by Fritz's energetic mate Enno.

"EAT!"

A dish of herrings is placed before my face. Again I do as told and eat like a dog. My bed is wheeled out of the room and the heat is turned up. Once I have licked the plate clean I need water—buckets of water! The herring was loaded with a sack of salt. But drinking is strictly forbidden. Fritz and Enno stand laughing as they watch me choking. My tongue soon clogs my mouth like a rasp as I melt beneath the burning globe in the flaming heat.

After an indeterminate period of time the door is opened—I hope for water. Instead of water my face is pushed into another dish of salted herrings.

"EAT!"

My stomach heaves. I can eat no more and vomit onto Fritz's boot. When his boot retaliates I pass out—to dream of drowning in a cool mountain pool.

I open an eye. The dull light of a winter morning is coming between the vertical bars to the window. My throat is set like cement. My head is thick.

"Get up!" yells Müller, kicking me in the side of the head.

"Water!" I plead.

"Get up you arsehole!" he yells again.

Fritz hauls me onto the chair. Müller grips my raw scalp and slams my head from side to side.

"You can have water when you tell me the NAMES!" he yells after he stops unscrewing my head.

"Names?"

"The names of those who told you to plant the bomb, you little runt."

"I was the sole instigator," I croak.

"Fucking LIAR!" he shrieks, butting his elbow into my temple to send me flying.

"Ask Nebe and Kappler. They believed me," I plead from the floor.

"Shut up you deadshit! I give you one last chance! Tell me the names of your accomplices and you can have a bucket of WATER!" shrieks Müller.

After a moment of contemplation I murmur, "Did Himmler make that cheeky remark on Kappler's report?"

Müller looks livid.

With his eyes sparking like welding electrodes he flies out the door, as Enno lands his boot in my ribs for good measure.

Another day passes without water. I am saying the Lord's Prayer over and over hoping I will be taken to Heaven before my brain fries, when Fritz and Enno pull me from the floor. They drag me along the passage to a small windowless room and sit me down on a chair.

A man with the look of a loony professor is sitting on the other side of the desk.

"I can handle the prisoner by myself so please get out," he snaps at my guards.

"Dr. Schäfer is my name. I want you to look on me as your friend."

I nod.

"I am told you have not drunk water for some time. That is not wise. Water is important if you want to survive. Do you want to survive?"

I shake my head.

"This is not good at all. And how did you get those bruises on your head?" he asks.

"A boot," is all I can muster as my lips are blistered and glued together.

"Is there something I can do for you?"

"A glass of — water?"

"Wait here."

In less than ten seconds Dr. Schäfer returns with a glass of water for me to drink.

"Don't mention to anyone I did this for you," he requests.

I shake my head.

"Drink slowly, take your time. No need to rush, feeling any better?"

"A little," I whisper.

"Good. Now you can do something for me — something very easy. Look into my eyes — look deep. Do you see in my eyes deep pools of water?"

I nod, as I have nothing to lose.

"Now close your eyes and think of Switzerland. Think of pure white glistening peaks — think of snow melting, think of water dripping — think of streams flowing — think of torrents tumbling into rocky ravines — think of rivers running in valleys to the Bodensee. Are you thinking of these things?"

I nod again.

"Good. Now I want you to concentrate and think back to the night you were about to cross the border into Switzerland. The same night you planned to meet someone on the other side of the wire fence. Think very carefully, and tell me the name of the person who was waiting for you there."

"There was no one waiting for me," I manage to say with a good deal of pain.

"Are you certain as this is very important?"

"I am."

"Maybe there was no need to meet that person on the other side of the border fence as that person had already made a payment into your secret Swiss bank account. Was this the way things were arranged?"

"Nay. I was totally self-funded."

"Are you certain?"

"I am."

"Then I believe you."
When I hear Dr. Schäfer click his fingers I open my eyes.
"How do you feel?"
"Thirsty. Can I have another glass of water?"
"No way! Do you want to have me shot?"

34

December 7-10, 1939
Berlin

DURING the next twenty-four hours a strange wave of kindness sees a return to normal rations, though diarrhoea from the salty herring restricts my intake to bread and water. In spite of my free flowing ailment I have appointments with no less than five more shrinks, all on the same day. Those in high places will not be amused by their negative reports. But is that my fault?

Next day I get more time to myself, though Fritz or Enno or some other goon is always around to send me up the wall — or to answer a question.

"Who was that high ranking officer sitting beside Müller the other day?"

"Heh? You mean the blond, long nosed one?" asks Fritz.

"I do."

"Him Heydrich, but we call him the 'blond beast'," giggles Fritz, like a naughty schoolboy.

With this information tucked into my brain, I roll over and face the wall. I hope to get a measure of undisturbed sleep after the trauma of the last few days. But a few minutes later I hear a knock on the door. Fritz farts as he gets off his arse to attend to the caller. A little man with the tragic look of Max Ehrlich is ushered in, followed by three chairs, a table, and a typist.

"Do you know who I am?" the sad little man asks me with great expectations.

"Count Dracula?" I joke, expecting him to blow his stack.

"You are close. I am Dr. Max. I have come to learn everything there is to know about you."

"Everything to know about me is already in Herr Kappler's lengthy report," I insist.

"That report is useless. There is no mention of your co-conspirators."

"Do you want me to say things that are not true?"

"If you could that would be most helpful. Let me explain. When you are in the witness box at the big trial you will want to say only things that are helpful to the Führer and the Fatherland and not say negative things that will only play into the hands of our enemies."

"What if I refuse?"

"I will ask Frau Roland to leave the room while Fritz freshens up your bruises."

"Then I refuse."

"Frau Roland, please leave the room."

Even before the well-rounded typist is out the door Fritz swings into me.

KrrrACK!

The butt of his pistol leaves me sprawled on the floor, until Fritz helps me back to the chair.

"Here—use my handkerchief to wipe the blood off your face," says the good doctor.

I do as I am told.

"Are you ready to proceed?"

"You win," I say, sick to death of being on the losing end. I might as well play their game. Besides, this 'big trial' may never see the light of day.

"Shall I begin my life story now?" I inquire.

"Wait till Frau Roland has returned. Would you like Fritz to give you a cigarette?"

"I would. Smoking never hurt anyone."

With a cigarette burning between my zither playing fingers and once Frau Roland has taken up her shorthand pad and licked her pencil, I commence.

"I was born in Munich and when I was quite small my mother died while giving birth to my dead sister. In the same week my father was killed in action. An uncle, my only relative who was a childless railway guard, took charge of me and raised me in a rough and ready fashion. I ran wild in my youth and had two clashes with the police. As a result I was sent to a reformatory for a year. At school I was exceptionally bright, though it was only my teacher in handicrafts who recognised my potential. When I was fifteen or sixteen, I cannot remember which, my uncle died leaving me only a small sum. This was quite insufficient to further my schooling and I was placed under the charge of the Munich municipal children's officer. I was soon apprenticed to a joiner who acted as my guardian. Despite my insubordination, and being a frequent cause of trouble, my intelligence and aptitude to my work made me a valuable assistant and my master tried to retain me in his service at the end of my apprenticeship. But once I was free of him nothing could hold me down. I packed my tools and other possessions into a shoulder bag and set off like the traditional German wanderer.

"My travels took me through most of southern Germany, even into Switzerland and for the first time I had little trouble in finding work. I had a responsible job as a model maker at one of the biggest Bavarian engineering firms—BMW cars. But unfortunately my employment was terminated after I started a row with an immediate supervisor. This was not the first or last time this happened. In 1937 I found myself back in Munich without a mark to my name, and with my tools sold or pawned, I had little hope of getting a job. And with the Nazis having a firm grip on labour organizations it was virtually impossible for someone who hated the Nazis to find employment. It was only natural I got mixed up with a band of Communists. Though I never joined the party, I helped in the printing and distribution of leaflets. I was accepted as one of the group and I enjoyed the element of danger being actively engaged in a fight against authority. All went well until one evening the café where we met was surrounded by the police. We were all taken to the police station where no definite evidence was found against us, but being out of work we were labelled 'anti-social' and 'work-shy' and sent direct to Dachau concentration camp for re-education. For the very first time in my life I felt the full force of irresponsible authority crushing every trace of individuality in me. Like other newcomers, I worked with pick and shovel, until my talent as a cabinetmaker was discovered and I was put to work in the camp furniture workshop. Before long I was making fine furniture for the camp commandant and all his friends. Though I gained many privileges I longed for my freedom. One day in early October 1939 I was called to the office of the commandant, where I was interviewed by two men who asked me questions about my antecedents and my friends. As for the former I said I had none and I knew only the first names of my Communist friends. A week later I was met again by the same two men. On the first occasion I was questioned while standing to attention, but this time I was taken to an office, told to sit down, and given a cigarette to smoke. The men were extremely friendly. The commandant had shown them my fine work and they said it was a shame such a good tradesman was wasting his life in a concentration camp. 'Would you like to regain your freedom' they asked me. I said I would. They replied this would be possible if I did a small job for them and once the job was done I would be financially rewarded and sent to Switzerland. There I could live as I liked and hold whatever opinions I pleased. What else could I do but say, 'yes'. If I had refused the job I would have gone up the chimney that evening. In the first week of November 1939 I was twice fetched at nightfall by the same two men and taken by car to the Bürgerbräukeller. I was shown a pillar into which a bomb was to be built. This pillar was covered with wood panelling, so all I needed to do was remove some panels and extract a couple of bricks, insert the explosive, an alarm clock and a fuse. The whole thing was child's play.

"The two men took me back to Dachau to wait for my reward. On November 9 the same two men called and drove me to the Swiss border near Bergenz at the eastern end of the Bodensee. When the car stopped short of the customs post I was handed an envelope with a large sum in German and Swiss notes, and given a postcard of the Bürgerbräukeller on which the pillar where I had inserted the bomb was shown with a cross. The two men assured me that if I showed the postcard to the frontier guards they would let me through without asking for my papers. I did as I was told but the frontier guard knew nothing about me, nor the meaning of the postcard. When the large sum of money was found I was charged with currency smuggling. But someone must have connected the postcard with the bombing in Munich. I was promptly handcuffed, taken to the nearest airfield and flown to Berlin. The next morning I was taken by lift to the top floor of Gestapo Headquarters where I spoke with the same two men. They were most sympathetic and told me my arrest was due to the unfortunate fact the guard who had instructions to let me through had been taken ill and was not on duty. After this I was taken to an office where there was a high-ranking officer of the SS___."

"Shut Up!! I think you are making all this UP!" explodes Dr. Max.

"Nay, this is the truth!"

But the good doctor is not able to handle the truth and bolts out the door.

"Do you want to finish your last sentence, Herr Elser?" inquires Frau Roland.

"Why not? After this I was taken to an office where there was a high-ranking officer of the SS and another man with duelling scars. He asked me whether I understood that my life was forfeit, and that I was nothing more than a candidate for death—however I had no need to worry as everything will come right in the end as the Gestapo always keeps its word."

"Is that all?"

"Yes, Frau Roland. That should speed my execution."

Nursing my damaged face I manage to get a few hours sleep overnight. Next morning, low and behold, Dr. Max is back. He has been working through the night and has come up with his own version of my life, condensed to two typed pages. He leaves me with the strict instruction to learn this version by rote by tomorrow morning—or else. If I fail Fritz will come to my assistance.

The boots and elbows in the face I have copped from Müller, plus Fritz's contribution have left me black and blue in the region of the cranium. So when four visitors come to visit next day I am in my best anti-social mood. Seeing Müller and Dr. Max at my door is no surprise. But the sight of the blond beast escorting my greatest love turns me into a quivering mess. Four thugs from Heydrich's personal bodyguard have also been invited to stand in each corner of the room like wax figures in a museum with their Lugers drawn. Heydrich must think he is next on my hit list. Other goons carry in five chairs so my guests can rest their arses. I perch on the central chair like a prized parrot. Once everyone is comfortably seated Müller is given the nod by Heydrich to get on with the show.

"Frau Härlen, is this the man you had in your bed as a married woman?"

"Yes, this is Georg, though I am now divorced from my husband Hermann."

"When did you first meet Elser?" Heydrich asks coldly.

"In 1933. I was twenty two."

"So you were only a new bride when Elser came between you and your husband," comments Müller.

"You could say that."

"Is it true you have remarriage plans?" asks Heydrich.

"Yes, to a good man, Karl Votteler."

"Did Elser ever ask you to marry him?"

"We talked about getting married, but as time passed by I realized Georg was far from thinking of marriage. He was very stubborn. If he did not want to talk about something he could not be moved. I told him I could not live with uncertainty and that I would find an honest man instead."

"Did he tell you of his assassination plans at the Bürgerbräukeller?" asks Heydrich.

"No never! I am convinced he could never have thought of doing such a thing by himself."

"Why is that?" asks Heydrich.

"Georg is harmless. He could not hurt anyone."

"See—even your ex-lover knows you did not commit your barbarous act without the help of others. Will you now confess?" insists Müller.

Dr. Max makes gestures in my direction, which I take to mean I should now commence my recently learnt recitation.

"Err—for a long time I have had a relationship with Otto Strasser. Going to Switzerland in 1938 I called on him at Hotel Bauer au Lac in Zurich where he introduced me to the Englishman, Best. I was told to take orders from this Captain Best, who was a spy in the employment of the British Government. I made contact with Captain Best in September 1939, meeting him in Venlo in The Netherlands. He gave me instructions for planting a bomb in the Bürgerbräukeller, promising me 40,000 Swiss francs. I refused at first but Best put the screws on, leaving me with no choice but to do as I was told. I___"

My mind goes blank. I cannot remember what comes next. Dr. Max jumps to his feet and comes up behind me.

"I___I___" I repeat, trying to remember the next line without success.

K-Thump!

My ugly shaved head rocks forward.

"Leave him! He has said enough!" Heydrich orders Dr. Max.

I look up to see tears flowing down Elsa's chubby cheeks. The only other time I have seen Elsa cry was the day she told me she could not live with me.

"Frau Härlen, do you have any questions for the fornicator?" asks Heydrich.

After more tears Elsa asks me, "Did you really do what you said you did, Georg?"

Our eyes meet. The day we first met Elsa had a spirited shine in her eyes. Now her eyes have dulled. What we had once has been lost. Had I not been so obsessed with planting my bomb we might now be husband and wife.

"Elsa___" I start to say, not really knowing what I want to say.

In the corner of my eye I see Dr. Max sneaking up behind me once more.

"Leave him be," orders Heydrich.

"He is an IMBECILE!" declares Dr. Max.

Too true, I think.

Without another word being uttered the blond beast leads the funeral procession from my room.

35

December 9-10, 1939
Sachsenhausen

WITH handcuffs clasped to his wrists and a hood pulled over his head Best is taken down to the courtyard of the Reich Security Main Office to the waiting car. Grothe and Dr. Schäfer sit each side of the prisoner in the back seat. From Prinz-Albrecht-Strasse the black sedan turns left into Friedrichstrasse and heads north through the city, crossing the river Spree. A Horch is ahead leading the way on the twenty-kilometre drive to Oranienburg. From Schlossplatz, in the heart of the ancient city, the two cars continue for another three kilometres passing large villas and fine gardens before turning up a drive to a pristine white double storey building with central gateway. After passing through the main gate and an inner gate both cars draw up at the door of a long low single storey building.

"Heil Hitler!" bark the guards, raising their arms, as Heinrich Müller and Walter Schellenberg step from the Horch. Best is led inside where the nauseous smell and shrill sounds are unmistakably those of a prison. He must stand with his face to the wall as if sent to stand outside the headmaster's office awaiting his sentence before the two men walk him to his cell. Perhaps to make his new home more palatable his bed has been made up with a blue and white checked cover. Müller tells Best to sit on the stool beneath the high window as a crowd of warders gathers to see their first English prisoner. Like a rare animal in a zoo he is a curious creature.

When the camp commandant arrives he moves a small table in front of Best.

"That is your place. You are to stay there," commands Hans Loritz.

When someone suggests he take off his coat a warder is sent for a coat hook to fix to the wall.

Once Müller is satisfied with the provisions made for his prisoner he takes the opportunity to warn Best to behave or regret the day he was born. After Müller has said his piece, Schellenberg steps up to speak, telling Best to be less cheeky in this place than he has been with him in the past.

After the two men depart and the prisoner is left to consider their wise advice Best stays motionless on the stool—unable to move. To be imprisoned in this place even for one day is something he cannot yet contemplate.

The torment of a burning light globe and the stench of his live-in guard chain-smoking ends when Drexl, a warder, swings open his door at 5 am next morning. With towel and soap in hand he is escorted to the latrine in the slippery wake of seventy other prisoners carrying their night buckets.

Though he is being held in isolation Best is not forgotten. Later in the day the camp commandant calls in to assure him he can ask for anything he wants. Whether he gets it or not is another matter. In the afternoon Grothe brings his personal belongings, spare clothes, soap, comb, hair lotion and other items seized in Düsseldorf. Though his razor must be held by a warder and dispensed only when needed in order to safeguard his life.

When asked to sign for his possessions Best is told his name is now 'Wolf'.

"Wolf! Be damned! I have never gone by a false name," Best declares, but signs nevertheless.

As his first full day at Sachsenhausen drifts towards the darkness of a long winter's evening, Drexl tells Best he needs to get some exercise outside. Given two ill-fitting boots to save the wear and tear on his spats, he is escorted to a yard of dirt criss-crossed by narrow concrete paths. An enclosing wall of concrete blocks topped with two electrified wires separate the yard from the main camp. Obvious to the 12,000 or more terrorised prisoners on the other side of the wall, Best makes a number of circuits. Realizing he might be living in this facility for some time — at least until his life is terminated or the war is decided — he has a vision of a flower garden. But his vision is premature. The parched yard will remain a venue of state-sanctioned torture of political prisoners for some time yet.

36

Late December, 1939
Berlin

NEBE came to see me yesterday. Seeing him once again brought tears of joy to my eyes. To be visited by him and to know there is at least one good man left in the world is truly something to weep over. As usual he promised he is doing the best he can for me, but not to set my hopes too high.

Nevertheless he also came with startling news. Müller has agreed I reconstruct my apparatus. This is something I could not have imagined with Müller being so pig-headed normally. Obviously Nebe wants to vindicate his findings in Munich and Kappler's findings in Berlin that I was the sole perpetrator of the crime and I received no help from anyone in my attempt to wipe the slate clean in Germany—politically speaking. I suspect the madman in the highest place is the only fool left standing, believing the two British spies and, or Otto Strasser had a hand in the bombing.

Today I have been making an exhaustive list of everything I need for the reconstruction, including materials, hand tools and basic workshop equipment. I presume everything will need to be purchased in secret and smuggled into the building. Should word get out the Gestapo is procuring angle grinders and electric drills, the man in the street could jump to the conclusion instruments of torture have entered a new era of terror.

After weeks of intense work, yet before my reconstruction is completed, I have visitors. I do not know exactly the day or the month, as I have lost track of time when the smooth faced blond beast, Reinhard Heydrich, arrives with his scar-faced soul mate, Walter Schellenberg. They have not travelled far as my workshop is on the top floor of the Reich Security Main Office.

Heydrich, wearing skinny-legged cord struck trousers with a bulky black leather flight jacket, looks a rare bird ready to peck out my heart, while Schellenberg has come looking cool in corduroy. As they circle my reconstruction examining at close quarters the smallest intricate details, I stand like a shag biting my fingernails, dreading the thought of negative reactions.

"This is amazing. I had no idea how much machinery is inside one time bomb," drools Schellenberg.

"The workmanship is excellent, almost as good as the airframe for the Messerschmitt Bf 109," remarks Heydrich.

"Have you made this to full size?" enquires Schellenberg.

"To the last 0.5 of a millimeter," I mumble.

"I see you've also built a replica of the pillar in the Bürgerbräukeller," Schellenberg observes.

"Apart from there being no brickwork my replica is exactly the same as the pillar I hollowed out in order to place the explosives inside," I explain.

"But are these *real* explosives?" queries Heydrich.

I delay my answer as I notice a drip of sweat about to drop from the tip of his long beak.

"It would have been nice to blowup the Reich Security Main Office and everybody inside. But Herr Nebe suggested I use plasticine."

"Nebe is wise," hisses Heydrich, wiping perspiration from his high brow.

"Seen enough?" asks Schellenberg.

"I have. Will you report back to Himmler?"

"No sweat."

"I need a drink," squeaks Heydrich.

Once the two Nazi playboys have disappeared to crash the nearest Berlin wine bar, I sit for hours — listless. Now I have passed my practical exam and proved myself I have no incentive or any desire to finish my reconstruction.

For the next few days I am overtaken by a bout of the black dog until Fritz brings an envelope stamped with the seal of the Reich Security Head Office. When I open the envelope I find inside a 12.5 cm x 7.5 cm photograph of my greatest love, Elsa Härlen. I recall the photo was taken on a hike in the Swabian hills, possibly in 1937 when our love was at a high point. On the back Elsa has penned a message in her neat hand.

Dear Georg,

Since we last meet under testing circumstances I have married Karl Votteller. He has now joined the battle to save Germany from her enemies. On the same day your family appeared before the Special Committee I had a friendly talk with Herr Himmler instead. He was most generous in arranging for all your family members and myself to come to Berlin in the comfort of a special train carriage and to stay in the luxury of the Kaiserhof Hotel a short prison van ride from Reich Security Main Office.

While I was in Berlin I had the wonderful honour of an audience with our Führer. He went out of his way to show me over the New Reich Chancellery. He told me the architect, Herr Speer, is a genius who interprets wisely the ideas of his client. Did you know the Chancellery lobby is double the length of the Hall of Mirrors at Versailles? Furthermore our Führer's private office is larger than any European ruler's in history including the Pope in Rome!

Relaxing with our Führer later in the evening he told me I was a brave woman to have suffered so terribly by having an affair with someone as evil as you. This will be the last time I ever write.

Heil Hitler
Elsa Härlen

These words bring no joy and I do not emerge from a long period of darkness until December 1940.

37
Sachsenhausen
1940

THE northern winter of 1939-40 is one of the coldest on record. With snow filling the exercise yard well into the new year, Best is confined indoors. The steam radiator beside his bed operates nonstop — while 100 metres away 140 prisoners die one day when paraded for hours in the icy weather.

By April Best is able to return to exercising outside in the yard. One day he is stopped in his tracks when he comes across words scratched in the dirt. A concise message from Stevens informs Best his colleague is alive and is being held in the same prison building — commonly called the Bunker.

Adapting to prison life would have been a little easier had someone in high places not given the order the two Englishmen are never to be locked in their cells — perhaps for some political reason. Loritz sees no sense in this order that only makes his life more difficult. He gets around the problem by using a leather strap to tie the prisoners' wrist to an eyebolt fixed to the wall by their bed to stop the pair wandering at night.

The monotony of daily life is eased when Loritz brings Best two books to read. One book is *Mein Kampf*. The other is a trashy novel, according to Best. A month later Loritz makes another concession. Best is permitted to smoke in his cell and given a daily ration of ten cigarettes. And when Grothe calls in from Berlin with a pack of cards Best can play the game that kept him sane while on the Western Front: Patience.

In June Best is taken from his cell to the interview room, not knowing what to expect. He finds Schellenberg with the camp commandant, Loritz. Both are in a jovial mood. After plying Best with a cigarette Schellenberg pushes a bundle of German newspapers across the table. Bold headlines tell of the bewildering success of the German invasion in the west, with France asking for an Armistice, the British Army defeated and evacuated from Dunkirk, and with 'millions' of Allied troops taken prisoner.

"Now you will see the war has been won! England will be totally destroyed," gloats Schellenberg.

"You should never underestimate the British. We're a dogged people and are at our formidable best in this sort of backs-to-the-wall situation," boasts Best.

Schellenberg draws deeply on his cigarette. Shifting uneasily on his chair he asks, "Do you think the British will refuse to surrender and will continue to fight the war from Canada?"

"You'll need to make up your own mind about that," Best responds.

"I will, Captain—I will."

"Is that the only reason you have come—just to ask me one stupid question?" asks Best.

"You're a wise and intelligent man, Captain. And I admire the British intelligence service having a tradition of three hundred years," returns Schellenberg.

"It would be equally wrong of you to think the British intelligence service is infallible. Like most organizations the top is marred by greedy men and sheer heavy-handedness."

"Do you only say this because of you were told to join hands with the Passport Control Office in The Hague against your better judgement?"

"Did Stevens tell you this?"

"Stevens has informed me of many things, though much of it we already knew—like the big house from where he operated in The Hague was so well known even local children would point it out as the British intelligence office."

"I hardly think this sort of intelligence will win you the war."

"You might be right. With Churchill now in the saddle anything is possible," concludes Schellenberg.

Best leans forward to ash his cigarette before he continues with the conversation.

"I presume you visited both Stevens and Lemmens while you are here today," probes Best.

"Stevens — yes. As for your Dutch driver I am doing my utmost to have him returned home. It may be possible to show some compassion in this matter."

"I hope so for the sake of his wife and children."

"Now Holland is occupied territory things are easier to arrange."

"And can you inform me on the health of Captain Coppens?" asks Best.

"Excuse me — but I must get back to the office. I have more pressing work to manage at the brickworks," announces Loritz, rising abruptly from his chair.

"Like another cigarette?" Schellenberg asks Best once they are alone in the room.

"I would, but I would also like you to answer my question."

"Unfortunately the man you refer to is dead."

"Poor Klop."

"But he did not die in vain as he made a full confession that he was in fact Lieutenant Dirk Klop assigned by Dutch Intelligence to collaborate with the British in encouraging a revolt by misguided military officers."

"So Klop regained consciousness in Düsseldorf just long enough to make a confession before he died?"

"Do you think we would forge his confession and falsify his death certificate?" asks Schellenberg.

"Anything is possible."

"I detect a degree of cynicism. I should mention that your colleague Major Stevens has already provided excellent information on the close cooperation between British and Dutch Intelligence. This material was appended to the Memoranda Foreign Minister Ribbentrop sent to the Dutch and Belgian governments a day before we invaded in the west.

Also appended to the Memoranda was the full confession made by the Dutchman, Klop."

"It is good to know all the paperwork is done before the dogs of war are let off the leash. But it sounds too good to be true. You ended up with the proof you wanted of a breach of Dutch neutrality while having both the body and the confession of poor Klop. Your masters must have been ecstatic."

"Hitler was," grins Schellenberg, fondling the Iron Cross around his neck.

"Did you receive that for kidnapping Stevens and me at Venlo?"

"I did. Alfred Naujock's and Helmut Knochen received the same decoration."

"I've had the pleasure of meeting Major Naujocks, but who the hell is Helmut Knochen?"

"Knochen had been receiving low grade intelligence reports from Dr. Fischer for some time — until he enticed you from your retirement."

"Fischer! I always had my doubts."

"Too bad you could not follow your instinct," replies Schellenberg, flicking ash from his cigarette. He might have gone on to tell how Fischer had rung Knochen in Berlin to report he had established contact with a Best and how Knochen had reported this to his boss, Reinhard Heydrich who thought this was a good opportunity for a young SS lawyer-officer to gain experience in a real life intelligence operation. Instead he says, "From an intelligence angle I thought it would have been better to continue the phoney negotiations with you and Stevens. But when Elser's bomb exploded in Munich any indecision Hitler had ended."

"Elser? Do you mean the home-grown assassin Stevens and I were falsely accused of backing?"

"I do. I was phoned by Himmler in the early hours of the morning with the order to bring you and Stevens to Berlin. I then told Naujocks to do the dirty work. Last September he'd done an excellent job faking the attack on the Gleiwitz radio station, leaving behind corpses disguised as Poles."

"So Major Naujocks is quite a high performer in SD ranks," remarks Best, not quite sure in which direction to lead Schellenberg next.

"Was Hitler kept fully informed of our covert meetings?" he asks at length.

"He was, even though all reports going to him have to be retyped on a special typewriter with a font three times the normal size due to his poor eyesight. Though this is nothing compared to his other debilitating health issues."

"Is that so?"

"My friend Professor Max de Crinis — who you met playing in the role of Colonel Martini — is a psychiatric consultant of some reputation and has expressed misgivings regarding Hitler's health coupled with his petit-bourgeois inhibitions — though I must say he was extremely nice to me when I dined with him."

"You dined with Hitler?"

"I did. Like another cigarette?" offers Schellenberg.

"Danke."

"Of course I was not the only one invited to the Führer's table. I accompanied Heydrich and Himmler to the new Reich Chancellery, the showpiece his architect Speer had designed down to the last stick of furniture and carpet. I was seated next to Himmler, with Heydrich on the other side. Across the table sat Field Marshall Keitel and Bormann. At the end of the table sat Hess, looking somewhat out of sorts. The meal was on the day after I had submitted my report on Venlo. Hitler opened the conversion by complementing me on my intelligence reports before he complained about the low atmospheric pressure as he had a heavy cold. I felt a tad sick myself as I watched him eat his specially prepared vegetarian food: a cob of corn drizzled with melted butter followed by an enormous plate of kaiserschmarren, a type of Viennese pancake with raisins, sugar and a sweet sauce. I hope I'm not boring you with too much detail on food?"

"No, not at all. This is all very interesting. Was any mention made of Stevens and myself?"

"I am not at liberty to say, though I can recall most of the discussion concentred on Elser."

"Elser!"

"Himmler said Elser admits he was connected with two unknown men. And closely following the conclusion I had reached in my report Himmler added there was only one other clue — being our technical men were certain the parts used in the time bomb were all manufactured abroad."

"And what did Hitler have to say about that?"

"He said he thought that all sounded quite possible, but he was more concerned to know what type of person Elser is, from the standpoint of criminal psychology. As he hoed into his pancake he sanctioned the use of every possible means to induce the criminal to talk, suggesting hypnosis and drugs and every other means that modern science has to offer — insisting he must know who the instigators are behind the plot to kill him."

"Did Elser implicate Stevens and myself after the implementation of Hitler's prescription to arrive at the truth?"

"I am not a liberty to disclose that information to you. All I can say is when Heydrich and I inspected Elser's reconstruction of his explosive apparatus we where highly impressed with his technical knowledge and workmanship."

"So the front page newspaper stories that connected Stevens and me with Elser were only to dupe the man in the street," Best surmises.

"What else are newspapers for? In war truth is the first casualty, Captain."

"So Aeschylus said."

"I'll take your word for it. But I fear I've already divulged too much to you."

"You can trust me not the rat on you. Locked up in here what chance do I have?" quips Best.

"You will be better off being here than cowering in a London subway once our bombardment begins. But for now I must be getting back to the witches cauldron," Schellenberg announces glancing down at his Phenix wristwatch.

"To Berlin?"

"Where else? Who knows what my next assignment will be?" muses Schellenberg as he stubs his cigarette in the ashtray and rises from his chair.

"Perhaps you will be sent to Spain and Portugal to abduct the Duke and Duchess of Windsor."

"Don't be so ridiculous, Captain!"

With Schellenberg's departure Best is returned to his cell to play Patience for the rest of the year.

Back in Berlin, and before going to Spain and Portugal, Schellenberg finds time to finalize his manual prepared for *Operation Sea Lion*: the invasion of Great Britain. Schellenberg and his staff have spent months on the manual that is to be used by the German administration after the occupation. Included in the document is information on: geography, the economy, political and legal system, military, education, museums, press, radio, religion, emigrants, Jews, Freemasons, police and a whole chapter devoted to the workings of the British secret service. In addition there is 'Special Search List, G.B.' containing the names of 2,300 prominent persons to be arrested and imprisoned, from political figures to intelligence personnel, plus writers, editors, journalists, publishers. Amongst the suspect writers designated to have their freedom fettered are: H. G. Wells, Virginia Woolf, E. M. Foster, Aldous Huxley, J. B. Priestly, C. P. Snow and Noel Coward. 20,000 copies of the manual are printed and stored in a room alongside Schellenberg's office awaiting the invasion.

During December 1940 the usual morbid noises give way to the sounds of tradesmen. At one end of the head passage in the 'T' shaped Bunker three cells are being combined into one. Best suspects a palatial suite is being prepared for him after his recent protests to Loritz over his living conditions. But Best is not going anywhere. Through his guards he learns the work is being done for a Todeskandidat—a man condemned to death.

Months pass before Best gets his first glimpse of the man who not only attempted to assassinate Hitler and other Nazi leaders but also caused the death of innocent bystanders and injured scores of others. One day while Best is taking a shower in the ablutions, Elser rushes in pursued by two agitated guards. Years later Best will describe him with these words:

He was a thin, pallid little fellow with very bright eyes and a stock of unbrushed dark hair; his clothes hung loosely upon him as though he had lost a lot of flesh.

38

June 30, 1942

Sachsenhausen

SINCE my expulsion from the top floors of Reich Security Main Office I have been whittling away my life in a space referred to as cell no.13. When the builders combined three cells into one they could have made this cell No.11 or No.12. Nay! They choose No.13—exactly the number of minutes Hitler and his rat pack escaped the wrath of my bomb. Fritz, my No.1 guard told me this. Fritz is a pig but I must trust him in something, even this.

But why would those in high places bother combining three cells into one for my sake-a failed assassin? Is the reason to make me feel better about myself? Is the reason to exploit my considerable woodworking skill? Or are they rewarding me for giving them more reason to 'hate', as Herr Hess so eloquently expressed the notion in his fine oration at the Feldherrnhalle?

But getting back to my present habitation, by combining three cells into one the space created has the internal dimensions of 7.9 m by 4.0 m. This may sound a heap of space, even generous for a confessed assassin, but with personal guards and my workshop to accommodate, it is like stuffing a hog into a handbag. Try squeezing a bed, dresser, closet for clean and soiled clothes, table, desk with swivel chair and guest chair, workbench, storage shelves for hand tools and materials, a bed and two chairs for two guards on duty, night buckets, a snooker table, a map of Europe and a Volksempfänger. I admit the last two items need no floor space but fitting all the other junk into a space this size is impossible. Nevertheless I have.

Though I am entitled to double rations and an unhealthy allowance of 120 cigarettes per week, being alive is not my preferred state of being. But I confess I still enjoy tinkering at my workbench and I do like being back on the tools — while doing my level best to torment my live-in guards by drilling, hammering and sawing at any infernal hour, day or night.

But I need to keep busy in my state of suspension between life and death — for my black thoughts when awake match my nightmares when I sleep. My darkest hour comes at 9.20 pm — inside the Bürgerbräukeller.

K-BOOOOOM!!

I see the blinding flash. I hear the roar. I feel the rush of burning air. Black acrid smoke peels skin from my throat. The dust cloud settles over a mass of masonry, twisted steel, splintered wood, pulverised plaster, shattered chandeliers, fragments of glass — a waitress with a missing face!

Nay!

I must hit my temples with my fists to knock this last image from my head!

When I am able to resume at my workbench my mind returns to my present state — living on a treadmill of self-recrimination. But while licking my wounds I am not exactly living in total isolation as amongst other things Fritz keeps me informed of the doings of the two Tommies. Stevens has long gone to Dachau, while Best is still here, forever making a nuisance of himself with the warders and the camp commandant. From what I hear Best is a regular pest.

I had a close shave with him in the latrine one day. I suspect he would like to make contact and pry into my private affairs, maybe to write a book one day. But I prefer to stay isolated, living in my own demented world, doing the things I do best rather than trawling over old ground, being repeatedly reminded of my past horrific mistakes. I can do all my own self-flagellation left to my own devices, either day or night without his help.

Axel, my No.2 guard is now asleep, snorting like a hog. He is meant to stay awake to watch I keep the sharp ends of chisels away from my throat—what a joke! I have been making fine furniture for the camp commandant and others since I arrived. There is a high demand for exquisite timber goods at rock bottom prizes. Though one day I will do something for myself. Making something I have only ever dreamt of making—zithers.

When Fritz returns from stinking out the latrine he wakes Axel and they vamoose like a pair of mutes. I wonder what is going on. But I have a rough idea when the short-arsed guy who did me over in Munich creeps into my quarters trailed by his bodyguards with their Lugers drawn. Herr Himmler moves about as if he is walking in a minefield. When his insipid eyes peer through his stupid pince-nez glasses, I peer straight back at him.

"You must know we are trying to do as much as we can for you. Have you any complaints? Do you lack anything?" he asks.

"Nay, Reichsführer."

"Good. I was told you had bronchitis and you were not eating your food. Naturally I was concerned you might die on us before we can prove to the world the pure motives of the Führer when the final victory is ours and the glorious one thousand years rule of the Third Reich will commence."

"I did have a deadly cough recently and was hoping to die to avoid being around for the one thousand years rule."

"You show no gratitude Elser! You do not appreciate what I am doing for you, and I take extreme exception to you encouraging Frau Roland to place a fatuous story spewed from your stupid imagination on your official file. I only learnt of this when the auditors came last year. If such a spurious story was to ever fall into the hands of the enemy there could be serious repercussions all the way down to the front line. Do you understand?"

"Yes, Reichsführer."

Herr Himmler slaps his thigh, turns and marches out without saying another fraudulent word.

Everything is back to normal when Fritz and Axel return, apart from having Fritz in my ear.

"Err—the Tommy 'Wolf' has put in an order for a shelf to hold his atlas. Here are the dimensions."

"Show me," I say, snatching the cigarette paper from the hands of the monster.

I take one look. "No problem Fritz, provided the camp commandant coughs up the lumber."

This is not my first foreign order from Best aka Wolf. His first order was to make a wooden frame to hold his treasured skittles set. I am informed Best loves to plant flowers and play ball games with one of his guards in the yard—that is whenever he has not got his head stuck inside a book.

Perhaps I could communicate with him using the bookshelf he has ordered. Who knows what tommyrot might spew from my imagination?

39
Sachsenhausen

June 30, 1942

NOT only is the man who attempted to assassinate the Führer living under the same roof as Best, associates of Rudolf Hess have now been brought to Sachsenhausen. After being sidelined by Martin Bormann and after opposing the invasion of the Soviet Union, Hess climbed into a Messerschmitt Bf 110 and flew solo to Scotland on his own peace mission—only to spend the rest of the war incarcerated in comfort in England.

Apart from his daily cut and thrust with the warders and exercising in the yard, Best has seen little action so far in 1942. Though he did receive a long delayed letter from May to say she left The Hague before the German occupation of The Netherlands and is living in Devon.

To add to that good news Grothe came one day bringing a large parcel of shirts, ties, jackets, trousers, shoes, socks, underwear, braces, linen as well as an assortment of his books. All have come from his home in The Hague where Maud has been holding the fort. A few days later Best has more excitement when his typewriter and his electric shaver arrive. Though he is less cheered by the news Stevens was transferred to Dachau concentration camp last December.

Stevens is not alone in being relegated from Sachsenhausen. Hans Loritz, the camp commandant, though he has overseen the expansion of the brickworks to be the largest in the world for the reconstruction of Berlin to the megalomaniacal plans of Hitler and his architect Albert Speer, has fallen from grace. His private projects that include a game park and a houseboat are put on hold due to his illegal use of prison labour and materials. He is relegated to command a concentration camp in Norway.

Since early June Best has been forewarned of a visit by Himmler. All ashtrays must be hidden away as the Reichsführer is a devout non-smoker. Best is one of the privileged prisoners to receive the venerated visitor.
"I am sorry to see a man like you living in such circumstances. But we are doing as much as we can for your personal comfort. Do you have any complaints?" asks Himmler.
"No Reichsführer."
"So you can see for yourself the stories of atrocities spoken of in the British White Paper are nothing but lies and the inventions of the Jews."
"I am sorry Reichsführer, but from what I have seen and heard the conditions are far worse than described in the paper you mention," Best answers.
Himmler looks gloomier than normal and leaves without saying another word. Against the dire predictions of the warders and guards Best suffers no consequences for his cheeky remark, apart from his weekly cigarette ration being increased to one hundred.

40

February 15, 1943

Sachsenhausen

___With burning hearts and cool heads we will overcome the major problems of this phase of the war.

A terrible screeching interrupts my fitful sleep. I turn on my cot to see Fritz and Axel standing to attention beside the Volksempfänger like two rabbits.

We are on the way to final victory! That victory rests on our faith in the Führer!

I see in my mind's eye the audience fizzing with anticipation.

This evening I once again remind the whole nation of its duty.

The Führer expects us to do that which will throw all we have done in the past into the shadows.

We do not want to fail him. As we are proud of him, he should be proud of us!

The audience is ignited! The cacophony of the 'Heil Hitlers' pierces my eardrums.

The great crises and upsets of national life show who the true men and women are___

The nation is ready for anything!

Every fool roars in agreement, "WE ARE READY!"

The Führer has commanded, and we will follow him!

The deluded chant, 'WE WILL FOLLOW HIM' over and over and over.

In this hour of national reflection and contemplation, we believe firmly and unshakably in victory. We see it before us. We need only reach for it. We must resolve to subordinate everything to it!

That is the duty of the hour!
Let the slogan be: Now, people rise up — and let the storm break loose!!

Brainless hysteria explodes as ten thousand outstretched arms slice the foul air in the Nazi salute.

Once the radio racket has receded to a crackle I have a half — intelligent question for Fritz.
　"Who was that?"
　"Err — him Dr. Goebbels, coming live from the err — Sportpalast in Berlin."
　"I might have guessed."

I shut my eyes and turn over to face the wall. The German people's love affair with Adolf Hitler is far more reckless than any love affair I have had, I decide. I hate to think what horrors will come before the breakup.

Footnote: A few weeks earlier the Wehrmacht had been defeated with over half a million casualties at Stalingrad. Goebbels bombast in Berlin was the Nazi panacea to this disaster.

41

1943

Sachsenhausen

THE arrival of the new camp commandant, Anton Kaindl, in September 1942, immeasurably improved life for the Englishman in 1943. When Best put in a complaint about Loritz's nighttime leather restraint Kaindl immediately phoned Heinrich Müller in Berlin. The fetter and eyebolt were removed the same day when Kaindl took full responsibility for the prisoner.

Best's persistent complaints have also resulted in relocation. His old cell No.51 beside the latrines was nothing less than an acoustic torture chamber with every gurgle being megaphoned through the wall. His new cell No.43 has a south-facing window that admits sunlight while providing a view of the perimeter wall without standing on a stool. The orientation of the window also aligns with the flight path of formations of Allied bombers en route to Berlin—a heartening sight for Best both day and night.

Though still living in isolation, Best has come to learn the names of some others living in the Bunker. Through loose talk by his guards he has learnt pastor and theologian Martin Niemöller is languishing in a cell due to his sermons that upset the Führer. Another prisoner is Martin Luther, a public servant and whistler blower who upset the Minister for Foreign Affairs, Joachim von Ribbentrop, by exposing his extravagance. And a Russian airman, Wassilly Kokoris, the nephew of the Foreign Minister Molotov, is sharing his cell with the son of Joseph Stalin who is suicidal.

Best is not immune to the grim reality of Sachsenhausen as whenever he is escorted to the camp dentist for removal of his teeth in exchange for dentures he must pass the semi-circular roll call area. The chilling sight of a group hanging, the brutal treatment meted out to prisoners by sadist guards for trivial offences are recorded in his diary for future publication. At the main gates Best also sees the lineup of new arrivals, the majority from Russia and Poland. Early in the year a remnant of Red Army prisoners, survivors from the Eastern Front are admitted, only to be shot or die of typhus.

Every new arrival must sew a coloured triangle onto their striped costume to designate the crime, race, religion, homosexual orientation, asocial or the work-shy behavior of the prisoner. But the prison clothing is not worn by Best. Nor does he work in the SS enterprises of joinery, woodcarving, tailoring, shoemaking, bookbinding, pottery, electrical and light engineering. Nor is he required to run himself to death on the purpose built track testing military footwear or dodge death daily in the brickworks.

Nevertheless Best keeps up appearances. Every day after he has been served breakfast he dresses in suit, collar and tie, unless he is taking a sunbath in the yard. He is condemned daily to relax in his cell in the armchair given to him by the officer in charge of the Bunker, Eccarius. From the armchair he can scrutinize the two self-portraits by May, as well as one of her sketches of her farmhouse in Devon, that hang on the fleshly painted walls of his cell. Beside the small table where his guard normally sits is a larger table for typewriter, a few books and some newspapers, while a table lamp allows his guard to read at night without disturbing his sleep. On a stool is an electric cooker with an asbestos lined cover made to order by Elser. The cooker allows him to keep food warm to suit his preference for dining late. Nearby is his radio that was also supplied by Eccarius after Best kicked up a stink when he found out another VIP prisoner had one. A double wardrobe not only contains his extensive range of clothes, but his reserve of provisions that are stored in a special glass-lined cupboard. Beside the steam radiator stands a three shelved bookcase holding many of his favorite tomes. On top of the bookcase is the shelf, also made by Elser, to hold his Stieler Atlas in the open position for ready reference. On his bed is a rug and a bolster against which he can lean when reading during the day. A bowl of edelweiss, picked from the garden in the yard completes the scene of prisoner paradise.

It was via the shelf made for Best's Stieler Atlas that Elser began to do the exact opposite of what Himmler would want. Upon taking delivery of the completed top shelf Best found attached beneath a tiny piece of paper covered with an almost indecipherable script. Best, being familiar with secret coded messages, soon realized Elser was communicating his life story — the first installment beginning:

I was born in Munich and when I was quite small my mother died while giving birth to my dead sister. In the same week my father was killed in action. An uncle, my only relative who was a childless railway guard, took charge of me and raised me in a rough and ready fashion. I ran wild in my youth and had two clashes with the police. As a result I was sent to a reformatory for a year. At school I was exceptionally bright, though it was only my teacher in handicrafts who recognised my potential. When I was fifteen or sixteen, I cannot remember which, my uncle died leaving me only a small sum. This was quite insufficient to further my schooling and I was placed under the charge of the Munich municipal children's officer. I was soon apprenticed to a joiner who acted as my guardian. Despite my insubordination, being a frequent cause of trouble, my intelligence and aptitude to my work made me a valuable assistant and my master tried to retain me in his service at the end of my apprenticeship. But once I was free of him nothing could hold me down.

In time, after being fed a series of handwritten messages, Best will have a history of Elser's life — without a single word of truth. Unwittingly, Best will use this fictional version of Elser's life almost word for word in his future book he will title, *The Venlo Incident*. This fallacious biography of Elser will be taken as gospel for many years to come.

42

July 20, 1944
Sachsenhausen

JUST as I get busy fitting the frets to a fret board of my fourth concert zither, I have an unexpected visitor. For some odd reason the weird eyed one with the bad haircut has come all the way from Berlin to molest me. Fritz and Axel are told to buzz off so we can confront each other in private.

"Kaindl phoned. He told me you are depressed and have thoughts of killing yourself," says Müller.

"Nay. I will let one of your boys do that job."

Müller casts his toxic eyes about as if thinking of sub-letting my workshop.

"What is this?" he asks lifting up a coil of wire.

"Wire for a thirty-seven string zither."

"Just don't use this stuff to string yourself up. Do you play the zither?"

"I was lead zither at the club in Königsbronn."

"Huh."

"Do you play an instrument?" I ask to be sociable.

"Not me."

"Your boss Heydrich looks a good Catholic boy with some music left in him."

"Heydrich is DEAD!"

"Dead? How did this happen?"

"Some bastard shot him in Prague almost two years ago. You must be the last one to hear — though I guess newspapers are scarce in here. But you were right about him having some music in him."

"I was?"

"Reinhard Heydrich was no novice on the violin. His father was of some repute, being a composer in the style of Richard Wagner. In fact the night before Heydrich was shot down he took his lovely wife, Lina, to a concert of his old man's music performed in Prague town hall. Himmler was by Heydrich's bedside in hospital just before he passed away. He told me later the last thing Heydrich did was to mutter a line from one of his old man's operas. It was something about the world being 'a barrel-organ where we all have to dance to the tune on the drum'."

"Poetic. Did you go to the funeral?'

"Everyone went — either to Prague Castle where Himmler gave the eulogy or back in Berlin where Hitler called Heydrich the man with the 'iron heart'. What exactly he meant by that expression is still open to debate."

"Did he receive a special Nazi badge for his dedication to the Nazi cause?"

"Hitler loaded him with every award he could dig up including the Blood Order Medal. Later he said in private Heydrich was an idiot for exposing himself to danger. But as I saw it — that was Heydrich's style. He went from being a submariner to being an ace fighter pilot. Did you know Heydrich flew almost one hundred combat missions for the Luftwaffe?"

"Nay. I did not know about that. But perhaps I've been too busy stringing zithers to know exactly what a fucking mess our country is now in. Sorry to use coarse language, but when you've been living with deadbeats for as long as I have you slip into using their words just to make yourself heard."

"Would you prefer not to have them under your feet?"

"I would."

"Done. We need every slacker we can find to hold the line with the Americans and the Russians closing in."

"I guess you strung up the guy who shot poor Heydrich."

"What a mess! I was ordered to Prague to pull in the assassin when some smartarse gave the order for two villages, Lidice and Ležáky, to be erased. All the men were massacred, most of the women were deported, while the children were gassed in Chelmno extermination camp—except for those we thought could be 'Germanized'."

"Who is taking the rap for that atrocity?" I ask foolishly.

"Don't ask me!"

I return to tinkering with the metal frets I am attaching to my ivory fret board, hoping Müller will get the hint and scoot back to Berlin. But he stays watching me working—his eyes burning holes in my sound box.

"Did Heydrich have ambitions to be leader?" I inquire, to kill the silence.

"Heydrich had the breeding—at least once we hushed up his Jewish ancestry. His unusual intellect was matched by the watchful instincts of a predatory animal, ever alert to danger and always ready to act ruthlessly. Yes, I believe he did have his eyes on the top job. He was an exceptionally gifted person. The way he organized coordinated attacks on the Jews and dealt with other threats to German security was pure genius. I recall the highly successful conference he organized in January 1942 held in the waterfront villa by the Wannsee. He spoke in a cool, calm way, outlining our deep problems and his deft solutions. There was barely a question during question time. The meeting was over in less than sixty minutes—giving us ample time to drink Cognac and smoke the cigars."

"What was the topic at this lakeside conference?" I ask stupidly.

"The final solution to the Jewish question."

"Forgive me, but I have been out of circulation since about November 1939. What do you mean by 'the final solution'?"

"The final solution boils down to extermination."

"Extermination! I knew Jews were being dispossessed and sent to concentration camps, but this is news to me."

"Heydrich said we had no other option. The initial plan was to work the Jews to death in Siberia, but this plan became untenable when our advance on Russia was snowed under at Stalingrad. It was imperative the Jewish question be put to bed in Poland and in other occupied territories. Of course Heydrich was only carrying out the orders of Göring and the decision reached at the Wannsee Conference was little more than a formalization of the processes Hitler had instigated years in the past."

"Was Herr Himmler at the Wannsee Conference?"

"I understand he was either too busy impregnating his secretary or having a massage to attend."

"Himmler strikes me as an individual cursed by repressed leadership aspirations."

"Who knows what Himmler is repressing? Being a shy Munich boy like me his devout mother and his upright school headmaster father raised him a good Catholic. But after studying agriculture he turned away from the Church to become obsessed with looking for proof of Aryan and Nordic racial superiority and more interested in selective breeding, the occult, mysticism and being a vegetarian than in being the fucking Führer. He is so devoted he would kill his parents if the Führer ordered him. Now he wets his pants whenever he sees Kaltenbrunner coming."

"Who is Kaltenbrunner?"

"Heydrich's replacement. Hitler brought him in from Austria, being someone he could trust."

"Kaltenbrunner has big shoes to fill."

"You bet—but being over two metres tall he has a head start. Hitler gave Kaltenbrunner the plum job of assassinating Churchill, Roosevelt and Stalin at their conference in Tehran last November. He called the project the *Long Jump* Operation. Turned out to be a long shot. A Russian spy learnt of the plot by plying one of our men with liquor. Hitler foamed at the mouth when told."

"At least grog is good for something," I point out.

Müller makes no comment on my intelligent remark. I keep working on my zither, thinking he must shoot through soon. But he seems determined to torture me by his presence. Without prompting he starts up again.

"In the first war I was a pilot for an artillery spotting unit. I was decorated for bravery winning the Iron Cross 1st and 2nd class, plus a few other badges. And what was lance corporal Adolf Hitler? He was a message runner at regimental headquarters a long way from the front, a job a dog wouldn't piss on. I was top cop in Munich while he was navel gazing writing *Mein Kampf*. He could not even get the title right. He wanted to call his book *Four and a Half Years Against Lies, Stupidity and Cowardice,* until Max Amman, his publisher, persuaded him to give the book the pithy title, *My Struggle*. Now he's sold over four million copies and made a mint—the bastard!"

"You sound bitter."

"My job is to sound bitter. If I don't sound bitter someone is bound to report me for going soft, putting me in the mire with those in high places."

"What about Heydrich's scar-faced mate. Is he a contender for the top job?"

"I presume you are referring to young Schellenberg. He is now commanding all our intelligence outside the Fatherland. We got rid of military intelligence, the Abwehr, and we sacked that mischief-maker, Admiral Canaris. Though if the top job ever become vacant Schellenberg would be too smart to accept it. The way this war is going with the enemy slipping into Normandy two weeks ago, the gloss is going off being leader. Being Führer may soon become a poisoned chalice. So Schellenberg has his head screwed on properly. I should not tell you this, but he has two automatic guns built into his desk he can fire in all directions simply by pressing a button."

"There could be a big market for lethal furniture in the Third Reich," I reason.

"Your cynicism is disturbing."

"Not as disturbing as the evil of the Third Reich."

"Now don't make things hard for yourself with wisecracks like that. Is there anything you need?"

"Just remind Kaindl of the electric motor for my lathe he promised months ago."

"I will. But before I go I have a question for you."

"You do?"

"Why did you set the detonation time of your time bomb at 9.20 pm and not 8.45 pm, for instance, halfway through the Führer's normal ninety minute address? Did you not know that the start time for the meeting at the Bürgerbräukeller had been moved back from 8.30 pm to 8.00 pm?"

I avoid Müller's dicey eyes, yet my fingernails dig deep into my fret broad. This is the exact question I have never dared to ask myself. But why is Müller asking me this question four and half years after the event? What is he trying to prove? Is his aim to send me insane? But Müller is right. If I had checked the start time in a newspaper things would have turned out differently — so differently in fact, it is reasonable to conclude the Final Solution would never have been implemented.

As I sear inside with guilt after this realization Müller continues to rave.

"The fact the Führer cut short his address and left early to catch a train rather than a fucking aeroplane due to the fog in Munich would not have been a factor in the equation — had you done your fucking HOMEWORK!"

I am redeemed from trying to extrapolate Müller's last convoluted condemnation when one of his men rushes in as if Judgment Day is upon us.

"A message has just been received a bomb has exploded in the Wolfsschanze!" he yells into Müller's ear.

"Oh shit! Not another mad bomber for me to investigate!" snorts Müller.

He grabs his cap and is about to disappear when he stops in his tracks to pull a brown envelope from his top pocket and hands it to me saying, "I almost forgot — this is for you from Himmler. Open it at your leisure."

As Fritz and Axel pack their bags for their fatal departure to slow down the Russians, I go to the far corner of my workshop to open the envelope. What can it be, I wonder. A late birthday card? An apology? A pardon? Nay. What I am holding in my hand is a personal voucher for Herr Himmler's latest initiative: complementary entry into the camp's Special Task Force facility where only 'pure breed' and 'disease free' ladies are employed. On the back is listed the four house rules: 1. No service to exceed fifteen minutes, 2. Shoes must be removed, 3. No talking permitted beyond that which is absolutely necessary. 4. Only the missionary position is to be employed. As I slip the voucher into my pants' pocket I wonder what else will the Nazi regime want to control. Not only do they control the hearts and the minds of the German people — now they want control over their genitals!

43

February 20–April 2, 1945
Sachsenhausen-Buchenwald

___We are living through the greatest crisis of occidental humanity. The crisis has been caused by the Western-democratic-plutocratic world and is carried on today by them despite the fact that they themselves are the prime sufferers of the alarming events. No one can say that the Führer did not make every attempt to find a peaceful way out, because he knew from the beginning the terrible consequences that war would have. The Western camp hindered his efforts, and today is paying a huge cost for its stubbornness. England is already complaining about the loss of all the wealth it built during the Victorian era, and who knows what a devastating position it will be in when this gigantic struggle ends.

But what good does this knowledge and these predictions do us when the enemy leadership holds stubbornly to its decision to carry on the war at any price, with the goal of destroying Germany and___

Best jumps up to turn off his radio. Replays of Goebbels' speeches on the RRG are no longer a novelty. Over the last six months he prefers to disobey orders and listen to the BBC. This way he has been able to follow the latest advances of the Allies, using his atlas on top of his bookcase to mark the relative positions of the armies on the battlefield of Europe.

Best is about to reach for his copy of *Ulysses* when he finds Eccarius at the door of his cell.

"Herr Best, you are leaving us."

"What! When?"

"Now, at once. Your transport is at the door waiting for you. You are to pack all your things as quickly as possible, within the hour if that is not too much trouble."

Only this morning Best asked commandant, Kaindl, if he would be allowed to stay until the Russians had overrun the camp, or would he be evacuated to a place further from the battle line. Kaindl replied he had no idea, shrugged his shoulders and walked away. Now the task of uprooting seems beyond him, being so deeply entrenched with so many possessions.

But his guards rally around him. They find five cardboard boxes and help him pack. Eccarius returns to give him his rations for the day plus two loaves of white bread and a pound of tobacco. After he packs his reserve food supplies into his handbag, Best takes his last look at his refurbished cell. Leaving is not easy.

Best finds the waiting transport is a prison van and not a sedan, like the car he arrived in with Grothe and Dr. Schäfer from Berlin over five years ago. He climbs into the back of the van after Kaindl has shaken his hand and said, "I wish you a safe return to your wife in England, Herr Best."

There are two others in the van but they are locked into the tiny cages. All Best knows they are airmen: one Russian, one an Englishman. After the intact villas surrounded by unscathed farmland comes the city — a city bearing little resemblance to the one Best entered with Major Naujocks after driving from Düsseldorf in 1939. On both sides of the Spree the empty shells of buildings stand in silent witness to the thoroughness of the Allied bombing. The prison van crawls through the mountains of rubble before coming to a stop in Prinz-Albrecht-Strasse. With windows blown out, floors missing, gaping holes through the roof, the labyrinth where Best and Elser endured long days and nights of interrogation is now abandoned, apart from the basement prison of the Reich Security Main Office. Best is escorted down to a dank cell not knowing his fate. The wail of the air raid sirens twice during the night brings a warder to his cell to take him via a zigzag entry into a huge bombproof shelter. He sits out the raid with a remnant of Berlin citizens—their morale still unbroken. The next day two guards who remember him from his sojourn in Berlin in 1939 are amazed to see him still amongst the living. The SS paper, *Schwarze Korps*, had reported his beheading years ago.

On his third night in Berlin, Best is transported further south towards Leipzig and Weimar. The overnight journey terminates at midday the next day. With other prisoners in the prison van he is hustled into the cellar of a building outside the gates to Buchenwald concentration camp. Apart from the dire shortage of food, the only thing Best can find to quibble over is being separated from his five cardboard boxes. After an altercation with two warders he succeeds in having his boxes brought to his cell.

Forever alert to instances of mistreatment of fellow prisoners and breaches of the Geneva Agreement, Best takes the management to task over there being no exercise yard. He prevails and the prisoners are permitted the use of the central passage of the cellar at set times to maintain separation of individuals. Within a day or so this rule is flouted and Best is able to mingle with the other prisoners almost as if he is hosting a dinner party in his own house. He lists the occupants in his diary:

Cell No.1: General Friedrich von Rabenau and Pastor Dietrich Bonhoeffer.
Cell No.2: Dr. Hermann Pünder and Commander Franz Liedig.
Cell No.3: Dr. Erich and Mrs. Margot Heberlein.
Cell No.4: Count von Alvensleben and Colonel von Petersdorff.
Cell No.5: General Alexander von Falkenhausen.
Cell No.6: Squadron-Leader Hugh Falconer.
Cell No.7: Wassilli Kokorin.
Cell No.8: Dr. Josef Müller and Captain Ludwig Gehre.
Cell No.9: Miss Heidel Nowakowski.
Cell No.10: Dr. Sigmund Rascher.
Cell No.11: Myself.
Cell No.12: Dr. Hoeppner.

Best sets himself the task of interviewing his fellow prisoners to discover how each has come to be in this perilous predicament—living with trigger-happy warders, armies approaching from two directions, Allied air raids day and night, sudden death a distinct possibility. To soften up his cellar-mates Best opens up his five cardboard boxes. Anyone missing a belt, a tie, a shoe, a sock, a dinner jacket or in need of a complete outfit has only to ask and Best will supply free of charge. Even anyone in desperate need of tobacco can expect a free handout—within reasonable limits.

The first person Best collars is Dr. Hermann Pünder, a man of his own generation and sporting a fashionable Charlie Chaplin moustache. Best tracks him down in the washroom early one morning.

"This is an odd place to talk I know, but I happened to notice you are not wearing a tie."

"So what, Best?"

"Let me give you my finest grey silk tie suitable for any diplomatic occasion."

"Well thank you and goodbye!"

Pünder snatches the tie, leaving Best stranded by the wash trough. Best might already know Pünder is a German politician. But how he ever got caught up in the July 20 Plot in 1944 to assassinate Hitler is a mystery. Best suspects he will not confirm or deny anything anyway, like a true politician.

The next person to be intercepted by Best is Commander Franz Liedig, Dr. Pünder's cellmate. Best finds him doing deep breathing exercises in the central passage.

"Musty in here, isn't it?" says Best.

"Incredibly so. I was interned at Scapa Flow in 1919. That was a picnic—this is a nightmare."

"So how did you become beached such a long way from blue water, Commander?"

"I rejoined the Kriegsmarine at the instigation of Admiral Canaris in 1936. I knew what I was getting into however. There was a plot to arrest Hitler that turned into a plot to shoot him. When in 1938 we had one of our meetings at Hans Oster's house in Berlin, Captain Heinz and myself were asked to form an assault group to arrest Hitler, though after Field Marshall Witzleben left the meeting, we decided to shoot Hitler instead.

But our plans were scuttled after the signing of the Munich Conference. It was the weak-kneed British Prime Minister, Chamberlain, who saved Hitler."

"Maybe, but did I hear you say a field marshal was at your meeting?" asks Bests.

"I did. Erwin von Witzleben. He was to take over supreme command of the Wehrmacht had we succeeded in destroying Hitler on July 20, 1944."

"So what became of him?"

"Witzleben was in the first group of conspirators to be brought before the Peoples' Court in August 1944. Though he was brutally beaten by the Gestapo, he approached the bench giving the Nazi salute, only to be jeered by judge, Roland Freisler. Witzleben was hung from a meat hook the same day."

"I am sorry to hear that Commander. But how did you come to be here?"

"I was arrested in November last year after the discovery of our plans to sideline Hitler back in 1938. I've survived this far and hope to walk free."

The next day Best comes across a military man standing by the grillage at the end of the central passage. Colonel von Petersdorff is easy prey.

"This is a fine pickle we are in," remarks Best.

"You can say that again. I was wounded six times in the last war, but all the in-fighting and the back-stabbing in the Nazi Party was the worst cut of all."

"How's that Colonel?"

"I was in the running to be the leader of the SA in 1931, but the Stennes revolt in Berlin put the cat amongst the pigeons. When Hitler intervened and gave the job to Ernst Röhm, I resigned in disgust from both the Nazi Party and the SA. I was lucky to miss the bloody purge of 1934, but could not resist the call to arms in 1939 and a chance to invade France. I was put in command of an armoured reconnaissance unit and won the race to the English Channel. For men like me the blitzkrieg was a buzz. For my heroic deeds I was awarded the Knights Cross of the Iron Cross."

"So how come you are here, Colonel?"

"I wish I knew. The People's Court acquitted me of complicity in the

July 20 Plot, but the Gestapo disagreed with the verdict and slammed me into Laehrterstrasse Prison in Berlin. I would be fighting fit had a bomb not come through the roof burying me in the debris with my ribs pinned to my lungs."

"Have you received any medical treatment?" asks Best.

"Not as yet, but I'll be fine," he says as he limps back to his cell.

Seventy year-old Count von Alvensleben buttonholes Best whenever he gets the chance, ever keen to relive his hunting exploits in Canada. Best thinks the man is senile and may not have heard him say he was in the inner circle of Reich Chancellor Kurt von Schleicher who was shot dead in his living room, along with his wife in July 1934. The Count escaped a similar fate by hiding out in a hunting lodge, but is now serving two years imprisonment for 'defeatist' talk. This is a light sentence. In 1943 Erich Remarque's sister was arrested and convicted of the same offence. She was beheaded.

Next Best tackles Alexander von Falkenhausen, the taciturn sixty-six year-old General.

"What do you want to know Best? Do you want to know about my time as military advisor to Chiang Kai-Shek of Nationalist China or about my time as an Infantry General on the Western Front before I was the Military Governor of Belgium? For Heaven's sake make yourself clear man!"

"I was just wondering if you were involved in the July 20 Plot?"

"Would I be that stupid? Just because I had close friends who turned out to be anti-Hitler conspirators should I be implicated?"

Captain Ludwig Gehre is a different proposition, evading Best whenever he sees him coming. Little wonder Gehre is deceptive. In 1928 he wrote a book on Clausewitz and worked in military intelligence. Being in the circle around Hans Oster, he was involved in an assassination attempt on Hitler in March 1943 with Henning von Tresckow, who wanted to 'shoot Hitler like a mad dog.' But nothing came to fruition. Gehre with his wife hid from the Gestapo for months until November 8, 1944. Fearing arrest he shot his wife dead before he turned the gun on himself, but only succeeded in seriously injuring his right eye. His fate now hangs in the balance.

Gehre's cellmate, Dr. Josef Müller also shied from Best's advances. Using the identity "X", Müller made a number of trips to Rome in 1939 and 1940 with documents seeking co-operation in a coup to replace the Nazi regime. Once Pope Pius XII had given his blessing to the documents they were forwarded to the British Foreign Office. The Gestapo arrested Dr. Müller in 1943 when copies of the documents were found in the home of Hans von Dohnányi, brother-in-law of Dietrich Bonhoeffer. Müller has already endured two years in Flossenbürg concentration camp.

The Heberleins are next on Best's hit list. Margot is a vivacious lady. Best chooses his moment and pins her to the wall when her husband is not around.
 "Frau Heberlein. I have heard your name is Margot."
 "That is correct Mr. Best."
 "Whenever I hear the name Margot I'm reminded of Margot Fonteyn, the up-and-coming prima ballerina," sparkles Best.
 "Mr. Best, my kidnapping was far more exciting than any ballet you might have seen."
 "Kidnapping? Perhaps you could elaborate?"
 "As you may know my husband was the Ambassador to Spain. Erich declared himself an opponent of the Nazis when they came to power in 1933, but he was prepared to work on under the rogue regime for a number of years thinking they would come undone. But they clung to power like leeches. After a few years when Erich took leave he could not stomach returning to his post in Madrid and ignored an order to return to Berlin. We thought we were safe living with my relatives. How wrong we were, Mr. Best! One night four men broke into our bedroom as we slept. Erich was whacked on the head while I was rolled up in a blanket to stifle my screams. A thug slung me over his shoulder and carried me down a ladder at the window to a waiting car in the street. Dressed only in our night attire we were driven to an airfield at Bordeaux. From there the Gestapo flew us to Berlin. We have spent the last three years at Sachsenhausen."
 "Sachsenhausen! But I never saw you there. What a pity our paths have not crossed until now."
 "Do you think we will get out of this alive, Mr. Best?"
 "My dear lady, I promise I will do everything in my power to see you do," replies Best to allay the fear he sees in the woman's eyes.

A few days later Best runs into a gingery man washing his hands in the washroom.

"Guten morgen. I'm Dr. Rascher," says the Munich educated medical doctor who arrived a few days after the others.

"Morgen. I'm Best."

"Ha! You would be the famous English prisoner."

"In person."

"I expect you would like to know all about me?"

"Not before I wash, have a shave and have some breakfast, old boy."

"I will be around for a while yet, Mr. Best."

"How nice."

Later that day Dr. Sigmund Rascher catches up with Best doing knee bends in the central passage.

"We meet again, Mr. Best.

"Eh!"

"It may come as a surprise to you I worked for Herr Himmler until recently."

"Good for you," says Best, returning to his imperious height.

"I had an important job responsible for medical research."

"And what did that entail?"

"I was doing ground-breaking research work into humane ways of extermination."

"Extermination!"

"Herr Himmler is a kind hearted man and was anxious prisoners be exterminated without worry or suffering. Great pains have been taken to design death chambers to camouflage their true purpose and to regulate the flow of lethal gas so patients fall asleep without knowing they will never wake. But sadly we have not succeeded as people have a different resistance to the effects of poisonous gas. Some survive longer than others and the vast numbers to be exterminated compounds the problem as the chambers are invariably overfilled and simultaneous death is impossible to achieve."

"Are you pulling my leg?" asks Best.

"No, no! Research into extermination is just the tip of the iceberg. For instance I worked on ways to save lives when people are exposed to extreme low temperatures such as airmen who ditch in the sea and must wait for rescue. Experiments using expendable persons have proved to be most valuable."

"Sounds diabolical."

"Not so. I discovered human warmth is different to artificial warmth. In freezing experiments I have laid a frozen hypothermic victim between two naked Romani women Himmler had sent direct from Ravensbrück concentration camp with promising results."

"If your experiments were such a success how is it you are here?"

"I upset Herr Himmler when I attempted to publish the results of my work in a Swiss medical journal. I wanted to share my findings so even British seamen waiting for rescue after U-boat attack might benefit from my research."

"That was noble of you. But please excuse me. I need to return to my quarters," mutters Best, his mind reeling and his knees shaking from hearing such evil.

For the next few days Best enjoys his isolation, not daring to run foul of Dr. Rascher. The only time he ventures out is on trips to the washroom. This requires him to pass cell No.1 where the door is invariably closed. But one day while making his toilet visit Best finds the door enticingly ajar.

"Hello, I'm Best," he says, sticking his head through the gap.

"Bonhoeffer," responds, the plumpish-faced man looking up from a handwritten page.

"Not Pastor Dietrich Bonhoeffer?"

"Guilty."

"This is indeed a pleasure I did not expect. I purchased your book, *Act and Being*, over ten years ago. Never got beyond the first page I'm afraid. Theology is an unforgiving pursuit from a layman's perspective, but I promised myself I would make time one day to get back to eternal questions."

"I hope you are given the opportunity," replies Bonhoeffer.

"So do I. As they say — time and tide waits for no man."

"And time is the most valuable thing we have, as time is the most irrevocable," counters Bonhoeffer."

"I see you are using your time here wisely to write your sermons," quips Best.

"I am writing letters to friends, not sermons."

"Though I presume you are explaining why God allows evil men like Hitler to run amuck in the world?"

"I wish that I were. Both St. Thomas Aquinas and Martin Luther confronted the problem of the existence of evil. Both came to the same conclusion—only God knows the answer. All I can offer you is my belief that He can and will bring good out of evil, even out of the greatest evil."

"After speaking to Dr. Rascher I wish I had your faith. But on a less theological question—are you like others in our midst implicated in the July 20 Plot?"

"My arrest and imprisonment predates that assassination attempt. I was delivered to Tegel Prison in Berlin in April 1943—the same month Hans and Sophie Scholl were beheaded in Munich for their pacifist leaflets. So I am thankful I can do a little of what needs to be done to end fascist evil."

"Is your cellmate in the same boat?"

"He is ultimately. General von Rabenau is a professional soldier with unshakeable Christian convictions and has played his part for the sake of sanity."

"But how can you condone the killing of any man, even a man as evil as Hitler?"

"As a follower of Christ I believe in non-violence, even though I once said 'as German Christians we are not to simply bandage the wounds of victims beneath the wheels of injustice. We are to drive a spoke into the wheel itself.'"

"You appear to be on the horns of a dilemma—but is the General about?"

"The General is taking a shower. He said it could well be his last."

"That is a flippant thing for a man in his position to say."

"Absolute seriousness is never without a dash of humor."

"I heartily agree. Cheering up people when the chips are down is half the battle."

Best is still at the door mulling over whether General von Rabenau might have been one of the generals Fischer or Solms were referring to in 1939, when he hears heavy footsteps coming down the passageway. He turns to see a wild-eyed warder bearing down on him with his pistol drawn.

"I had better scarper," Best gasps, ducking into the washroom.

44

March 7, 1945

Dachau

I HAVE been shunted out of Sachsenshausen and brought to Dachau. A warder named Franz Lechner is hanging around my cell like a bad smell. He keeps pestering me about Ernst Thälmann as if he is a hero of his.

"Why did you plant the bomb?" Lechner asks me for the umpteenth time.

"If I tell you will you leave me in peace?"

"You have my word."

"The reason is pure and simple. I had to do it because Hitler meant the downfall of Germany. I am not some dyed-in-the-wool Communist. I did have some sympathy for Ernst Thälmann, but getting rid of Hitler just became an obsession of mine. But, as you can see I got caught and now I have to pay the consequences for my act. I would have preferred to be executed right away, rather to be pestered by people such as you. Now, have I answered your question?"

"I think you have."

"Then piss off!"

No sooner is Lechner out the door I regret my meanness towards him. Like Nebe, he is basically a good person, doing his best to make life bearable in this Nazi necropolis. He comes by my door whenever he hears me playing as if I am a Pied Piper who plays the zither instead of the pan flute. Last week I sent him away to buy sheet music and he spent 30 marks from his own pocket at a music shop. He came back with a stack of Viennese folk songs tucked under his paralysed arm. Lechner can thank the gypsy dictator he will never play the zither or flute with that dud arm, though after his stint in the Wehrmacht fighting for nothing he is lucky to be still living.

I light up another cigarette. I must smoke forty a day so my ration will not be cut back. With a gram of luck I will smoke myself to death. I already have one foot in the grave. As in the other place they converted three cells into one so I can tinker. They could have saved the expense and sent another V2 flying bomb over the English Channel. But in this Nazi bureaucracy crazy things happen every day. Lechner is a prime example. He is such a good-hearted soul he lets the prisoners roam up and down the passageway when his masters are not at home. One day I ran into Pastor Niemöller. If he smiled he would crack his face. To cheer up the unrepentant preacher I told him my 'wife' had once read his stupid U-boat book. And he believed me! I laughed all night at that one. But my real fear is Lechner will be caught out one day and go up the chimney leaving me to wallow in my misery. And what Müller said to me at Sachsenhausen about my critical chronometric miscalculation still haunts me.

As I lie on the bunk like a lazy jerk, I dig my soiled hand inside my pants' pocket. At the very bottom I find a crumpled card and pull it out. The card is the voucher bequeathed to me by Himmler. Bringing the relic closer to my face I can make out the expiry date is November 8, 1948. Nazi optimism springs eternal—but as far as I am concerned this voucher expired six months ago in the Special Task Force facility hut in Sachsenhausen. Only the memory of my agonizing sadness survives.

The matron's grey streaked hair was pulled back into a bun. She sat behind a reception counter built in haste of cheap Baltic pine. To her credit a vase of white snowdrops sat on her desk to make things look almost civilized. After she repeated the four house rules, she asked if I had used the disinfectant cream. When I said I had she issued me with the No.6. A guard then escorted me along the passageway to a freshly painted blue door with spyhole and No.6 neatly sign written on the doorframe. Once the door was opened and I stepped inside I noticed the new china basin, the lavender towel, the floral curtains hung over the frosted glass window. I also noticed the young woman perched on the edge of the bed sucking a cigarette. She was wearing an oversized grey army shirt and nothing else, as far as I could see. I stood like a novice apprentice at the foot of the wrinkled bed sheets while she stubbed her smoke on the windowsill. She then turned her head to land her leaden eyes on me.

"Hello," I said as cheerfully as I could.

"You must take off your shoes before you get on the bed," droned the young woman.

As she laid her close-clipped skull down on the pillow, I fumbled with my buttons as if my hands were in fact the hands of Orlac.

"Tell me your name?" I asked as I kicked off my shoes.

"Do names matter any more?" she answered, as if I was a fool for asking.

"Tell me anyway."

"If you must know my name is Gerda."

"Gerda? But Gerda was the name of a waitress I once met at the Bürgerbräukeller."

Her head jerked up. Once our eyes met she laid her head back on the pillow and twisted her body to one side.

"Are you Georg Elser?" she purred.

Hearing her say my name I sat down on the bed and took hold of her ankle. She tried to pull away but I firmed my grip.

"I remember you were the pretty waitress who served me on the first night of my work."

"Was I?"

"Were you there on November 8, 1939?" I asked.

"If you mean the night your bomb went off—I was not, thank God."

"Was that your night off?"

"No. I called in sick. How do you think I ended up here?"

"I don't follow you."

"If I must explain everything your fifteen minutes will expire before you're satisfied."

"Explain to me what you mean anyway."

"You may not know this but all the Bürgerbräukeller managers and the staff were arrested the next morning. The fact I was not there on the night cast added suspicion on me. I did not help my cause when I was rude to an official. He made a complaint and I was labelled 'asocial'. Though I am not even part gypsy, I was sent direct to Ravensbrück concentration camp."

"I have never heard of Ravensbrück."

"Believe me it exists! Just ask the ten thousand women and children who live there — if 'live' is the right word."

"So why are you here now? Did they force you to do this work?" I asked.

"I expect you will look down on me if I say I volunteered."

"Nay. I would not be so mean."

"Many women volunteer. Few are selected. I was selected because I looked healthier than the rest. This was my one big chance. Here at least they feed you. To tell the truth I am terrified of going up the chimney," she said as tears flooded her eyes.

"We all must die sometime," I said like an imbecile.

"But I am only twenty two!"

I gave her ankle an extra squeeze as she buried her head in the pillow.

As her body quivered I wondered if I should act or let her be? One half of me wanted to act. The other half hesitated.

"What are you waiting for?" she asked after a senseless minute of inaction.

A moment later Gerda parted her legs and I eased myself into her. It was as if we were made for each other. Time stood still and every external thought was suspended as I lost myself inside her — pleasuring myself with a gradual acceleration in the tempo. For almost six long years I have been denied the joy of lying between a woman's thighs, though I've only my pigheaded fucking self to blame for that unnatural deprivation.

I knew my time had expired when the guard rattled the door handle.

"Will you come again?" Gerda asked as she reached for the towel.

"I will," I said once I realized what she meant as I slipped on my shoes and did up my buttons.

I gave myself a month to think over what I might say to Gerda next time we met. To my shame I had never found out the name of the waitress who was killed by my bomb — the one who has given me nightmares for over five years. Was she one of the three waitresses I photographed in the beer garden using the camera I received as a Christmas gift from Maria Schmauder? Was she the one I posted the photograph and wrote a letter but have never received a reply? Gerda would know who she was, though I was reluctant to ask in case the dead waitress happened to be her friend.

These thoughts were an utter waste of time as I was to learn when I went to visit Gerda again.

"May I see the same lady as last time in room No.6?" I asked the matron.

"No.6 left yesterday. The replacement comes tomorrow."

"But how can this be?"

"When she had her medical examination the doctor deemed her to be pregnant."

"But where has she gone?"

"Back to Ravensbrück for an abortion."

"Will she return?"

"I *doubt* it!" the matron laughed, letting me know I had asked another stupid question.

Every bone in my body groaned as I walked back to the Bunker. I had no nightmares that night. I wept all night instead.

45

April 3-8, 1945

Buchenwald-Schönberg

ONE week before the full horror of Buchenwald concentration camp is revealed to the world by the international press and the newsreel cameras, the VIP prisoners in the cellar are ordered to evacuate. Best and fifteen other prisoners are crammed into the back of a prison van, a space designed for eight. The crush of bodies could have been far worse had Best not reduced his cardboard boxes from five to three as a result of his garment redistribution.

    The prison van is powered by a wood-burning generator and takes time to warm up and get going. But even before the vehicle has gone one hundred metres there is trouble. Dr. Rascher panics, thinking the vehicle is a gas van as used in 1940 to euthanize Polish mentally ill children and later to transport thousands to extermination camps, saving time and fuel by delivering the passengers dead on arrival. But Rascher is wrong and Regensburg is reached at dusk the next day with all those inside the van still with air in their lungs. Though during the day two prisoners in the van were diverted to Flossenbürg concentration camp.

At Regensburg Allied bombing has reduced the railway goods yard to a tangle of rails and a jumble of upturned wagons. In the adjacent over-crowded Regensburg prison Best and his group must spend the night packed into two cells. Next morning the prison passageways are awash with another group of prisoners—men and women as well as children—all relatives of those executed for their suspected part in the July 20 Plot. The wife of Colonel Claus von Stauffenberg is not amongst them however. A pregnant Nina has been sent direct to Ravensbrück concentration camp.

Among those Best greets in the passageway is the industrialist Fritz Thyssen and his wife, Amélie. In September 1939, before leaving for Switzerland, Thyssen sent Hermann Göring a telegram bluntly saying he opposed the war. His opinion was not appreciated. He was instantly expelled from the Nazi Party and the Reichstag. His mining and steel company was nationalized. Three years later he was arrested in Vichy France and from 1943 he has been in hibernation at Sachsenhausen, where his wife joined him voluntarily. He may now regret donating a considerable sum to the coffers of Adolf Hitler shortly before the Beer Hall Putsch in 1923 and in being influential in the crowning the dictator in 1933.

While Best is telling Thyssen something of his own ordeal a twenty-seven year old woman is observing him. Isa Vermehren, the accordion playing German cabaret artist, will later describe the tall Englishman with mirth in her aptly titled book, *A Journey Through the Last Act*. She found herself in Ravensbrück and Buchenwald after her brother and his wife defected to the British while he was serving as a diplomat in Ankara. Isa, her parents and other family members, are guilty by family association.

The village of Schönberg in the Bavarian Forest is reached later that day by Best and his fellow travellers. In a classroom of the village school with windows overlooking the surrounding fields and forest, neatly made beds are ready for the tired and hungry VIP prisoners. The congenial accommodation puts everyone into a state of delirium as beds are allocated and bags are unpacked. Dr. Rascher, the man ever happy to immerse dispensable people in freezing water until they turn purple, amuses the others by writing witty things over the bed heads. Heidel Nowakowski has other vices. From the moment Best laid eyes on her in the cellar at Buchenwald she has been a person he has avoided. But in this situation with everyone mingling in one room he is trapped when she pounces.

"Will you pull off my boots Mr. Best? I'm totally whacked."

Seduced by her luminous blue eyes, Best goes down on his knees. Heidel rests her heel on his thigh and pulls up the hem of her dress quite needlessly. She wriggles her foot in his groin as he tugs at her doubly knotted laces.

"I love your monocle, Mr. Best."

"Do you dear?"

A moment later Heidel is lying flat on her back. She has fallen through the bed to the floor. Others have the same problem. The thin plastic battens used in the bed bases are simply not up to the job. Best retreats to leave Heidel to deal with her predicament. He has heard all sorts of distressing rumours about this short, thickset blonde in her early twenties. All agree she was in Ravensbrück charged with spying for the Allies and was tortured by the slow removal of teeth. Others say she boarded in Sachsenhausen concentration camp brothel. Best is relieved when she redirects her advances to the little Russian airman, Wassilly Kokorin.

Next morning there would have been no breakfast had Dr. Rascher not shared a loaf of bread he was holding in reserve and Best had not contributed his supply of peppermint tea. But the sharing did not end there. Ten men queue to use Best's electric shaver and later in the day the villagers come good with freshly baked loaves of bread and a large bowl of potato salad, even though there is little food left for the locals.

The following day the word is spread Bonhoeffer will speak. Thirteen individuals, who have already had a taste of Hell, gather to hear what the pastor has to say. Bonhoeffer puts aside his half smoked cigarette and begins.

"I am humbled by this opportunity to say a few words as I know many of you belong to the Roman Catholic Church. Though at Easter time both Catholics and Protestants remember that our salvation comes through the death and resurrection of Jesus Christ. As Isaiah prophesied, 'by his wounds we are healed'. But rather than read from the Old Testament let me read to you from the Gospel of Mark:

> On that day, when evening had come, he said to them, "Let us go across to the other side." And leaving the crowd, they took him with them in the boat, just as he was. And other boats were with him. And a great windstorm arose, and the waves were breaking into the boat, so that the boat was already filling. But he was in the stern, asleep on the cushion. And they woke him and said to him, "Teacher, do you not care that we are perishing?" And he awoke and rebuked the wind and said to the sea, "Peace! Be still!" And the wind ceased, and there was a great calm. He said to them, "Why are you so afraid? Have you still no faith?" And they were filled with great fear and said to one another, "Who then is this, that even the wind and the sea obey him?"

After he returns his pocket sized New Testament to his top pocket, Bonhoeffer closes his eyes and prays: "We have been silent witnesses of evil deeds; we have been drenched by many storms; we have learnt the arts of equivocation and pretense; experience has made us suspicious of others and kept us from being truthful and open; intolerable conflicts have worn us down and even made us cynical. But we have a God who sent His Son, the Alpha and the Omega, the Beginning and the End. Amen."

The praying man has barely reopened his eyes when two men in plain civilian clothes come through the doorway on official business.

"Prisoner Bonhoeffer! Get ready to come with us," orders one of the men.

Seemingly unperturbed Bonhoeffer takes his time to shake the hands of those gathered around him. After Heidel Nowakowski and Frau Heberlein kiss his cheek, Bonhoeffer approaches the Englishman with a bulky envelope.

"Would you deliver this to the Bishop of Chichester for me, Captain Best?"

"I will, and I pray everything ends well for you."

"This *is* the end, but for me it is the beginning of life," Bonhoeffer declares.

After shaking Best's hand Bonhoeffer takes up his suitcase and is escorted from the room by the two men.

46

April 7, 1945

Dachau

MY live-in guard nods off every time I look his way. All day he sits slumped on a wooden stool by my cell door. Now that every pimply youth and grey-haired professor has been given a gun and sent out to defend the Fatherland only a grandpa can be spared to guard the evil assassin.

"Hey you!" I call out, causing him to come out of his stupor like a startled hedgehog.

"What you want?" he asks.

"What is your name old man?"

"What's it to you?"

"I like to know who I am talking to."

"Günter Knop."

"What did you do to deserve the plum job of guarding the satanic beast?"

"Everyone must do his bit for our Führer."

"The Führer is fucked in my humble opinion."

"You might be right, but that is hard for me to digest. I gave my life to the Party."

"What was your job?"

"A clerk in the service of Wilhelm Frick."

"I've not heard that name before. Is Frick someone important?"

"He certainly is, being the Reichsminister of the Interior from 1933 to 1943."

"He must have had his wits about him to stay that long in one job. I never did that."

"You are right. Frick is an intelligent man. He studied philosophy at Munich University and then law in Heidelberg and Berlin, taking his doctorate in 1901. The Reichstag Fire Decree was his baby, giving the Party power over the states, to start the process of Nazifying the whole country."

"If he took his doctorate in 1901 he must be a fossil like you."

"We are the same age — sixty eight."

"So how did Herr Frick climb up the political ladder?"

"I guess Frick's first break came when the Munich Chief of Police, Ernst Pöhner, introduced him to the Führer, probably after one of his charismatic orations at the Kirkus Krone in Munich around 1922. Pöhner had already helped with permissions to hold political rallies, giving the Führer a platform to air his lucid thoughts on the criminals in the Weimar government and the Jewish question. Frick worked as a lawyer in the Munich police department and with Pöhner he was given the task of keeping the police out of the way on November 8, 1923. After gate crashing the Monarchist meeting at the Bürgerbräukeller, the Führer got the attention of the inebriated audience by jumping onto a table and firing his pistol at the ceiling, yelling: 'The National Revolution has just BEGUN!'"

The old man needs to take a minute to catch his breath before he can continue.

"The next day the Führer called for a propaganda march into the city from the Bürgerbräukeller. The crowds in Marienplatz cheered wildly as the jubilant Führer with General Ludendorff at his shoulder led the march with Strasser's armed storm troopers bringing up the rear. Everything was going brilliantly until the Feldherrnhalle was reached. A line of Bavarian State Police stood in th way in Odeonplatz. Without warning they opened fire — spilling the blood of fifteen martyrs. It was fortunate the Führer was flattened to the ground by the man falling beside him — and if anyone tells you differently they are lying."

"I thought there were sixteen blood martyrs?" I interject.

"Err — there was once the Führer added the name of an innocent bystander shot dead — to round up the number. After the melee at the Feldherrnhalle and after the high theatre of the trial where Herrs Hitler, Hess, Röhm, Frick and others were charged with treason, the Führer was happy to cool his heels in prison. Herr Frick told me later the Führer talked incessantly in Landsberg and to shut him up his fellow-prisoners talked him into writing a book, which he did with help. After his release from prison Frick was elected to the Reichstag on a National Socialist Freedom Movement ticket, though his anti-Semitic, anti-Bolshevik stance soon returned him to the Nazi Party. Upon the Führer's release things moved ahead with industrialists, Kirdof and Fritz Thyssen bankrolling the Party. Frick was the Nazi Party leader in the Reichstag and associated mainly with another Bavarian, Gregor Strasser, the Party's propaganda specialist before Dr. Goebbels gained the blessing of the Führer."

"Was Gregor Strasser the brother of Otto Strasser?" I ask, as I recall the name from the distant past.

"He was, though Gregor Strasser expended too much energy arguing the toss on Party policy and fell foul of the Führer. For the sake of party unity he was liquidated, as was Ernst Röhm — and a den of other traitors. Otto Strasser had already kick-started the Black Front and fled to Prague to continue his futile fight against the Führer. Now he is hiding out in Canada with a heavy price on his head. Dr. Goebbels tarred him, 'public enemy No.1.'"

"Lucky fellow. Your story is intriguing, but what exactly did you do working for Herr Frick?"

"I worked in the legal office drafting the decrees for crime prevention and the protection of the people's community against parasites, asocial and work-shy individuals — all those who pose a threat to our national purity — and of course dangerous individuals who are an Enemy of the State."

"Little wonder the concentration camps are overflowing, and I guess you drafted the necessary decrees to legalize the extermination of the Jews."

"Not me! The 'Jewish question' was the responsibility of others. My work was related to the implementation of other necessary measures, such as sterilization—a measure we used to stem the Gypsy plague."

To let the old man rest his conscience I take time out to light another fag.

"Did Herr Frick work for Himmler?" I ask before he nods off to sleep again.

"No—he was Himmler's boss, even though Himmler's appointment as Reich police chief effectively united the police with the SS and made it virtually independent of Frick's control, as the SS was responsible only to the Führer."

"That is too confusing for me to understand."

"To be honest, we all have difficulty in understanding the methods of the Führer. He seems to survive by creating overlapping responsibilities, perhaps to keep every one at each other's throat and not at his throat. I think Machiavelli would approve of his use of the dictum 'divide and rule'."

"You sound as if you are having misgivings over the methods of the Führer."

"After what my grandson told me I no longer know what to think."

"What do you mean?"

"I would not want to burden you with the terrible things that have happened in this war."

"I am already as depressed as I can possibly be. So have a smoke and unload on me."

"Danke."

The old man reaches out for one of mine and once I have torched his fag he is set to let fly.

"My son's Waffen-SS unit was assigned to Minsk in August 1941. Himmler had put General Nebe in charge of mopping up operations after the advance of the Wehrmacht into Russia. One day Nebe was ordered to hold a mass shooting of one hundred local people—purely as a demonstration. But when Himmler vomited after he witnessed the shooting he told Nebe to come up with a better means of killing—something less distressing for the SS men. In the next few days Nebe experimented by killing mentally ill patients with explosives and later using automobile exhaust. My son said the idea came from Nebe's own experience, when one night after a party he drove home drunk and fell asleep with the car engine running in his garage, almost killing himself.

After testing the effectiveness of connecting the exhaust from a large truck they had backed up to a barn, Nebe and his technical experts took their proposal to Reinhard Heydrich who approved the exhaust gas method without a twitch."

"I think you're making this up."

"Nein! This is exactly as my son told me."

"Then you must be talking about someone other than Arthur Nebe, the head of Kripo."

"I am not."

"But Nebe is a good man — he always looked out for me!"

"Maybe he was good deep down."

"Why do you say — he was?"

"Because Nebe is dead."

"DEAD! How can this be?"

"You may not have heard of the foolhardy attempt on the Führer's life at the Wolfsschanze headquarters last year — on July 20 to be exact. A time bomb in a brief case left under a conference table killed four and injured 20. The Führer was shaken but his life was preserved. Back in Berlin Nebe was waiting, ready to lead his men to assassinate Himmler to complete the filthy business. But when he heard the Führer was alive he took flight, going into hiding on an island in the Wannsee. Since that day 7,000 suspected of involvement in the plot have been rounded up. 4,500 have been executed to date. As for Nebe, he was tracked down when his ex-girlfriend betrayed him. Two weeks ago — on the express orders of the Führer — he was hanged with piano wire suspended from a meat hook."

The old man leans forward and snuffs out his butt on the leg of his stool.

"You were right, Knop," I say.

"About what?"

"I did not need to hear of these terrible things."

"I could tell you more."

"Don't bother. It seems to me the Führer is a far worse person than I ever imagined he could possibly be."

"If I told you he had the cleric killed who helped him write his book, would you believe me?"

Knops eyes have turned to water. He has the doleful look of that Anglo beauty on a bike.

47

Schönberg–Dachau

April 9, 1945

ON the edge of a dark forest at Flossenbürg concentration camp six prisoners are woken early on a bitter morning. They are stripped naked and led in single file from a wooden hut to the execution yard. The six to be hanged are Admiral Wilhelm Canaris, General Hans Oster, General Karl Sack, Theodor Strünck, Ludwig Gehre and Dietrich Bonhoeffer.

A prison van leaves Flossenbürg camp a short time before the dawn execution. After a drive through rolling farmland edged by beech and spruce forest, the prison van reaches Schönberg before midday. Best, General von Falkenhausen and the Russian airman, Wassilli Kokorin, are separated from the others billeted in the Schönberg village school and ordered to board the prison van just arrived from Flossenbürg. After willing volunteers load his suitcase and his three boxes, a guard breaks the good news to Best their destination is not back to Flossenbürg. The prison van is heading 180 kilometres southwest to Dachau concentration camp—just 20 kms north of the centre of Munich.

Best is magnanimously sharing his last shreds of precious tobacco and fragments of cigarette paper with Wassilli Kokorin and General von Falkenhausen, when laughter erupts from a prisoner already inside the prison van.

"Pardon my mirth, but please try one of mine," offers the elegant woman holding out her red leather cigarette case.

"Well—thank you. I don't believe I have yet had the pleasure," Best reciprocates.

"I'm Vera von Schuschnigg and sitting over there is my husband, Dr. Kurt von Schuschnigg. He is nursing our daughter, Sissie."

"Your daughter?"

"Yes, Sissie was born in Sachsenhausen four years ago."

"Were you really at Sachsenhausen with an infant and I never knew or heard?"

"For six years we were locked away in a small hut separated from the hordes."

"Really. Von Schuschnigg? Now that name rings a bell," Best admits.

"Up until March 1938 my husband was Chancellor of Austria," says Vera.

"My apology for not recognising you. How have you ever endured this ordeal?" asks Best.

"Our life underwent a metamorphosis when Kurt was placed under house arrest in March 1938 due to his noble efforts to keep Austria independent of Nazi Germany. But Hitler and the National Socialists somehow got the upper hand. At least we were spared bloodshed in Austria, unlike France. We have been hoping to meet up with Léon Blum and his fiancée, Jeanne. Have you heard or seen anything of them, Mr. Best?"

"Are you referring to the first Jewish Prime Minister of France?" queries Best.

"I am Mr. Best. We had good information they were being held in Buchenwald."

"If they were there I am sure I would have noticed, though there is quite possibly more than one compound at Buchenwald for people such as us."

"Please excuse me Mr. Best. Looks like Sissie is waking," Vera replies, turning her attention to her daughter and her husband.

Best switches his attention to the three men in uniform sitting almost opposite. The man with the hardened face and crew-cut instigates the conversation.

"Halder—General Halder."

"I am pleased to meet you General. Best is my name, Captain Best. I'm British."

"I know who you are, Best. You don't need to elaborate. I saw your handsome mug shot on the front page alongside that Elser fellow over five years ago."

"The suggestion I aided Elser is false of course," protests Best.

"I won't admit to that either."

"But will you admit to why you are inside this prison van bound for Dachau?"

"I don't mind telling you something of my spats with Hitler. Though I planned the invasions of Czechoslovakia and Poland he consistently ignored my advice on strategic matters. I warned him Stalin had 1.5 million men ready to pour into Stalingrad. Instead he listened to his lapdog Keitel with devastating results. I quit my post as Chief of Staff in protest. Almost two years later the Gestapo knocked on my door and slung me into prison. Some reward for all my years of hard work and effort!"

"I presume you were also mixed up in the July 20 Plot."

"Like hell I was! Have you spoken to Field Marshall Brauchitsch?"

"No—not yet."

"Good. He would probably tell you we planned to dispose of Hitler on November 5, 1939, just three days shy of your mate's bomb going off in the Bürgerbräukeller."

"As I said before, Elser was not a mate of mine."

"I understand. Stick to your guns! Don't let those Gestapo bastards get the upper hand! Did you ever run into that Müller fellow with weird eyes in Berlin?"

"I did have the displeasure, General, but what is this I hear about your assassination plan in November 1939?"

"Hitler had fixed X-day as November 12, 1939, for the invasion of France. Brauchitsch and I thought this crazy. For a week or more I took a loaded gun in my pocket planning to shoot him but I never had the courage or the opportunity—one or the other. Then in our meeting with Hitler on November 5, Brauchitsch begged him to put off X-day, saying morale in the Wehrmacht was worse than it was in 1918. There was icy silence before Hitler flew into a rage. He accused the General Staff, Brauchitsch and me of disloyalty, cowardice, sabotage and defeatism. He vowed to destroy us! I returned to headquarters at Zossen shaken to the core, a total nervous wreck. We told Karl Goerdeler we wanted to abort the coup attempt we had planned with him. As things turned out it was not the end of the world. Hitler deferred X-Day due to the heavy snowstorms on November 7. From then on it was one delay after the other before we invaded."

"You mentioned Karl Goerdeler. I recall he was a Finance Minister under Hitler."

"He was briefly—as well as being the mayor of Leipzig. Goerdeler was in the running to be Chancellor in 1932, but lost out to Franz von Papan. He was an autocrat by nature and took everything terribly seriously, even refusing to pull down the statue of Felix Mendelssohn, the Jewish composer, in Leipzig—but my young colleague here, Colonel von Bonin, can divulge more about Goerdeler," suggests Halder. "Wake up Bonin!" he snaps, giving the man slumped beside him an elbow in the ribs.

"Huh! I don't know much more about Goerdeler. I know he resigned as mayor of Leipzig in 1937 and had an offer to work for the industrialist Krupp, but Hitler stood in his way. Instead Goerdeler joined the Bosch Company and travelled around Europe as their representative. Who knows what deals he did in Britain, France and Sweden? He said the Munich Agreement only encouraged Hitler to think the English would not resist him."

"You can add," interjects Halder, "Goerdeler contacted Brauchitsch and told him if we attacked Poland the result would not be the limited war Hitler expected, but a world war pitting us against Britain and France. Goerdeler insisted a putsch was the only way to save Germany. But Brauchitsch was not interested and told Goerdeler to get stuffed as he shared Hitler's belief we could invade Poland without risking a world war."

"How did Goerdeler react to that?" asks Best.

"He remained as zealous as ever—perhaps because he hated the guts of Ribbentrop. After the drama of November 5, I met with Goerdeler and gave him five good reasons to drop his putsch ideas. But he persisted in holding secret meetings, drafting peace terms, conferring with men like

Bonhoeffer, Beck, Hassel, Popitz, Oster and others, while writing fervent letters to anyone he thought he could convert to his dangerous way of thinking."

Halder pauses to look into the palms of his trembling hands before he continues.

"When Goerdeler came at me again in April 1940 I told him straight to his face — my oath to Hitler and my belief in Germany's inevitable victory precluded me from acting against the Führer. I ended by saying bluntly — 'It was Britain and France who declared war on us! We have to see it through'!"

"I expect you regret saying that now," murmurs Best.

Halder's lips move, but no words come out.

"I recall," von Bonin resumes, "when Goerdeler failed to drum up enough support for staging his putsch he had the wild idea of meeting Hitler face to face to explain why his leadership is defective. Goerdeler hoped Hitler would see the light, resign and appoint him as his successor. He was lucky to have a few friends left to talk him out of this idiotic plan!"

"I presume Goerdeler was involved in the July 20 Plot?" probes Best.

"He was — he was sweating on becoming Chancellor," asserts Halder.

"So what became of him?"

"Dead of course. Hung at Plötzensee Prison two months ago after five months of interrogation and torture."

"Another good man cut down in his prime," sighs Best. "And what was your crime, Colonel?"

"My misdeeds are more recent. As Chief of the Operational Branch of the Army General Staff, I gave permission for a retreat from Warsaw in January, ignoring a command from Hitler."

"Good for you!"

Best then turns to meet the eye of the man sitting on the otherside of Halder.

"Don't expect to get anything out of me, Best. With my rational, yet radical Hunger Plan for Russia I'm a far more duplicitous character that either of these two men," admits General Georg Thomas.

48

9-11pm, April 9, 1945
Dachau

ANOTHER mind crippling day comes and goes. I smoke a packet while hoping Lechner will come so I can play him a tune. He loves to see me weep when I sing. But I know my time is running short from what I have heard.

Knop is sleeping like a good sentry on his stool by the door. Without disturbing the old man I rise from my bunk. I go to my workbench to take a chisel from my leather pouch. The madmen in high places have now gone to ground, sucking the Fatherland dry, hammering in the last nail—intent on total devastation. No wonder oil is hard to come by, I muse as I spit onto the oilstone and make a figure of eight with the chisel blade. This act only reminds me once again that the eighth day of the month is the day of my fatal miscalculation. But from what Knop has told me I am not the only imbecile who can foul up exploding a fucking time bomb!

With this thought grinding inside my mind I continue to sharpen every chisel in my deadly collection. When I have finished they will be sharp enough to shave the shame from my soul. Once I pack away my tools I return to my bunk to go through my regular ritual at this hour of my infernal existence. I pull off my right shoe and withdraw the folded photograph I have concealed inside the sole since my time in Berlin. The edges are now wearing thin and what is preserved under my foot is surely on its last legs. The hand written message on the back is now an illegible inky smear, though the image of my greatest love is not yet obliterated.

Is there anything to forgive?

Nay. There is nothing to forgive. I know the things she wrote were not her words. They were the words of someone else. They were words dictated to her by the dictator himself—unless some other prick was in on the act. Whatever is the case my love for Elsa can never be erased. Though I know the time is near when I need to say—Auf Wiedersehen.

I lay her image down on my bed—as if to make love again—and reach for my zither. With the instrument resting on my overworked knees I begin to play. I have only played two or three bars when I hear the familiar clang of the steel grille door in the passageway. I continue to play even though I hear jackboots stopping outside my door. When the door is unlatched and opens wide I see Lechner has not come tonight. Instead head warder SS officer Stiller is standing outside, looking dead eyed.

I stop playing in the middle of the phrase and lay my zither by my side. I begin to remove the plectrum from my thumb—but decide to let it be. After one last glimpse I return my keepsake to the sole of my laceless shoe and stand to show I am ready to do what must be done. The killer of two waitresses and countless other innocent vicitims cannot delay his execution.

Stiller comes inside without waking the old man on his stool. He tells me to put on my coat. Once he has the handcuffs pinching my wrists we take the long walk along the length of the passageway, our footsteps echoing until we reach the farthest door. When we pass out into the cold night air the sky is inky black, yet no enemy plane will disrupt what must be done tonight. We walk without speaking. There is no time to talk. There is no turning back. We crunch across the gravelly expanse of the roll call square and go up the side alley passing the ends of eighteen wooden huts. After the huts of misery we pass through a gate in the electrified fence. On the other side stands a brick building with a tall brick chimney and a pungent smell. But before we reach the edifice of the Final Solution we slow our pace and come to a stop in the dark yard. Stiller pushes me forward. A man steps out of the shadows. He could be the Prince of Darkness for all I know, though I see he has a gun in his hand.

"Get down on your knees," he groans.

I do as I am told.

All I have left to do is what my mother taught me.

Our Father in heaven
Hallowed be thy name
Thy kingdom come
Thy will be done on earth as in heaven
Give us today our daily bread
Forgive us our trespasses
As we forgive our debtors
Lead us not into temptation
Deliver us from____

END

49   April 9-May 2, 1945
Dachau-The Alps

WELL after dark a prison van arrives at Dachau concentration camp. The VIP prisoners aboard are immediately unloaded, but they must wait several hours in the cold of the reception hall for some arcane reason. Amongst those waiting is the prisoner Hjalmar Schacht, once President of the Reichsbank and Minister of Economics during the rise of the Third Reich.

    As the weary prisoners stand about wondering when and how the Nazi nightmare will end, Schacht and the English prisoner, Best, engage in conversation. The German is expounding his forthright views on how to resurrect the post-war economy of Germany, as the dead body of Georg Elser is being stretchered into the crematorium. And shortly after the same fully clothed body is fed into an oven the camp commandant, Eduard Weiter, waddles into the reception hall to welcome the new arrivals.

    "Sorry distinguished people to keep you waiting out in the cold, but camp accommodation is in short supply. Nevertheless we now have room for you. I hope you find everything to your satisfaction."

The new arrivals are accommodated in individual cells within the camp prison building that stretches almost fence to fence on the south side of the concentration camp. Best is sick with dysentery for a week but recovers in time for his 60th birthday on April 14. SS officer Edgar Stiller, the man in charge of the prisoners in 'special protective custody' at Dachau, brings bottles of wine to help Best celebrate. The party lasts for two days, with Best's VIP friends consuming a cask of beer ransacked from the camp canteen. To add to the celebration a zither-playing guard, a friend of the warder Franz Lechner, contributes to a musical evening for the Englishman. Later on the same night, in secret and against strict orders, warder Lechner, brings Richard Stevens to Best's cell for a brief reunion.

Three days later, in the middle of an Allied air raid, Best, Stevens and other VIP prisoners leave Dachau in a convoy of buses and trucks. They are escorted by Stiller with a strong force of SS guards. After passing through Munich, now a devastated city from three years of Allied aerial bombing, the convoy heads south to the Alps. Other convoys leave Dachau on other nights to rendezvous near Innsbruck, swelling to 133 the number of Austrian, Hungarian, Russian, French, Lettish, Danish, Norwegian, Swedish, Polish, Czechoslovak, Greek, British, Yugoslav, Italian, Swiss, Dutch and German VIP nationals fleeing from the Third Reich.

Even when billeted in the idyllic mountain-lake setting of the Hotel Pragser Wildsee in South Tyrol, the lives of the VIP prisoners are still in peril as their SS guards have specific orders. And if press reports are to be believed, such as the one that appeared in the *New York Times* on May 8, 1945, Best did all he could to keep his promise to Margot Heberlein.

DOBBIACA, Italy, May 7 (AP)---One hundred thirty-three political hostages of the Germans---many of them internationally known---have been freed by American soldiers. The captives had narrowly escaped execution by the Gestapo and the Elite Guards ordered to kill them rather than permit their liberation. Like voices from the dead, such men as Léon Blum, one time Premier of France; Dr. Kurt Schuschnigg, the Austrian Chancellor who opposed Germany's grab of his country, and the Rev. Martin Niemoeller, who defied Adolf Hitler, told today the story of their escape.

They and the others, including Hjalmar Schacht, former head of the Reichsbank, and Alexei Kokosin, a nephew of Foreign Minister Vyascheslaff M. Molotov of Russia, were rescued from a resort hotel eight miles southwest of this highway town, less than fifteen miles west of the Austrian border. Troops of the American Eighty Fifth Infantry Division of the Ninth Army took the hotel and rounded up the garrison of 150 German soldiers. All the hostages were in surprising good condition.

Briton Saves Group
Credit for saving the group from death was given to Sigismund Payne Best, a Briton whom the Germans seized as a spy in 1939 in a foray into the then neutral Netherlands, and Gen. Georg Thomas, a former German commander, arrested when he advised Hitler against invading Poland. Mr. Best saw an official order directing the Elite Guards and the Gestapo agents wipe out the hostages if the Allies threaten to free them. He told Gen. Thomas, who got permission to see the German commander in this sector. Through him a company of regular German soldiers was dispatched to protect the group. Mr. Best, in a magnificent bluff, notified the Gestapo leader that he was taking command under the German Army and, to his surprise, the scheme worked. The Gestapo and Elite Guards left, then the hostages had only to sit and wait for the Americans. Until five days ago they were all in Dauchau."(sic)

US forces reach Dachau concentration camp on April 27. In the railway siding near the camp they find 39 boxcars filled with bodies, all in an advanced state of decomposition. Moving deeper into the camp more bodies are found—naked or barely clothed, piled in heaps. The stench of death is overpowering. By early May over 60,000 emaciated prisoners in the Dachau main camp and the sub camps, including the 7,000 who were ordered to evacuate on a 'death march', are liberated.

In the distant north other human dramas are being enacted. A remnant of Sinti and Roma people are transported from the extermination camp of Auschwitz-Birkenau to Sachsenhausen, while 15,000 Scandinavian prisoners are bused to safety in a humanitarian mission instigated by a Swedish count and agreed to by Himmler. In April 33,000 prisoners are marched out of Sachsenhausen towards the Baltic prior to liberation by Polish and Soviet forces. Camp commandant, Anton Kaindl, will later testify at a war crimes trial many prisoners on the march would have starved to death as there was no food to feed them, therefore they had to be shot.

Also in the north in a candle lit room of the Danziger Hof Hotel, Lübeck, Major General Walter Schellenberg hovered at the shoulder of

Heinrich Himmler as he penned a declaration of German capitulation to be sent via the Swedish Government to General Eisenhower.

The Allies reject Himmler's belated offer with contempt. The Führer, bunkered down in Berlin hears of Himmler's unilateral action on the BBC, sending him insane with rage. Being betrayed by his close friend, architect Albert Speer — in not carrying out his narcissistic and vindictive order to totally destroy whatever remains of the Fatherland — is one thing — but hearing the treachery of his most faithful sycophant is the END.

On May 2 Berlin radio station broadcasts the last lie of the Nazi regime:

The Führer met his end in his command post in the Reich Chancellery fighting to his last breath against Bolshevism.

50   May 5, 1945
Naples-Isle of Capri

BEST'S war ends in Italy. After a nightmarish road trip through the Dolomites to Verona, he is flown to Naples. He is not the healthiest man alive when he arrives, having lost a lot of weight, though he was always as skinny as a rake.

    In Naples, Best comes into the care of the US Army GHQ and in particular into the care of Senior Commander Olive Grant. With Best's red Ford Lincoln Zephyr now in all probability a burnt out chassis on the side of a distant autobahn, Olive, with her glossy red lipstick, gleaming white teeth, curvaceous body, could be misconstrued as the replacement model—and the very latest off the showroom floor.

When Best and Olive board a motor launch to cross the Bay of Naples, the purpose of the trip is not for pleasure or for romantic interlude. Best boards solely to visit his good friends, the VIP former prisoners now convalescing in relative luxury on the Isle of Capri.

After doing whatever he can to assist his fellow survivors, Best's next assignment is to return home to England. There he will need to pick up the pieces with his Dutch wife May, now living in Devon. This might be his toughest assignment yet. But before crossing that bridge Best has one last scene to play.

A new moon is rising over the Mediterranean. Olive has abandoned her hair to the cleansing sea breeze as she lingers on a balcony of the Hotel Eden Paradiso at Anacapri. Best has spent the better part of the day soaking in a hot soapy bath before he shaved and slipped into a velvet bathrobe. He now sits in a soft armchair nursing a singed Nazi kitbag on his lap.

Like a new age Venus de Milo, Olive comes in from the balcony in flowing chiffon. Still holding her glass of Marsala she pokes her head over his shoulder.

"What are you doing, Honey?" she asks.

"Trying to undo this damn knot."

"Need my manicure clippers?"

"I do indeed."

"What's inside?"

"Who knows? A disaffected SS man in South Tyrol gave me this kitbag the day before your lot came on the scene. He said he rescued the contents from a bonfire at Dachau. No doubt the fellow is hoping I will like what I find inside and put in a good word for him when the war trials begin."

Once the knot is snipped, Best spills the contents onto the terracotta tiles like a paper avalanche. He goes down on his hands and knees to sort through the pile. Everything appears to be only routine Nazi orders until he comes across something different—a brown envelope with a curious handwritten instruction:

May be opened only by SS Unstuffy. Edgar Stiller or by seeking a person commissioned by him. Must Be Destroyed unopened in case of Unstuffy. Stiller's death.

Best returns to the armchair to extract the contents from the envelope. With his monocle in place he studies the two-page document. His bony hands begin to quiver as he reads:

THE CHIEF OF THE SECURITY POLICE AND THE SD
Berlin SW 11, Print-Albrecht-Str.   Date: 5 April 1945

Express Letter

To the Commandant of the KL. Dachau
SS-Obersturmbannfuhrer Weiter.   Personal!
[in pencil]

On the orders of the R[eichs] F[ührer] SS and after obtaining the decision of the highest authority the prisoners scheduled below are to be admitted to the KL. Dachau immediately.

The former General Halder,
 "   "   General Thomas,
Hjalmar Schacht,
Schuschnigg with wife and child,
The former General v. Falkenhausen,
The Englishman Best [Wolf],
Molotov's Nephew Kokorin,
The Colonel, General Staff. V. Bonin.

As I know that you only have at your disposal very limited space in the Cell Building I beg you, after examination to put these prisoners together. Please, however, take steps so that the prisoner Schuschnigg, who bears the pseudonym Oyster under which name kindly have him registered, is allotted a larger living cell. The wife has shared his imprisonment of her own free will and is therefore not 'prisoner-in-protective-custody'. I request that she may be allowed the same freedom as she has hitherto enjoyed. The RF-SS directs that Halder, Thomas, Schacht, Schuschnigg, and v. Falkenhausen are to be well treated. I beg you on all accounts to ensure that the prisoner Best [pseudonym Wolf] does not make contact with the Englishman Stevens who is already there. v. Bonin was employed at the Fuhrer's Head Quarters and is now in a kind of honorable detention. He is still a Colonel on the Active List and will presumably retain this status. I beg you therefore to treat him particularly well.

The question of our prisoner in special protective custody, 'Eller', has also again been discussed at highest level. The following directions have been issued: On the occasion of one of the next Terror Attacks on Munich, or, as the case may be, the neighborhood of Dachau, it shall be pretended that 'Eller' suffered fatal injuries. I request you therefore, when such an occasion arises to liquidate 'Eller' as discreetly as possible. Please take steps that only a few people, who must be specially pledged to silence, hear about this. The notification to me regarding the execution of this order shall be something like:

'On .... caused by a Terror Attack on .... the prisoner in protective custody 'Eller' was fatally wounded.'

After noting the contents and carrying out the orders contained in it destroy this letter.

Signature: ????

"Look at this!" Best quakes with excitement.

"Steady, Hun."

"This document is nothing less than the execution order for a prisoner at Dachau. They refer to the prisoner as 'Eller' but I know this is the code name for Elser. They refer to a 'Terror Attack'. This just means an Allied air raid. They wanted to call me 'Wolf'. I would not have a bar of it, but as you will notice on this order, they succeeded. Getting back to Elser, though the signature on the order is conveniently illegible, this document is *his* execution order. This order has come from the highest authority. This is the official order to liquidate a man—a man I barely knew. I only ever saw him once. He was only a little fellow—a zither playing cabinetmaker—who almost succeeded where many others had failed___"

"Why are you crying, Honey?"

"After the insanity of this war how else can I react?"

Footnote: While Best found the signature on the Express Letter illegible, in 1950 Anna Schmid recognized the signature to be that of Heinrich Müller. Anna was his secretary and longtime friend.

Destruction at the Bürgerbräukeller. Source: Bundesarchiv, Bild 183-E12329 / CC-BY-SA 3.0

Afterword

THE war Elser wanted to avoid cost 50-60 million lives worldwide. No one could have predicted the horror, misery, genocide and terror the Nazis would inflict by the time the Third Reich had passed into history. Not even Elser.

As a controversial figure Georg Elser ranks with Guy Fawkes of the 1605 Gunpowder Plot. But unlike Fawkes he was a lone wolf assassin, without fellow conspirators — as far we know. Out of the three leaders he targeted only Hitler and Goebbels were present at the Bürgerbräukeller on November 8 1939, while Göring was absent. Whether Elser would have stopped the war if his plot succeeded we will never know. All we know is his bombing of the Bürgerbräukeller was a propaganda windfall for the Nazis.

On the train after leaving Munich for Berlin, Goebbels recorded in his diary their escape appeared to be 'miraculous' and the fact the Führer had started and finished his speech half an hour early was the reason for their escape. Goebbels concluded that the Führer was 'still under the protection of the Almighty' and he 'will only die once his mission is fulfilled'.

While Goebbels was counting Nazi blessings, Hitler jumped to the conclusion Otto Strasser in collusion with the British was the culprit. Nevertheless other rumours of who was responsible spread like wide fire. Even Göring, due to his absence from the rally, was not ruled out as a possible perpetrator in the public mind. The press, under the control of Goebbels and his Ministry of Public Enlightenment and Propaganda, soon established Elser as being in the employment of Otto Strasser and the British Secret Service. This official Nazi version, together with other theories mentioned below, blotted the character of Georg Elser for many years.

A British leaflet dropped from the air on Germany in December 1939 and January 1940 to rebut British involvement, caricatured Georg Elser as being a pawn of the Nazis like Marinus van der Lubbe — the Dutchman executed for starting the Reichstag fire in 1933. Martin Niemöller also promoted the idea Elser was in the service of the Nazis in a speech to the Protestant Student Congregation in Göttingen in January 1946. Isa Vermehren, repeated rumours Elser had been lured by the Nazis with a bribe 40,000 marks to plant his bomb in a pillar in the Bürgerbräukeller in her 1946 book titled, *Journey through the Last Act*. In the *Sunday Times* of December 15 1946, responsibility for the Munich bombing was sheeted home to a secret anti-Nazi organization called Union Time Ltd. founded in London by people from British business and the press. In December 1949 Alfred Loritz, a member of Bavarian WAV party, claimed he was responsible for the bombing, while Elser was only a courier. According to the Austrian journalist and historian, Günter Peis, Wilhelm Schneider from Bamberg, a former member of the Polish underground movement, stated under oath the bombing was planned and carried out by his organization in collaboration with the SPD in exile in London and with British authorities. Walter Usslepp, who until the spring of 1944 was one of Elser's guards in Sachsenhausen concentration camp, came out with his story: *Finally the truth about the attempt to assassinate Hitler in Munich Bürgerbräukeller,* published in the weekly German magazine *Home and World* in 1956. Usslepp supported the theory that the Nazis had staged the Bürgerbräukeller assassination attempt and Elser was a member of the SS. In May 1964, in the magazine *Stern* under the three-part article titled, *The Assassin,* it was claimed Elser was a member of a Communist group lead by Karl Kuch a Swiss citizen, originally from Königsbronn. In another twist Georg Vollmer, owner of Königsbronn quarry, suspected Elser was caught in his work at the Bürgerbräukeller and Heinrich Himmler and Reinhard Heydrich forced him to continue, as they wanted to kill Rudolf Hess. Dutchman, Henri A. Bulhof, linked Payne Best with Otto Strasser and Elser in a book titled *Sigismund Payne Best-lead actor in Venlo Incident,* published posthumously in 2010. Relying on the diaries of Best and his wife May, Bulof claimed the three had met in the lounge of the hotel Baur au Lac in Zurich to plan the assassination attempt, where Elser received 4,000 RM as a down payment.

Regarding all of these theories Manfred Maier from the *Georg-Elser-Arbeitskreis-Heidenheim* has concluded:

Written sources and statements of witnesses lead to only one conclusion: Georg Elser was a lone operator but should one day evidence of backers for Elser show up unexpectedly, we will be the first to acknowledge he was a failed resistance fighter.

Not so long ago, I had not heard of Georg Elser. He only came across him reading *The Venlo Incident* by Captain Sigismund Payne Best. And it was only through the biography of Dietrich Bonhoeffer by Eric Metaxas, published in 2011, that I became aware of the Venlo Incident. Not only does Best's book provide a unique record of the last weeks and days of Bonhoeffer's life, it provides an intriguing account of his encounter with

Georg Elser while both were imprisoned in the Bunker at Sachsenhausen concentration camp.

Best portrays Elser as a hapless man caught up in the web of a bizarre Nazi plot. The notion Elser acted alone in his assassination attempt seemed improbable. How could anyone spend so many nights inside the Bürgerbräukeller without being detected? And how could anyone have the willpower? These were my initial thoughts, but in time I came to accept the view Elser had acted alone and was motivated by his own convictions.

Peter Koblank reminded me it was due in part to Best's misleading portrayal of Elser in *The Venlo Incident* that he remained discredited as the sole perpetrator of the Bürgerbräukeller bombing for many years. The discovery in 1964 of Elser's 1939 Berlin interrogation report in the German government archives in Koblenz began Elser's rehabilitation. When analysed by researchers such as Anton Hoch a more reliable truth was revealed. After the 1984 exhibition titled, *Resistance Against National Socialism,* Elser was included in the Gedenkstätte Deutscher Widerstand [German Resistance Memorial Center] in Berlin. Further recognition followed in 1995 when Peter Steinbach and Johannes Tuchel organized a special exhibition in Berlin titled: *I wanted to prevent the war.* The following year the Georg Elser Memorial was opened in Königsbronn, taking over the Berlin special exhibition and supplementing it with other historical material. Since then a Georg Elser postage stamp was issued in 2003, while many streets and places have been named in his honour and memorials erected in Königsbronn, Munich and Berlin.

However, to my mind there still remains an intriguing mystery. Did Best receive secret messages from Elser while in Sachsenhausen as Best claimed in his book *The Venlo Incident*? Koblank believes Best received no secret messages from Elser and that Best fabricated everything. He says his view is supported by Best having no material evidence of secret messages transmitted on tiny pieces of paper upon his return in 1945 to England, though he kept many other private documents, including his diaries from five years of imprisonment. While this is a strong argument I have gone out on a limb and taken a kinder view of Best. I find it hard to believe he would deliberately fabricate the secret message narrative, even to improve the sales of his book. Why would he risk being found out? But more to the point, why was Best's depiction of Elser's life in *The Venlo Incident* so outrageously erroneous from start to finish? And as an intelligence officer, presumably interested in factual information, how could Best get things so wrong?

Best's fictional biography is the same story Elser invents for Dr. Max in Chapter 34 of this book. Take for example the first sentence:

I was born in Munich and when I was quite small my mother died while giving birth to my dead sister.

In this statement there is not one word of truth, and reads like the birth of a character in a Charles Dickens' novel. Elser was not born in Munich. His mother did not die until 1960, and certainly not in childbirth. I doubt Best would have concocted this fanciful story from his own imagination. So where did the story originate? One explanation would be Best was repeating hearsay and did not bother to check one single fact before his book was published in 1950. I find this equally hard to believe, as Best had visited Germany often prior to the war and possibly had post-war contacts, while Elser's mother, three sisters and his brother were all still alive in 1950.

I am suggesting *only* Elser was capable of inventing his fictional biography that paralleled his life, while satirizing aspects such as: his contact with Communists, his brush with employers, working for BMW rather than for Dornier, his skill as a cabinetmaker, and finally his painstaking work in designing, manufacturing and installing his time bomb in the Bürgerbräukeller. Perhaps significantly, there is not one mention of musical ability in Best's account of Elser's life except for:

___having been given suitable wood he set to work and made himself a zither; he could not play it but it had always been his ambition to learn.

I contend this is Elser being self-mocking. I suspect he had a sardonic sense of humour that equipped him well to play a mischievous joke on Best by sending him misleading messages. Would Best have had any reason to suspect Elser's messages were not the truth? Best showed his gullibility in being deceived by Schellenberg, while Elser would be keen for amusement to break the boredom of his isolation, particularly if that involved disobeying his archenemy, Himmler. To add to my case, Eugen Rau, Elser's old school friend, when interviewed by members of the *Georg-Elser-Arbeitskreis-Heidenheim* in 1989 remarked: 'Georg could be very funny.'

And it appears Best was not the only victim of Elser's fun. In a letter from Martin Niemöller to Elser's mother in 1945, Niemöller states Elser told him in Dachau his 'wife' had read his book, *From U-boat to the Pulpit*. While it is strange Elser referred to his 'wife', as he had not married Elsa

Härlen, I suggest telling Niemöller that his 'wife' had read his book was Elser's way of being funny. There is irony here also as the book *From U-boat to the Pulpit* was praised in the Nazi controlled press in 1933 due to its patriotic ideas, as Niemöller at that time was pro-Hitler and shared with the Nazis a dislike for the Communists and for the Republic of Weimar.

Turning to Otto Strasser: he is the silent victim in this saga. Hitler would have good reason to accuse him of being the 'organiser' of the plot against him. In his book *Flight from Terror*, Strasser admits to his involvement in at least two assassination attempts on Hitler prior to November 1939. But regarding the Munich bombing Strasser denied all knowledge and responsibility. His response is included in the Appendix.

The kidnapping of Best and Stevens and the shooting of Dirk Klop gave Hitler his excuse to invade The Netherlands and Belgium, while the incident was an embarrassment for the British government and deterred any support of the German Opposition for the duration of the war.

Three weeks after the Venlo incident the British Foreign Secretary, Lord Halifax, still believed the SIS agents had made 'a genuine contact' with the German Opposition. Since then historians have debunked this as wishful thinking. However, Dutch historian Bob de Graaff has found contrary evidence, citing the recent discovery of an investigation carried out in January 1940 by Dutch national police detective W.C.J. Wooning into the criminal activities of Dr. Franz Fischer. It appears Fischer was entangled with a 41-year old Dutch woman named Rita Schuilenburg in the attempted transfer of money out of Germany and possibly in cocaine smuggling. Wooning found in Rita's possession letters between Fischer and other persons including Best, with one letter to Fischer being from German General Deichmann. These letters contain content and language that strongly suggests Fischer was in fact in contact with the German Opposition. [Graaff also notes the name 'Teichmann' in Cadogan's reports is a misspelling and should be 'Deichmann'.] Graaff's thesis is backed up by mention of General von Weitersheim in *The Venlo Incident*, and also in the memoirs of Field Marshall Wilhelm Keitel where there occurs a remark on Weitersheim's conflict with Hitler:

Early in August 1939 [Hitler] conceived the idea of addressing his ideas to the various army chiefs of staff by themselves, in other words without their Commander-in-Chief, at the Berghof. From the shadows I was probably in the best position to study its effect and I realized that he had failed to achieve his object: for while General von Wietersheim [chief of staff of the Second Army Group] was the only one to find his tongue enough to show by his questions how little he agreed with what Hitler had outlined, this in itself probably crystallized in Hitler's mind the suspicion that he was confronted with an iron phalanx of men who inwardly refused to be swayed by any speech they thought was just a propaganda speech.

In attempting to reconstruct the past, a portion of what I have written is speculation. For instance, Elser's chance encounter with Unity Mitford, and his visit to the 'honour temples' in Königsplatz, Munich. Elsa Härlen's letter to Elser is also my invention, though there are reports Elser had a photograph of her while he was in Sachsenhausen. Elsa's interrogation in Berlin by Himmler seems certain, though whether she met with Hitler in person is unclear. There is also the question of Elser's visit to the camp brothel at Sachsenhausen, though according to Best in *The Venlo Incident*, Elser was allowed visits twice a week.

On another matter Walter Schellenberg claimed in his memoir he attended the October 20 meeting with Best and Stevens and that he drove his own car to Zutphen and Arnhem. While his account is plausible, I stayed with Best's version that Schellenberg made his first contact with Best and Stevens at the meeting held in The Hague on October 30.

Peter Koblank has raised a grey area concerning Heinrich Himmler. He doubts that Himmler would have personally attacked Elser as this act would be 'out of character'. Nevertheless I have adopted the view of Hellmut G. Haasis who cites the evidence of an eyewitness, a Dr. Böhme, in his book, *Bombing Hitler: The Story of the Man who almost Assassinated the Führer*, even though Koblank considers Dr. Böhme to be an unreliable witness.

While the conversations are invented, content is often taken from other sources. For instance Best's talk with Schellenberg in Sachsenhasen uses content found in Schellenberg's memoir and his talk with Dietrich Bonhoeffer makes use of Bonhoeffer quotations. There is no evidence the protagonists patronized the Ratskeller, Hotel Kurhaus, Alter Simpl, Café de Korenbeurs, Den Bremer, Hotel American, and the Hemingway bar in Venlo, though all these establishments existed in 1939, and still exist to this day. Also I admit to a twisting of the truth in my romanticised ending as Best had read Elser's liquidation order long before he stepped onto the Isle of Capri with his American escort Olive Grant.

Peter Koblank has also called into question the *New York Times* report on Best's role in the liberation of the VIP prisoners in South Tyrol in 1945, as the article makes little mention of the significant part played by the Wehrmacht as outlined in *The Secret Surrender* by Allen W. Dulles. For this reason an extract has been included in the Appendix.

To end my meandering I return to Elser and ask: did he act morally? During the Berlin interrogation Elser inferred his act was not against Protestant doctrine. Martin Luther had little if any sympathy for the peasants in their fight against feudalism in the German Peasants' Wars of 1524-1526 and maintained the duty of a Christian is to 'suffer injustice, not to seize the sword and take to violence.' However, the Augsburg Confession of 1530, that became the primary confessional document for the Lutheran movement, did leave the door slightly ajar for unspecified acts against civil authority:

Accordingly Christians are obliged to be subject to civil authority and obey its commands and laws in all that can be done without sin. But when commands of the civil authority cannot be obeyed without sin, we must obey God rather than men (Acts 5:29) [from Article XVI]

In 1415, before the Reformation, the Council of Constance [Konstanz] considered a proposition in support of tyrannicide that read:

Any vassal or subject can lawfully and meritoriously kill, and ought to kill, any tyrant. He may even, for this purpose, avail himself of ambushes, and wily expressions of affection or of adulation, notwithstanding any oath or pact imposed upon him by the tyrant, and without waiting for the sentence or order of any judge." (Session XV)

This proposition, which would have given comfort and confirmation to Elser, was declared heretical and rejected. But leaping forward into the 20th century, Karl Barth gives a measure of support to Elser's action. The Swiss Protestant theologian, who was well acquainted with Dietrich Bonhoeffer's agonizing over the question of tyrannicide for some years, asked rhetorically in *Church Dogmatics III*:

____may not someone from the lower ranks of the political hierarchy, or even from outside it, take up the obviously abandoned cause of the state on his own responsibility for the salvation of the whole, and, since all other ways are barred, proceed at the risk of his own life to the elimination, i.e., the killing of this publicly dangerous person?

Elser's action may have become an obsession, as he told Franz Lechner in Dachau in 1945. Yet his decision to act was a choice between two evils, as revealed by his statement in Berlin during his interrogation:

I wanted to prevent even greater bloodshed through my deed.

Appendix

Notes on the cast

Georg Elser [Johann Georg Elser] The most recent memorial to Elser was unveiled in 2011: a 17-metre high steel sculpture in Wilhelmstrasse, Berlin, by German playwright Rolf Hochhuth.

In 2015 a feature film directed by Oliver Hirschbiegel was released in Germany titled: ELSER. The English version of the film was titled: 13 Minutes

Maria Schmauder was sent to work as a maid in the house of a prison warder on the orders of Heinrich Müller. Her father was subjected to lengthy interrogation due to Elser's evidence he listened to foreign radio stations in his home.

The Baumanns—fate unknown. The apartment building in Blumenstrasse no longer exists.

Alfons and Rosa Lehmann were interrogated but not charged with any offence. Their apartment building still exists in Türkenstrasse.

Jan Lemmens, Best's driver, was imprisoned in the Bunker at Sachsenhausen, but was released and returned home in October 1940. He was active in the Resistance to the German occupation in Holland.

Sigismund Payne Best returned to England in 1945. With the permission from the head of SIS ('C'), he published his memoirs in 1950 under the title *The Venlo Incident*. His book was a bestseller but his marriage to May ended in 1953. After the separation Best married his third wife Bridget. Best died in 1978 at the age of 93 in Calne, Wiltshire, England.

Richard Henry Stevens left the British Army as a Lieutenant Colonel having been promoted to that rank during his captivity in Germany. He worked as a translator at NATO in Paris and London between 1951 and 1952. He died of cancer in 1967 aged 74.

Gerda is a fictitious character.

Berta - fate unknown, though she survived the Bürgerbräukeller bomb.

Jörg Brög was interrogated by the Gestapo but was not charged with any offence. The building in which he had his workshop still exists as does the tavern Alter Simpl next door.

Georg Ludwig Elser, Georg's father, died in 1942.

Maria Elser, Georg's mother, when interviewed in 1950 continued to lay blame on others saying: 'I don't think my son would come up with anything like that on his own'. In March 1946, having received no news of her son since 1939, she wrote to Pastor Martin Niemöller: 'I have read in a newspaper that you were with my son in Dachau. I would be very grateful if you could write me just a little something about him.' Niemöller replied a month later that her son was very well treated, had disappeared at Dachau and must now be dead. In the same letter he added that he had spoken once with Elser in Dachau, who told him his 'wife' had read his book, *From U-boat to the Pulpit*. Maria Elser died in 1960 aged 80.

Leo Dannecker - fate unknown.

Maria Hirth, Georg Elser's sister, was considered an accomplice to Georg and spent one year in prison.

Karl Hirth, Georg Elser's brother-in-law was imprisoned for one year, being regarded as an accomplice of Elser.

Franz Hirth was sent to an orphanage while his parents were imprisoned.

Leonhard Elser, Georg Elser's younger brother died in 2004.

Mathilde Niedermann was interrogated over several nights by the Gestapo in 1939. She maintained that Elser was 'completely uninterested in politics'. Niedermann, the mother of Elser's son Manfred, married Hans Bühl, also a member of the Konstanz Zither Club. Bühl was killed in battle in January 1945.

Manfred Bühl, Elser's son, was seven when a schoolmate told him his father left his mother for another woman. Three years later [in 1940] the same boy informed him his father had wanted to kill the Führer. After years of doubt and after seeing a 1969 documentary film by Hans Gottschalk on Elser he said he was 'finally proud of my father'. Bühl spoke in praise of his father at the dedication of the Georg-Elser-Platz in Munich in 1997. He died the same year.

Eugen Rau, Elser's best friend, died in 1995 in Königsbronn. In an interview in 1989 he said Elser was 'a man who insisted on justice when he believed himself in the right, he suffered no rudeness, and could be very funny'.

Elsa Härlen married Karl Votteler, a machine worker from Mannheim, in December 1939. Drafted in 1940, he went missing in action in Russia in 1942. In 1954 Elsa married Silesian refugee Günter Heinz Stephan and lived with him in Jebenhausen, west of Königsbronn. Elsa had three children and died in 1994. In an interview in 1959 she said she did not want any restitution from the government of the Federal Republic as it was 'those gypsies that were there before' that had brought her harm, meaning the Nazis.

Unity Valkyrie Mitford was returned from Munich to a hospital in Oban, Scotland in 1939. Doctors decided it was too dangerous to remove the bullet lodged in her head. She died in 1948 aged 34. In 2007 there was speculation by an English journalist Mitford had returned home pregnant with Hitler's baby.

Dr. Franz Fischer was arrested and interrogated in Berlin after the Venlo incident. One of the things the SD took an interest was his sale in England of a portrait on behalf of Travaglio (Solms) to finance the German Opposition—according to a post-war statement by Travaglio. In

1940 after release he went to Paris as an assistant to the German Coal Commissioner, only to be arrested on orders of Helmut Knochen, then head of the Security Police and the SS in occupied France. In July 1942 he was sentenced to three years for embezzlement between 1933-1934. He was released on the condition he not leave the village of Altensteig in the Black Forest where he remained to the end of the war. He gave evidence at the Dutch inquiry into the Venlo Incident in 1948. In his memoirs Walter Schellenberg refers to him as agent F479 of the SD, though Fischer maintained he was never [knowingly] employed as an agent of the SD.

Solms was the alias of Major Johannes Travaglio, a Luftwaffe officer stationed in Division 1 Luft (Air Reconnaissance) of the Abwehr in Stuttgart. He was born in Frankfurt a Main in 1892. His birth name was Hans Burckelmann, as he was the adopted son of an Italian wine merchant, named Travaglio. Giving evidence at the Dutch inquiry in 1948 into the Venlo Incident he claimed he was never questioned or arrested by the SD.

Dirk Klop [Captain Coppens] was severely wounded at Venlo, suffering a shot to the head and a shot through an artery in the shoulder. He was transferred to the Evangelical Hospital in Düsseldorf where he died the same day without regaining consciousness on November 9, 1939. At the direction of Berlin his confession was fabricated as additional proof of violation of neutrality by The Netherlands. Best refers to 'Coppens' while others have referred to Klop's alias as being: 'Copper' or Cooper'.

Maud—fate unknown.

Lieutenant Grosch was the alias of Bernard Christensen, who was a long-serving SD officer trusted by Walter Schellenberg.

Captain von Seidlitz was the alias of [?] von Salisch, a long-serving SD officer trusted by Walter Schellenberg.

Walter Friedrich Schellenberg [alias Captain Schaemmel] rose to the rank of Major General in charge of all German Foreign Intelligence following the arrest of Admiral Wilhelm Canaris. In July 1940 he was sent to Portugal to intercept the Duke and Duchess of Windsor to persuade them to work for Germany. The mission failed. Schellenberg was in Denmark when the British took him into custody in June 1945. In the postwar Nuremberg Trials he testified against other Nazis. In 1949 he was sentenced to six years' imprisonment, during which time he wrote his memoirs that were published posthumously in 1956. He was released in 1951 on the grounds of ill health. The following year he died of liver cancer in Turin aged 42. Some think he was poisoned. During the German occupation of Paris Schellenberg is rumoured to have been a lover of Coco Chanel while engaging in failed peace plans with Britain.

Colonel Martini was the alias of Prof. Dr. Maximinus Friedrich Alexander de Crinis, an Austrian born doctor. He was involved in the Nazi euthanasia program "mercy killing" called Action T4 between 1939-1941. In 1938 he became Director of the Psychiatric Department of the Charité Hospital in Berlin upon the retirement of Karl Bonhoeffer [the father of Dietrich Bonhoeffer] and Medical Director of the Ministry of Education in 1941. De Crinis and his wife committed joint suicide on 2 May 1945 using cyanide capsules.

Alfred Naujocks was arrested at the end of the war on suspicion of being a war criminal. At the Nuremberg Trials he said the attack on the Gleiwiyz Radio Tower was ordered by Heinrich Müller and Reinhard Heydrich. He escaped from custody to work in Hamburg where he sold his story to the media as *The Man who Started the War*. He died of a heart attack in 1966 aged 54.

Georg Vollmer and his employees were severely beaten during Gestapo interrogations. Vollmer was sentenced to 20 years in Welzheim concentration camp for negligence in storing explosives at his quarry in Königsbronn. He was released in 1941 after his wife petitioned Rudolf Hess through an old connection. She started the rumour a Zurich music dealer named Kuch, with a group of three Communists, had commissioned Elser to carry out the bombing.

Arthur Nebe was involved in various plots including the 20 July 1944 plot against Hitler. He was sentenced to death by the Nazi People's Court and executed at Plotzensee Prison, Berlin, on 21 March 1945 by hanging with piano wire from a meat hook, as Hitler wanted all the July 20 conspirators to be "hanged like cattle". Born the son of a schoolteacher, Nebe was wounded twice by gas in WW1. In 1920 he joined the Berlin detective force [Kripo] and attained the rank of Police Commissioner in 1924. In 1941, prior to Operation *Barbarossa*, Himmler selected Nebe to command the paramilitary death squads following the Wehrmacht, and responsible for the mass killings of civilians.

Hans Lobbes was a member of the Criminal Police from 1920 and joined the NSDAP in 1933. He was expelled in 1944 and sentenced to two years imprisonment for participating in the July 20 plot by aiding his friend Arthur Nebe. In post-war years he continued undercover police work.

Franz Josef Huber was appointed head of the State Police in Austria in March 1938. He worked out of the Hotel Metropole in Vienna with a staff of 900, the largest security office outside of Berlin. Huber was also the formal chief of the Central Agency for Jewish Emigration in Vienna, responsible for mass deportations until December 1944. The Allies took him prisoner in1945. After a trial in 1949 he was released and worked as a bookkeeper in a Munich office equipment company. He died in Munich in 1975.

Frau Krantz—fate unknown.

Heinrich Himmler. Following Hitler's suicide Himmler went into hiding with a forged pay book under the name of Sergeant Heinrich Hitzinger. When he was stopped at a British checkpoint he boasted who he was and demanded to be taken to General Eisenhower, but was refused. On May 23, 1945, during a medical examination he bit into a vial of cyanide concealed between his teeth and was dead within minutes. Himmler's secretary Hedwig Potthast from 1939 had two children by him. When tracked down in Baden Baden by a journalist in the 1980's, she claimed she had persuaded Himmler to negotiate with the Allies. Himmler's wife Marga died in 1967.

Dr. Max may have been the alias of Dr. (Ernst) Schambacher 'the England specialist', on the basis of evidence given at a Dutch post-war hearing into the Venlo Incident by Heinz Jost, SD Chief of Foreign Intelligence1939-1942. Ernst Schambacher committed suicide in May 1945.

Heinrich Müller was last seen in Berlin on the evening of 1 May 1945, the day after Hitler's suicide, according to Hans Baur, Hitler's pilot. He later quoted Müller as saying, "We know the Russian methods exactly. I haven't the faintest intention of being taken prisoner by the Russians." But Müller's fate remained a mystery with various explanations: he was killed or committed suicide during the chaos of the fall of Berlin and his body was not found; he escaped from Berlin and made his way to a safe location, possibly in South America; he was recruited and given a new identity by either the U.S. or the Soviet Union, and employed by them during the Cold War. Walter Schellenberg stated in his memoirs, "In 1945 he [Müller] joined the Communists, and in 1950 a German officer who had been a prisoner of war in Russia told me that he had seen Müller in Moscow in 1948 and that he had died shortly afterwards." However, in 2013 the head of the Memorial to the German Resistance, Johannes Tuchel, claimed Müller was buried in a mass grave in Berlin in August 1945, his body being found by a work crew cleaning up corpses and buried along with about 3,000 others on the site of a Jewish cemetery on Grosse Hamburger Strasse, a cemetery that the SS had destroyed in 1943.

Dr. Schäfer—fate unknown. Walter Schellenberg states in his memoires that a Dr. Schäfer was the Personnel Director at the Reich Security Main Office, in Berlin.

Reinhard Heydrich was interned in Berlin's Invalidenfriedhof, a military cemetery. The exact burial spot is not known. A temporary wooden marker disappeared when the Red Army overran the city in 1945, precluding Heydrich's grave becoming a rallying point for Neo-Nazis. West Germany awarded Heydrich's widow, Lina, a Federal pension. The couple had four children. Lina wrote a memoir, *Living With a War Criminal*, published in 1976. She remarried and died in 1985.

Herbert Kappler served on the Elser special commission in 1939. Later he was the Chief of Police in Rome at the time of the Ardeatine massacre. In 1947, he was tried in Italy and sentenced to life imprisonment in the military prison of Gaeta. He converted to Catholicism and at the age of 68 was diagnosed with terminal cancer. In 1977 his second wife, Anneliese, smuggled him out of the prison hospital in a large suitcase and they escaped to West Germany. He died aged 70.

Friedrich Seibold served on the Elser special commission in 1939. He died in 1997 in his hometown of Munich aged 88, after never once speaking of Georg Elser.

Friedrich Schmidt served on the Elser special commission in 1939. In 1945 he went into hiding under the name of Friedrich Schütte. He was convicted in 1969 of aiding and abetting the murder of Allied airmen and sentenced to two years imprisonment. He died a bachelor in Munich in 1983 aged 75.

Fritz, Axel, and Enno are fictitious characters.

Ernst Thälmann, a stoker on a freighter between 1903-1913, became leader of the German Communists Party. In 1933 when he called for the violent overthrow of Hitler's government he was arrested to spend over eleven years in solitary confinement. In August 1944 when in Buchenwald concentration camp he was shot dead and cremated. The Nazis blamed his death on an Allied bombing attack. He is listed at The German Resistance Memorial Center, Berlin.

Otto Strasser was a member of the NSDAP from 1925. He was on the left of the Nazi Party and published a number of Nazi newspapers in Berlin in competition with Joseph Goebbels. Hitler's association with industrialists caused him to leave the NSDAP in 1930. He formed the Black Front to fight against Hitlerism before fleeing Germany in 1933 to publish and broadcast anti-Hitler material in Vienna, Prague, Switzerland and Canada. He returned to West Germany in 1955 where he continued to propagate his socialist views until his death in Munich in 1974.

In his 1940 book *Flight from Terror* Strasser claimed his brother, Gregor, was shot dead in his cell in the basement prison of the Reich Security Main Office by Reinhard Heydrich after his arrest following the Night of the Long Knives on June 30,1934.

Martin Niemöller was a U-boat commander in WW1. He later studied theology and became a Protestant pastor. After early support of the Nazis he became the symbol of the Church's opposition to Nazism. Arrested in 1937, he was imprisoned to Sachsenhausen, then Dachau between 1941-1945. He was liberated in South Tirol with other VIP prisoners. From 1947 to 1965 he was President of the German Lutheran Church and Head of the World Council of Churches. He campaigned for nuclear disarmament during the Cold War and was awarded the Lenin Peace Prize. He died in 1984. He is listed at The German Resistance Memorial Center.

Anton Kaindl was captured by the British and handed over to the Russians. In 1947, with Kurt Eccarius and eleven other SS officers from Sachsenhausen, he was sentenced to life imprisonment with compulsory forced labor at the Vorkuta Gulag, where he died in 1948.

Ludwig Gehre, a Captain in the Abwehr [Military Intelligence] was executed at Flossenbürg concentration camp by hanging with five others, including Admiral Canaris on April 9, 1945. He was a member of the circle around Hans Oster and Hans von Dohnányi and was involved in preparing an assassination attempt on Hitler in March 1943 led by Henning von Tresckow. He is listed at The German Resistance Memorial Center, Berlin.

General Friedrich von Rabenau took part in the invasion of Poland in 1939 and acted as an intermediary for the resistance groups around Ludwig Beck and Carl Friedrich Goerdeler. In 1942 after being relieved of his post as chief of the Army archives, he studied theology in Berlin. He was shot without trial on the specific orders of Himmler at Flossenburg concentration camp on April 14 or15 1945 and is listed at The German Resistance Memorial Center, Berlin.

Dietrich Bonhoeffer was a German Lutheran pastor, theologian, and founding member of the Confessing Church that arose to oppose efforts to nazify the German Protestant Church. In 1933 he delivered a radio address in which he attacked Hitler and warned Germany against slipping into an idolatrous cult of the *Führer*. After working in London and New York he joined the Abwehr on his return to Germany in 1939. In April 1943 he was arrested and held without trial in Tegel prison. After a SS summary court-martial in Flossenbürg he was hanged the next day on April 9,1945. He is listed at The German Resistance Memorial Center. His involvement in assassination plots has been questioned in *Bonhoeffer the Assassin*, published in 2013.

His brother, Klaus, was sentenced to death by the People's Court on February 2, 1945. His brother-in-law, Hans von Dohnányi was executed at Sachsenhausen on April 9, 1945.

Franz Liedig was liberated in South Tirol with other VIP prisoners. After being military attaché in Sofia and Athens he was First Officer of the German cruiser Köln until February 1944. He was a founding member of the Christian Social Union of Bavaria in 1946. He died in 1967 in Munich.

Erich and Margot Heberlein [Stenzel] were liberated in South Tirol with other VIP prisoners and settled in Toledo, Spain in 1945. Living in a property named El Rincón in the old quarter, Erich played the pipe organ in Toledo churches, including San Juan Bautista. Margot died in 1967. Erich died in Toledo aged 90 in 1980. He was known locally as 'the German'.

Count Werner von Alvensleben was liberated from Magdeburg prison by American troops in April 1945. He died in Bremen-Vegesack in 1947.

Colonel Horst von Petersdorff was liberated in South Tirol with other VIP prisoners.

Alexander von Falkenhausen was liberated in South Tirol with other VIP prisoners. He was put on trial for his role in the deportation of Jews from Belgium, but not for their deaths in Auschwitz. In 1951 he was found guilty and sentenced to twelve years hard labour in Germany. In 1955 he was pardoned by Chancellor Konrad Adenauer and died in West Germany in 1966.

Heidel Nowakowski was liberated in South Tirol with other VIP prisoners.

Dr. Horst Hoeppner was a businessman liberated in South Tirol with other VIP prisoners.

Dr. Sigmund Rascher. When Dachau concentration camp was liberated by American troops on April 26, 1945, Rascher was found dead in his cell, possibly shot by Theodor Bongartz on the orders of Himmler. Rascher's wife was Karoline "Nini" Diehl, a Munich concert singer and a good friend of Himmler.

Isa Vermehren was liberated in South Tirol with other VIP prisoners. In 1933 she was expelled from high school for not offering the Hitler greeting out of sympathy for a Jewish schoolmate. She joined the Berlin cabaret 'Katakombe' were her first performance as 'Hanna Dose' was an instant hit, her signature song being a subtle mockery of Nazi officials. Goebbels shut down the cabaret in 1935. From 1940-43 she was a Red Cross entertainer for German troops. In early 1944 her brother Erich defected to Britain and the entire Vermehren family was arrested. As a prisoner at Ravensbrück concentration camp she arranged group singing of songs such as 'Die Gedanken sind Frei' (Thoughts are Free). Her book *A Journey through the Final Act: Ravensbrück, Buchenwald, Dachau: A Woman Reports*, was a bestseller. In 1951 she joined a convent and began a career as a teacher, public speaker, school director. From 1983 she hosted the German TV show 'The Word on Sunday'. Isa died in Bonn in 2009 aged 91.

Kurt and Vera Schuschnigg were liberated in South Tirol with other VIP prisoners. They emigrated to the United States where Kurt was a professor of political science at Saint Louis University from 1948 to 1967. Vera died 1959. Kurt's first wife had died in a car accident in 1935. He died at Mutters near Innsbruck in 1977 and is listed in The German Resistance Memorial Center, Berlin.

General Franz Halder was liberated in South Tirol with other VIP prisoners, including his wife Gertrud. He spent two years in an Allied prisoner of war camp from 1945. During the 1950's he worked as a war historian advisor to the US Army Historical Division and advised on the redevelopment of the post-war German army. He died in 1972 in Bavaria.

General Georg Thomas was liberated in South Tirol with other VIP prisoners, to die in Allied custody in 1946. In 1939 he became chief of the War Economy and Armaments Office in the High Command of the Wehrmacht, and was involved in the Nazi policy for the occupied Soviet Union that was designed to exploit the entire resources of the country for the benefit of Germany and the German armed forces at the expense of the deaths by starvation of 20-30 million people. This was the Hunger Plan. Nevertheless Thomas is listed in The German Resistance Memorial Center as he was involved in plans for a coup against Hitler in 1938-39 and had close contact with Ludwig Beck, Carl Goerdeler and Johannes Popitz.

Bogislav von Bonin was liberated in South Tirol with other VIP prisoners. He worked for Daimler Benz, the Federal Ministry of Defence, before journalism. He died in Potsdam in 1980.

Wassilly Kokorin, nephew of Molotov, was liberated in South Tirol with other VIP prisoners. He shared a cell with the son of Joseph Stalin, Yakov Iosifovich Dzhugashvili, at Sachsenhausen. When they attempted an escape in August 1944, Yakov grabbed the electrified wire on top of the wall around the yard and was shot dead by a guard. According to Best Kokorin joined Italian Communist partisans active in the Dolomites and died from frostbite in May 1945.

Franz Lechner was drafted into the Wehrmacht in 1939. After he was seriously injured in the winter of 1941-42 at Leningrad, he was assigned to work at Dachau concentration camp. He had contact with Elser and appeared in a 1969 Rundfunk documentary film titled, *The Assassin*.

Günter Knop is a fictitious character.

Edgar Stiller, an SS officer in Dachau concentration camp, served five years in Landsberg Prison. In 1951 he was tried for complicity in the murder of Georg Elser. Sigismund Payne Best wrote to the court in support of Stiller. The following is an extract from his letter:

__*He was just an unimportant subaltern snatched up in the Nazi machine under circumstances when his life and liberty depended on unquestioning obedience to orders. Even if Stiller knew of Georg Elser's end and even if he gave orders for his execution and was present when these were carried out, it was not he who committed murder but the man who signed the order and whose liberty is concealed by illegibility.*

Stiller was acquitted. The court concluded Elser was shot by SS Sergeant Theodor Bongartz, head of the crematorium at Dachau. Bongartz died of illness in an Allied POW camp in May 1945. In 2001 his gravestone in Heilbronn-Böckingen military cemetery was removed by the cemetery management. Since 2008 it has been at the Georg-Elser Memorial in Königsbronn.

Olive Grant was attached to the US Army Transport Services. [ATS]

Prominent Nazis at the Bürgerbräukeller on November 8, 1939

Amann, Max	President of Reich Press Chamber
Bormann, Martin	Head of the Party Chancellery
Brückner, Wilhelm	Chief adjutant to Hitler
Epp, Franz Ritter von	Reich Governor in Bavaria
Fiehler, Karl	Chief of NSPAD Main Office for local politics
Frick, Wilhelm	Reich Minister of the Interior
Goebbels, Joseph	Reich Minister of Public Enlightenment & Propaganda
Graf, Ulrich	Member of the Reichstag
Hesse, Rudolf	Deputy Führer
Hierl, Konstantin	Reich Labour Leader
Himmler, Heinrich	Reichsführer SS
Hitler, Adolf	Führer, Head of State, Nazi Party Chairman
Hoffmann, Heinrich	Hitler's photographer
Hühnlein, Adolf	Corps Leader of the NSKK
Kriebel, Hermann	Military Führer of the Putsch of 1923
Ley, Robert	Head of the German Labor Front
Rosenberg, Alfred	Reich leader of the NSDAP, Reich Minister
Schaub, Julius	Adjutant to Hitler
Schmundt, Rudolf	Military Chief adjutant to Hitler
Todt, Fitz	Plenipotentiary for the construction industry
Wagner, Adolf	Gauleiter of Munich Upper Bavaria
Weber, Christian	SS Brigade Commander
Weber, Friedrich	Reich Veterinarian
Wolff, Karl	Chief of Personal Staff to Himmler

Others not included in newspaper reports that may have attended.

Bouhler, Philipp	Chief of the Chancellery of the Führer of the NSDAP
Dietrich, Joseph 'Sepp'	Commander of Hitler's Personal Bodyguard
Frank, Hans	Governor General of occupied Poland
Ribbentrop, Joachim von	Reich Minister for Foreign Affairs
Streicher, Julius	Publisher of "Der Stürmer"

Source: Peter Koblank www.mythoselser.de

Maria Strobl*, recalls her ordeal in 1959

____The roar remains. It will always remind me of those awful minutes in time—as long as I live.

And the doctors no longer believe there will ever be quiet again inside my head.

The detonation of the bomb destroyed my eardrums. My left side of the head is like a blaring express in a tunnel. On this Sunday, November 8, there are exactly 20 years since this roar began. I will cry again this evening. Cry about my affliction caused by the attempt to assassinate Hitler in the Bürgerbräukeller.

When Hitler began his speech, we waitresses always went into the anteroom. We lit a cigarette and had a little chat. We had nothing else to do during the long speech.

When the Song of Germany and the Horst-Wessel-Lied were sung, we waitresses would go down to the toilet to fix our make up in front of the mirror. When we heard that the chairs were moved in the hall we waitresses then went back into the hall.

Immediately after the Horst-Wessel-Lied the Fuhrer is gone with his closest collaborators. He left the room directly through the main entrance. His car was waiting in front of our portal in Rosenheimerstrasse.

Most tables in the great hall had emptied. There was hardly anyone on the gallery. A total of about 150 men remained in the hall. They stood in smaller groups and discussed the speech of Adolf Hitler. They also drank something as they talked. I had twelve steins in hand as I stood right in front of the flag where Hitler spoke. I think this flag has not been washed once in 15 years. It was stiff with dirt. But again and again people came, especially women, who put flowers on the banner or they kissed it enthusiastically.

When I had the twelve beer mugs in your hand there was a terrible air pressure. It threw me through the swinging doors to the main entrance. Stones and filth flew around my head. And then I noticed nothing.

The explosion threw me out of the hall. When I came to my senses, I was between fragmented beer mugs, smashed tables, tattered flower garlands and bleeding men. I was covered with bricks and brick dust. Behind me, the heavy ceiling of the hall was thrown down with the five mighty chandeliers. The men whose steins I wanted to re-fill were buried underneath.

*Maria Strobl was a temporary waitress at the Bürgerbräukeller.

Source: Günter Peis, 1959 / Peter Koblank www.mythoselser.de

The dead and the wounded at the Bürgerbräukeller

Killed:
1. **Maria Henle**, 30, temporary waitress, married with husband and two small children.
2. **Eugen Schachta**, 32, technician in the Reichsautozug, married for eleven months.
3. **Wilhelm Weber**, 37, technician in the Reichsautozug, married with wife and two small children.
4. **Franz Lutz**, 53, long-time supporter of Hitler, SA captain.
5. **Michael Kaiser Wilhelm**, 50, long-time supporter of Hitler, SA captain.
6. **Emil Kasberger**, 54, long-time member of the NSDAP, flutist, married with wife and daughter.
7. **Leonhardt Reindl**, 57, since 1923 a member of the NSDAP, and an old fighter.
8. **Michael Schmeidl**, age unknown, NSDAP member, died a few days after bombing.

Injured and hospitalized:
1. **Richard Bach Fischer**, electrician, Munich.
2. **Anna Blank**, cashier, Munich.
3. **Josef Böswirth**, Munich.
4. **Maria Dietenberger**, cashier, Munich.
5. **Albert Eckebrecht**, Reichssender (radio station) engineer, Munich.
6. **Zenta Egger**, cashier, Munich.
7. **Emil Faetsch**, Blood Order, SA Regiment, Munich.
8. **Karl Fischer**, insurance employee, Munich, Blood Order.
9. **Anneliese Gawenat**, Munich.
10. **Anton Gruber**, SA soldier, bookbinder.
11. **Elise Heuschmann**, cashier, Munich.
12. **Christian Himmler**, technician in the Reichsautozug.
13. **Charles Hundt**, SA soldier, Munich.
14. **Bartholomew Ippisch**, sound engineer, Munich.
15. **Hans Lenz**, Munich-Pasing, Blood Order.
16. **Johanna Liesecke**, Cashier, Munich.
17. **Herbert Müller**, merchant, Munich.
18. **August Ortner**, teacher, soldier, Dunzweiler.
19. **Franz Reder**, Wehrmacht, Munich, permanent pass holder.
20. **Jakob Royer**, engineer, SA Regiment, Munich.
21. **Hildegard Schirmer**, gymnastics teacher.
22. **Wolfgang Schmuckert**, medical student, Munich.
23. **Max Schultz**, dentist, Munich.
24. **Theodor Thenn**, treasurer, Munich.
25. **Willi Tietz**, inspector, Berlin-Britz.
26. **Josef Werberger**, master electrician, soldier, Munich.
27. **Emil Wipfil**, Munich.

Thirty others were discharged from hospital with minor injuries, bringing the injured to 57.

Source: Peter Koblank www.mythoselser.de

Elser with Nebe. Source: Bavarian State Library in Munich (Photo Archive Heinrich Hoffmann)

Reconstruction of the 'apparatus' by Elser in December 1939. The Gestapo used the device for training purposes.

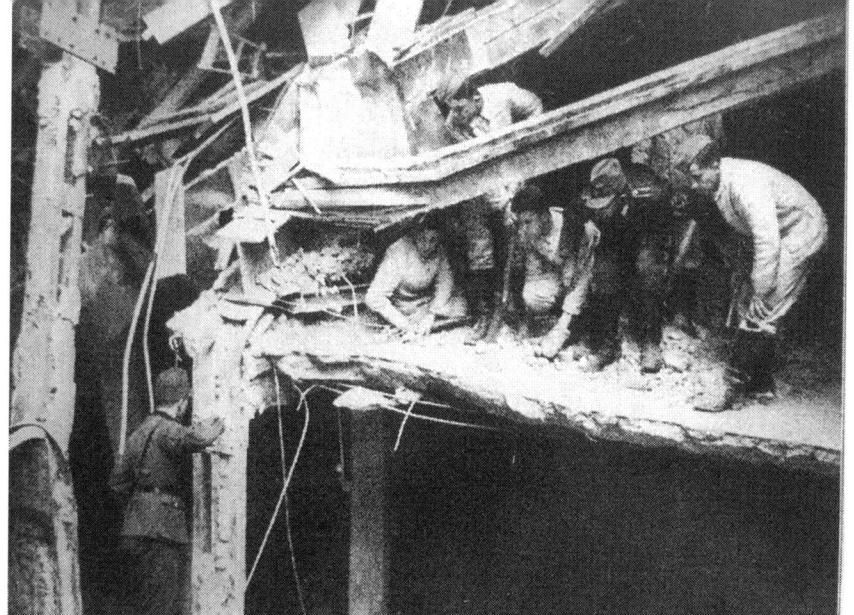
Inspecting the damage at the Bürgerbräukeller (Original Photo: Heinrich Hoffmann)

Images from *Illustrierter Beobachter* (*Illustrated Observer*) Nov. 1939, the illustrated propaganda magazine published by the Nazi Party from 1926 to 1945 in Munich, edited by Herman Esser. Photographed by the author at the Topography of Terror, Berlin, in 2015.

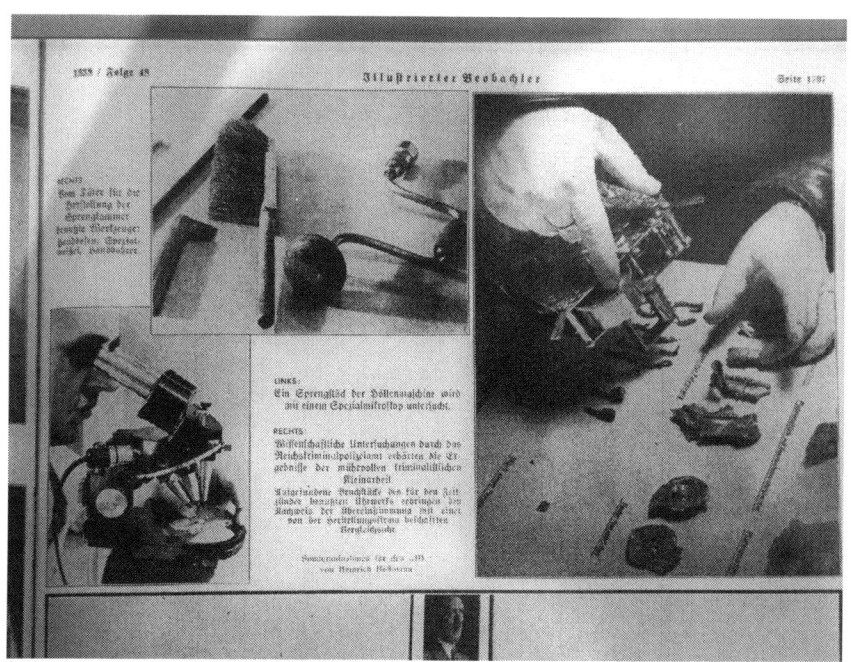
Shifting through the evidence (Original Photos: Heinrich Hoffmann)

Elser's reconstruction of the timing device

How Rosa Lehmann recalled Georg Elser in 1998

I had hung out a sign to say that a room was for rent from such and such a date. My husband said to me: "Have a good look at the people who come to inspect." My goodness, one cannot see into anyone. You have to take people how they come. We had to rent a room. You can't say I will look at twenty or thirty people and then pick one. You can't see what's inside people, and what makes them tick.

So he came, Herr Elser. He said he was a carpenter and an inventor. Well, I believed him. So he moved in with us. He had a pile of boxes, beautiful boxes, probably made them himself. And he asked my husband if he would help him carry the boxes to the cellar. What kind takes such a small room, if he has a pile of stuff? That's what my husband thought taking the boxes down. That was on August 1, 1939. [sic]

My husband has always called him a "house sneak", such a one forever sneaking around. Suddenly he was standing outside the door. You did not know if he had comes up from the ground or the devil, or from where else. He had the room close to the front door and moved quite softly. Almost three months, my God! The room was small, just room for a bed, a bedside table and a desk. At the back he had his things hanging. Four marks a week he paid. I never cared for the man. I am not one of those who look what other people do. Perhaps it would have been better. All rooms in the apartment were unlocked, because I made up the beds and had to clean the room. That's why you rented out your room, that's why you were paid. It was one Sunday afternoon, I still remember exactly when my husband and I came home and Elser was sitting on the edge of a wooden trunk with a domed lid studying a Leitz folder [possibly a tool brochure]. Really shocked he was when we unlocked the door. He threw the folder into the trunk, and he was off. At that time we thought nothing of it.

One fine day, when I had just cleaned the room, I saw an accumulator near the window. Why does he need an accumulator? Really strange, I told my husband to go there and have a look. And on the desk was a clock that was set up somehow. My husband looked at the accumulator and the clock, then at me, then he said: "He will certainly not build an infernal machine!" We then had a good laugh and went out. With that the case was closed.

On another day when I was about to clean the room, Elser was still lying in bed. I thought to myself, this is great, still in bed in broad daylight. He had a problem with his knees, he said. Probably from a lot of kneeling at night while he was building the thing in the Bürgerbräukeller. "What will we do with him?" I asked my husband, "Well," said he, "we can't allow him to starve. Take him soup." He took it to him and soon afterwards he got up.

On 12 October, I'm at the Red Cross to give birth, that's where the lad, Peter, was born. It was a difficult birth. I had to stay there fourteen days. That was a time when Elser had a free hand. During the day my husband was at work till six o'clock at night and on Saturday till two in the afternoon.

On October 15 he came to see me and said: "Just imagine, Elser has terminated." At that time one could not give notice from 15th (of the month) to the first, not the other way round. That's handy, I thought, I'm in hospital, and can't look for someone else and Elser moves out! "Don't get excited," my husband said, "we'll find someone." If we'd only known he'd stay such a short time, perhaps we wouldn't have taken him. But that's how it is, one can't look inside people.

Then there was the tale of registering the end of his stay. I had just got home from the hospital and could not leave the child. I then asked Elser if he could not deregister himself. He only had to take the completed forms to the police. We filled them out together and he went. However he did not deregister himself. Later someone from the police came and really told me off, asking if I could not read the fine print. He complained he had to give me the deregistration form. And then I also had to pay the penalty.

On November 1 he moved out with all those many boxes. Where to, we did not know. We didn't exchange a personal word with one another. We had our concerns and his head was full of his things. A few days later, it was a real rainy November day; at nine o'clock the doorbell rang. Elser was standing outside, small and stocky, with a big black hat that covered his face. I was terribly frightened he looked so scary. He only wanted to know if mail had come for him. "No," I said, "nothing is here." Then he went again. That was the last time I saw him. By the way, he only got mail once, as far as I know. And not one visitor.

On the 9th November the assassination took place. My husband had been to the zoo with my sister and my young niece. I was cooking and listening to the radio. Then they announced that they had caught and arrested a certain Herr Elser at the Swiss border. Because of the attempt to assassinate Hitler. For God's sake! For God's sake!

When my husband came, I said, "Hey, it's best you go to the Gestapo and report that Elser stayed with us!" Then he went to Wittelsbacher Palais on Briennerstrasse and told them. At that the matter for us was finished. But not for them. A few days later at five the doorbell rings. Huge SS men stand in front of the door, on the street a green Mercedes. "Is your husband there? No? Then we have to wait." Every day Gestapo came and interrogated me. Once even they had me go in for questioning. I could barely walk, as my knees trembled so much. I could only repeat that he had lived with us, Elser that is. I knew nothing else.

Source: Interview by Hella Schlumberger with 90 year-old Rosa Lehmann in 1998.

Translation: Vita Kristovskis.

Bürgerbräukeller Hall in 1930's   Source: German Resistance Memorial, Berlin

Otto Strasser on the Bürgerbräukeller bombing

An extract from *Flight from Terror*, by Otto Strasser, published in 1943.

For two months after that [the outbreak of the WW2] I remained in Switzerland, seeing in wretched helplessness the great nations of the world facing each other for the showdown, sparring, feinting, grimacing as they waited for an opening. Some people labeled it a "phony war"; I knew it wasn't. I felt like a man who must watch impotently as a sputtering fuse burns closer and closer to a powder keg while others stand about and comment on how little noise the fuse is making. But I was truly thankful for one blessing: my wife and children were in Switzerland, and I was with them. Then, with the characteristic abruptness of all events those days, even that small solace was torn from me.

On the evening of November 8 I was listening to European broadcasts, idly turning the dial as I picked up one country after another, when I suddenly became arrested by the unmistakable sound of Adolf Hitler's raucous, browbeating tones. It was a surprise, for no announcement had been made of any speech by the Fuehrer that night, and I left the set tuned in. He was broadcasting from the Burgerbrau Keller in Munich, evidently celebrating the anniversary of his beer-hall putsch of 1923. It was a typical Hitler speech, and when it was over I thought nothing more of it. It wasn't until the following day that I found out I was supposed to have been present at that celebration - very much present!

"Last night," the radio announced to me and my startled wife, *"a bomb explosion shattered the Burgerbrau Keller where our Fuehrer had just finished speaking! Fortunately indeed, the Fuehrer had left the hall - though it was but nine minutes before the explosion occurred! This base, cowardly attack killed seven loyal Nazis and wounded sixty-three!*

"Investigation has revealed that the yellow murderers who planned and executed this incredible outrage were Doctor Otto Strasser and a British intelligence officer. The guilt is clearly and indisputably traced to them. Attention, all Germans! These two men, and especially Strasser, must be made to pay for their crime! So anxious is our heartbroken Fuehrer that they atone for the dead that he is offering a reward ..."

I could scarcely believe my ears; but that evening, when I was able to buy the daily German papers, I found whole pages filled with my exploits, both actual and imaginary. I was described as the most dangerous criminal in Europe, and a reward amounting to $500,000 was offered for my arrest and surrender to the Gestapo! Half a million dollars! Although this was undoubtedly an out-and-out propaganda trick to whip up flagging German war spirit - as was the Nazi-planned explosion itself [1] - I knew it could have but one unfortunate result for me. Flight again.

The very next day Switzerland received a German ultimatum to surrender Otto Strasser - and I was given four hours to get out of the country. There was nothing I could do. Miserably I said good-by to my dear family and took the next plane for Paris. At that moment I felt it was as safe a place as Switzerland, though not nearly so comfortable to live in. Didn't the Maginot Line and the whole French army stand between Hitler and me?

For the next six months my existence was one of aniety, wild rumor and restless inactivity, but at least I was still at liberty. During that time, and the years before it, I had witnessed the tragedy of Europe. I had seen bloody oppression in Germany followed by bloody oppression abroad: the march on Vienna, the annexation of the Sudetenland, the violation of Prague, the destruction of Warsaw, the onslaught on Copenhagen, the occupation of Oslo, the burning of Amsterdam, the submission of Brussels.

The panic of the incompetent gripped France. Chauvinist politicians, short-sighted generals, treacherous members of Parliament staged the tragi-comedy of the agitation against the "emigrants"; imprisoned the convinced enemies of Hitler, along with Hitler's own Germans, in concentration camps; and celebrated this miserable farce as "a victory over the Fifth Column." I, who for more than ten years had been Hitler's enemy, who for seven years had been hunted from country to country by Himmler's Gestapo and Ribbentrop's foreign agents, was interned as a suspected fifth columnist! On May 14 1940 the French government seized me and put me in the Bufalo Concentration Camp, holding five thousand people, of whom ninety-five per cent were Jews. This had previously been a great sports arena and was located on the northern outskirts of Paris. Like the Yankee Stadium in New York, the arena was surrounded by closed stands, and it was in these stands we spent the night, the days being passed out in the open.

Footnote by Otto Strasser:

[1] Hitler and the other big Nazi leaders, contrary to custom, this night suspiciously rushed from the hall upon conclusion of the speeches, thus indicating knowledge of the coming explosion.

Best and the Venlo Incident

Sigismund Payne Best in The Hague, 1939.
Source: Bridget Payne Best

Office at Nieuwe Uitleg 15, The Hague
Source: Municipality archive Den Haag 1939

Café Backus, Venlo.

Source: Rijksinstituut voor Oorlogsdocumentatie Amsterdam

Translation of text from left to right: Dutch Customs border posts; Road where the Dutch car stood; The Cafe; German customs building.

The British White Paper

The British White Paper is referred to by Best in *The Venlo Incident* as well as in this book. The following is a related article that appeared in the *West Australian* newspaper on November 1, 1939, p 8-9.

NAZI BRUTALITY. A BRITISH WHITE PAPER. SHOCKING DISCLOSURES

Concentration Camp Horrors

LONDON, Oct. 31-The British Government published a White Paper yesterday containing details of the barbaric cruelty of the Nazi treatment of German inhabitants sent to concentration camps and various reports from British consular officials describing the Nazi vengeance against Jews and political opponents.

A foreword to the White Paper states: "Even after the outbreak of war His Majesty's Government was reluctant to take action which might inspire hatred, but the German Government's attitude and the unscrupulous propaganda it is spreading compel His Majesty's Government to publish these documents so that public opinion here and abroad may judge for itself. The German Government has complained of the maltreatment of German minorities in foreign countries and of 'Macedonian conditions' reigning there, but it will be seen from these documents that under the present regime the conditions in Germany itself and the treatment accorded to Germans are reminiscent not of Macedonia but of the darkest ages in the history of man."

Several documents reveal in detail the brutal conditions endured by prisoners in the notorious Buchenwald and Dachau concentration camps in Germany, including statements of the experiences of exprisoners in the Buchenwald camp communicated to the British Foreign Office by a charity organisation in Germany.

Buchenwald Barbarities

During working-hours of 16 hours a day for seven days a week, says the statement of a formerly well-to-do Jewish businessman, it was forbidden to drink even in the hottest weather. The food was not bad but was quite insufficient. While he was there, the work of Jewish prisoners was doubled and their rations halved. The work consisted of moving heavy stones far beyond the strength of even a normal well-fed man. The Jews were sneeringly told by the Nazi guards that they were only experiencing the same treatment as their forefathers in Egypt and that Pharaoh had not gone half far enough. Men were kept standing at attention for many hours on end. Floggings were frequent for such small offences as drinking water in working hours. The usual punishment was 25 strokes, given alternately by two guards. This often produced unconsciousness, but the Jews were told that Hitler had given orders that Jews might receive up to 60 strokes. Another exprisoner, a small businessman arrested in June, 1938, in a round up in the streets of Berlin without cause or pretext, describing the floggings, said that the normal punishment was 25 strokes on the seat carried out by two guards standing on each side with riding whips. The prisoner was lashed to a board. If he cried the strokes were increased to 35. The guards used all their force, sometimes springing into the air so as to bring the arm down with increased momentum. Another punishment was hanging up, three metres from the ground by the arms, which were violently bent back for the purpose. Special men were employed to carry out these punishments. The hanging lasted for ten to twelve hours and was in public. Another ex-prisoner described the Buchenwald camp as filth and mud knee deep. His face was unrecognisable owing to torn flesh. He said there were 100 straw sacks for 10,000 men, who were beaten if they lay on their backs and were ordered to lie on their sides. The sentries used their rifles without warning. One saying was: "A bullet costs 12 pfennigs, which is all a Jew is worth."

Eventually, the statement added, no Jews were accepted as sick. They could only be well or dead. Many who were unable to stand had to be forcibly held up at the roll call. Many virtually committed suicide by feigning flight in order to be shot down.

British Consular Reports

The former British Consul-General in Vienna (Mr. Gainer), reporting on November 11, 1938, on the anti-Jewish demonstrations in Vienna on the occasion of Herr von Bath's murder in Paris, said that when a large number of Jewish shops and houses and Jewish prayer houses and synagogues were fired, the police obviously received instructions not to interfere. Vienna presented an extraordinary spectacle, with fires raging all over the city and Jews being hustled along the streets, cursed at and assaulted by crowds of hooligans, whose pride it was to belong to one of the greatest and most civilised nations In the world.

The former British Consul-General in Cologne (Mr. Bell), reporting on November 14, said the anti-Jewish manifestations of November 11 were very thorough and systematic. He went on: "There is nervousness amongst the middle-class Germans, who in general disapprove, but they dare not voice disapproval. One German woman who did so in a tramcar which runs past my door was arrested at the first stopping place. I have been the more shocked by the cold-blooded manner in which the action was taken than by anything else. Yet I am inclined to think the Fuehrer knows his Germans. Amongst the masses who have nothing at stake there is observed a certain amount of 'schadenfreude.'" [pleasure derived by someone from another person's misfortune]

[two paragraphs have been omitted]

"The Times," in a leading article today, says:- "All civilised people must be appalled at the White Paper's account of the German treatment of prisoners. It was not generally realised that the barbaric cruelties of 1933-1934 still continued. Readers will be ashamed to know that the rulers of a nominally Christian country belonging to a continent which claims to be the nursery of civilization combines the savagery of the darkest ages with the subtler mental cruelties of a more advanced epoch. A most disquieting feature is the choice of guards from the Nazi elite; namely, the Black Guards, who provide the bodyguard for Hitler and the majority of whom are 20 years old or less. They have been deflected from the normal course of education and transformed into brutal ruffians. The old police whom Hitler and Goering took over from the Republic were not savage enough and they trained their own ruffians. The Germans must some day repudiate this ghastly tyranny. Meanwhile, the civilised countries must see that no foreign race is forced to submit a moment longer than is necessary to this blighting, paganising influence."

The Rescue of the VIP Prisoners by the Wehrmacht in 1945

An extract from *The Secret Surrender: The Classic Insiders Account of the Secret Plot to Surrender Northern Italy During WWII* by Allen W. Dulles.

During our stay General Lemnitzer asked Gaevernitz to go to Capri. Just arrived was a group of about one hundred and fifty former prisoners from various German concentration camps that had been housed by the Allies to clarify their future fate on the island. They belonged to an even larger group of prisoners of various nationalities, which had been held by the highest SS leaders, probably, in the absurd hope to buy impunity by their release at the last minute. From a variety of concentration camps in Germany and Austria they had been brought together and hauled over the Alps to Niederdorf in Toblach (Dobbiaco). It was a total of nearly two hundred prisoners, among them many well-known non-Germans, who had been partially in the hands of the Nazis since the war began. On Capri Gaevernitz learned of their individual fates and how close they escaped death.

Wolff and Röttiger had heard of this prisoner transport before the capitulation. As a prisoner, Colonel Bogislaw von Bonin, succeeded long enough to escape the SS guard, to get to a phone and call the Bolzano headquarters of the German Army Group. He had succeeded to contact Röttiger, an acquaintance from earlier times. Then Röttiger instructed the commander of his headquarters, Captain Wichard von Alvensleben, to explore the situation in Niederdorf. On his own initiative Alvensleben ordered the same night the arming of a Eingreifkommando of the Wehrmacht, consisting of 8 extra brave battle-hardened Unteroffiziere. On April 29 Alvensleben drove at dawn to Niederdorf and searched for the SS officer who commanded the SS escort of the prisoner transport. When questioned about the purpose of its mission he explained this simply: "My job is only done if the prisoners are dead."

Shortly after Alvensleben commanded the Eingreifkommando of the Wehrmacht to block off the market and drive the 86 men of the SS guard unit scattered throughout the village into the town hall. Two SS officers tried to breakout, but were prevented by the Eingreifkommando of the Wehrmacht. When the SS threatened to make use of their weapons, Alvensleben immediately ordered a 100-strong motorized Wehrmacht company from Toblach, which soon arrived. Fortunately the position ruled in favor of the armed forces and so saved the lives of the endangered detainees.

After a telephone agreement with General Wolff Alvensleben the SS were put in their own vehicles and sent towards Bolzano. He then ordered the resettlement of the liberated prisoners to the Hotel Pragser Wildsee. He was supported by his cousin Captain Gebhard von Alvensleben, who brilliantly organized their accommodation and meals until they were a few days later reached by Allied troops and brought to the island of Capri.

First page of Elser's Interrogation Report

Abschrift.

IV Z 1 Berlin, den 19. 11. 1939.

Vorgeführt erscheint

I 1, I 2
I 3, I 4
I 201, I 6

I 101

I 102

E l s e r, Johann Georg,
geb. 4. 1. 03 Hermaringen/Württemberg, Oberamt
Heidenheim, ledig, Schreiner, RD, zuletzt wohnhaft
München, Türkenstrasse 94/II bei L o h m a n n, Sohn
der Holzhändlerseheleute Ludwig und Maria E l -
s e r geb. Müller, in Königsbronn bei Heidenheim
wohnhaft, und gibt folgendes an:

A) Zur Person:

I 202

I 103

J 204

Ich wurde am 4. 1. 1903 in Hermaringen als
der aussereheliche Sohn der Maria M ü l l e r
geboren, die seinerzeit bei ihren Eltern, die
dort eine Wagnerei und einen landwirtschaft-
lichen Betrieb inne hatten, wohnhaft war.
Ein Jahr später hat meine Mutter den Kinds-
vater Ludwig E l s e r geheiratet. Durch die-
se Eheschliessung wurde ich legitimiert. Mein
Vater Ludwig E l s e r war in Königsbronn wohnhaft. Er hatte dort ein eigenes Anwesen und
hat sich ferner durch Holzfahren und land-

Source: Federal Archives Koblenz, signature R 22/3100

Acknowledgements

SEVERAL biographies of Georg Elser have appeared since 1990. I have attempted to retell his story not as a dry history written in the third person, but by stepping into his shoes. Nor did I want to tell his story in isolation, but in the context of the deeds of others who attempted to resist the Nazi regime, including those outside Germany who tried but failed to avoid what evolved into perhaps the darkest hour in European history.

To piece together this polygonal story I have relied on a numerous sources. A primary source was *www.georg-elser-arbeitskreis.de* of the Georg Elser Arbeitskreis [working group] Heidenheim, Germany, a website edited by Peter Koblank. This site has online the full text of Elser's interrogation report conducted in Berlin in 1939. This two hundred page document contains most of what is known about Georg Elser and his assassination attempt. The website of Peter Koblank, *www.mythoselser.de,* also presents essays on Elser and related topics. In my reconstruction of events much information has been sourced from Captain S. Payne Best's book *The Venlo Incident* as well as from Walter Schellenberg's memoir, first published in 1956. The book, *Bombing Hitler: The Story of the Man who almost Assassinated the Führer,* by Hellmut G. Haasis, together with an essay on the Venlo Incident by B.G.J. (Bob) de Graaff in *Battleground Western Europe: Intelligence Operations in Germany and The Netherland in the Twentieth Century,* were all useful references. Extracts of speeches were sourced from the *German Propaganda Archive* of Randall Bytwerk, Professor Emeritus, Calvin College, Grand Rapids, MI, USA, and BBC online Archive.

I am greatly indebted to Peter Koblank for his assistance in acting as consultant editor. Since I emailed an early manuscript to him *cold* in July 2014 Peter has been of great encouragement. His knowledge of the subject, his rigorous attitude to history, coupled with his meticulous attention to detail guided me to completion. For their willing assistance I also wish to thank: Monika Knop of the Sachsenhausen Memorial and Museum for providing details on Elser's living space at Sachsenhausen; Vita Kristovskis for her encouragement and translations; Angela Plant for her proofreading; Kim Davis for her encouragement, Professor Bob de Graaff for his permission to use his quotation, and Dr. Kirstin Frieden of NS-Dokumentationszentrum München for her permission to use the material in the Postscript.

Thanks again to Peter Koblank for meeting me in Munich and for his comprehensive tour of the Elser 'stations' on November 8, 2015, that included the annual wreath laying ceremony at the Elser memorial in Schnaitheim. I also wish to thank Joachim Ziller for showing me through the Georg Elser Memorial in Königsbronn.

Bibliography

Otto Strasser, *Hitler and I*, translated by Gwenda David and Eric Mosbacher, first published by Jonathan Cape Thirty Bedford Square London,1940 and *Flight from Terror*, translated by Michael Stern, published by AMS Press, 1943.

Hans Bernd Gisevius, *To the Bitter End*, Jonathan Cape, London, 1948.

Captain S. Payne Best, *The Venlo Incident*, first published in 1950 by Hutchinson & Co (London). Republished by Pen and Sword Books Ltd and Skyhorse Publishing, New York, 2009.

Walter Schellenberg, *The Schellenberg Memoirs* first published in 1956 in Great Britain by André Deutsch Ltd. Republished in 2000 by Da Capo Press, titled *The Labyrinth: Memoirs Of Walter Schellenberg, Hitler's Chief Of Counterintelligence*.

William L. Shirer, *The Rise And Fall Of The Third Reich, A History of Nazi Germany*, first published in 1960 by Simon and Schuster.

Albert Speer, *Inside The Third Reich*, first published in Great Britain in 1970 by Weidenfeld & Nicholson.

Helmut Hörtner, *The Lone Assassin, The Epic Story of the Man who Almost Killed Hitler*, published in 1993 in Germany. English edition by Skyhorse Publishing, New York, 2012, translated by Ross Benjamin.

Larry L. Rasmussen, *Dietrich Bonhoeffer: Reality and Resistance*, Westminster John Knox Press, 2005.

Beatrice de Graaf, Ben de Jong & Wies Platje (editor) *Battleground Western Europe: Intelligence Operations in Germany and The Netherland in the Twentieth Century*, Het Spinhuis Publishers, 2007

Keith Jeffrey, *Mi6: The History of the Secret Intelligence Service, 1909-1949*, Bloomsbury, 2011.

Hellmut G. Haasis, *Bombing Hitler: The Story of the Man who almost Assassinated the Führer*, first published in German in 2001. English edition by Skyhorse Publishing, New York, 2013.

Robert Sommer, *The Concentration Camp Bordello: Sexual Forced Labor in National Socialistic Concentration Camps*, published in German by Schöningh Verlag, Paderborn, 2011.

Gunter Morsch & Astrid Ley (ed.) *Sachsenhausen Concentration Camp 1939-1945 Events and Developments*, published by Metropol, 5th Edition 2013.

Postscript

Munich Documentation Centre for the History of National Socialism
www.ns-dokuzentrum-muenchen.de

Opened on May 1, 2015, the Munich Documentation Centre for the History of National Socialism at Königsplatz was conceived as a place of learning and remembrance devoted to addressing Munich's Nazi past and the origins, manifestations and consequences of the Nazi dictatorship. The Centre is on the site of the Brown House, the former headquarters of the National Socialists where Adolf Hitler, Heinrich Himmler, Hermann Göring, Rudolf Hess and other Nazi leaders had offices. On the plinth in the foreground stood one of the two 'honour temples' for the sixteen 'blood martyrs' before being demolished in 1947. The Director of the Department of Culture Dr. Hans Georg Küppers explains the contemporary relevance of the permanent exhibition of the Documentation Centre with these words:

The crucial questions posed by the exhibition are: 'Why Munich?' and 'What does this have to do with us today?' We can only take an active stand against exclusion, racism, anti-Semitism and discrimination if we develop an awareness of the past.

Architect: Georg • Scheel • Wetzel Architekten, BERLIN   Photo: Jens Weber

Doorway at Türkenstrasse 59 leading to the workshop where Elser assembled his 'apparatus'.
Photo: Author

Georg Elser plaque on the site of the Bürgerbräukeller [demolished in 1979]. Photo: Author

Georg Elser Memorial in Königsbronn
www.georg-elser-arbeitskreis.de

Königsbronn town centre. Rathaus is in the centre with Brenz River spring pumphouse on the right. The Georg Elser Memorial-Museum is located within the building on the left. Photo: Author

Elser's concert zither on display at the Georg Elser Memorial, Königsbronn. Photo: Author

Elser's work bench on display at the Georg Elser Memorial, Königsbronn. Photo: Author

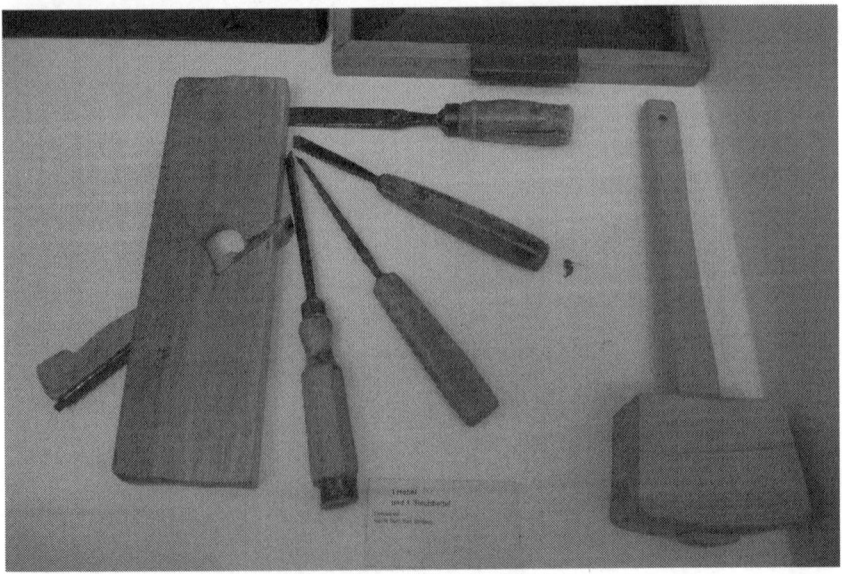
Elser's tools on display at the Georg Elser Memorial, Königsbronn. Photo: Author

The German Resistance Memorial Center, Berlin
www.gdw-berlin.de

Georg Elser occupies one room of the German Resistance Memorial Center, Berlin. Photo: Author

The 17m high steel sculpture by Ulrich Klages in tribute to Georg Elser in Wilhelmstrasse, Berlin.
Photo: Author

Georg Elser [in coat] and Elsa Härlen [seated infront] with friends at Wental, about ten kms from Königsbronn. Eugen Rau is seated at front. His wife, Emma, is beside Elser. Circa 1936. Photographer: unknown

TOM FERRY

Tom Ferry (b.1945 in Sydney, Australia) has previously written and published *Improbable Rendezvous,* a comic historical parody inspired by Haruki Murakami and the Japanese midget submarine attack on Sydney Harbour in 1942. Ferry has created and maintains the webpage georgelser.info.

PETER KOBLANK

Peter Koblank (b. 1952 in Berlin, Germany) is a writer and management consultant with an interest in history. Since 2005 he has been the editor of the website of the working group *Georg-Elser-Arbeitskreises*, the most extensive online archive that exists worldwide for a resistance fighter against the Third Reich.

Was this Georg Elser's escape vessel?

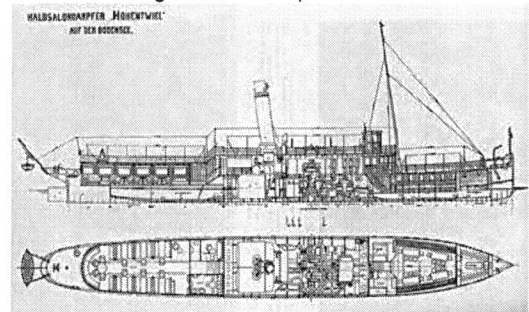

Image: www.kingswearcastle.co.uk

Paddle steamer, *Hohentwiel*, sailed on Lake Constance (Bodensee) between 1913—1962 and is now fully restored as a tour vessel.
www.hohentwiel.com.

Made in the USA
Middletown, DE
29 November 2018